The Rebels of Hastings

The Rebellion of 1837 is an early landmark in Upper Canadian history. Most Ontarians know about the dramatic uprising in Toronto, led by William Lyon Mackenzie, but the troubles elsewhere in the province are less well understood. Centring her account on Hastings County, Betsy Dewar Boyce explores the events of this period in eastern Ontario.

Although generally believed to have been solidly loyal, Hastings had its share of Reformers too, and the region was in fact bitterly divided over a number of issues. The story includes a Patriots' conspiracy to take Kingston, the pirating and burning of a passenger ship on the St Lawrence, the posting of a hundred-man guard to Belleville, the Battle of the Windmill (near Prescott), conflict between Orangemen and Catholics, and a strange case of bank robbers near Cobourg.

More than eighty men of the district were arrested and charged with treason during this period; some spent months in prison. In the end none was convicted, and the identities of those who actually participated will never be certain.

Drawing on provincial records, newspapers of the day, and the private papers of families of the area, Boyce reconstructs a turbulent time in Ontario's past, and sheds new light on the history of the province's eastern region.

BETSY DEWAR BOYCE is a writer living in Belleville, Ontario.

The Rebels of Hastings

BETSY DEWAR BOYCE

UNIVERSITY OF TORONTO PRESS
Toronto Buffalo London

© University of Toronto Press 1992
Toronto Buffalo London
Printed in Canada

ISBN 0-8020-5986-4
ISBN 0-8020-6920-7

Printed on acid-free paper

Canadian Cataloguing in Publication Data
Boyce, Betsy
The rebels of Hastings

Includes bibliographical references and index.
ISBN 0-8020-5986-4 (bound) ISBN 0-8020-6920-7 (pbk.)

1. Hastings (Ont. : County) – History.
2. Hastings (Ont. : County) – History, Military.
3. Canada – History – Rebellion, 1837–1838.
I. Title.

FC3095.H37B6 1992   971.3'58502   C91-095666-9
F1059.H37B6 1992   72799

This book has been published with the help of a grant from the
Social Science Federation of Canada, using funds provided by
the Social Sciences and Humanities Research Council of Canada.

Contents

Acknowledgments

It would not have been possible to do the research for this book without the help of many people in many places, and although there are too many to name here, I am grateful to all of them. The assistance provided by the Ontario Arts Council for carrying out the research is also gratefully acknowledged.

Almost all the material for such a history comes from libraries and archives, and wherever the material has been gathered, librarians have given their willing help. Those who have been called upon most often have been in the Reference Department of the Belleville Public Library. My thanks go especially to Elizabeth Mitchell, Betty Law, and Karen Peterson. Of all those who have helped along the way, a few have given time and effort that is here gratefully acknowledged. Dr Elwood Jones of the Canadian History Department at Trent University kindly read an earlier version of the manuscript and made valuable suggestions. While I could not follow all of them, they did result in changes of which I hope he will approve. The unknown readers who assessed the manuscript for publication supplied critiques that have helped immeasurably in correcting and improving it. Dr Colin Read of the University of Western Ontario was good enough to send information about sources at the beginning of my research on the subject. William Lamb, president of the Canadian Methodist Historical Society, supplied me with material not easily available elsewhere. Lois Foster of the Hastings County Historical Society, with her wide-ranging knowledge of Belleville history, its buildings and its people, has given me the benefit of her extensive files. I appreciate the detailed editing, as well as the encouragement, which Alice Grey provided out of her knowledge and experience. Other help has come from Nick and Helma Mika, F.G.F.

Skill, Robert Cupido in the Baldwin Room at the Metropolitan Toronto Reference Library, and Patricia Kennedy at the National Archives, who has more than once taken time to discuss some details. My son Robert introduced me to and instructed me in the use of a computer, without which this manuscript would never have been finished. Lastly, I owe a great debt to Gerald Boyce, historian, writer, and teacher. He is not related to me, but he must be considered the godfather of *The Rebels of Hastings*. Like any other godfather, he cannot be held responsible for how the infant has turned out.

(Sir) Richard Bonnycastle, British officer, acting commander at Fort Henry during the rebellion years

Anthony Manahan, Hastings MLA, colonel of Third Hastings Militia Regiment, and Elijah Ketcheson, Hastings magistrate, lieutenant in First Hastings Militia Regiment

Billa Flint, Belleville businessman, president of the police board 1836–40, and Marshall Spring Bidwell, Lennox and Addington MLA and Reform speaker of the house 1829–36

Nelson Reynolds, Belleville merchant, one of those accused of treason in 1837, shown in the uniform of the Prince Consort's Own Rifle Brigade, about 1855

George, Baron de Rottenburg, British officer in command of the Hastings and Bay of Quinte militia 1838–9

Louisa Ridley, daughter of Dr George Ridley of Belleville, married Baron de Rottenburg in 1839.

Edmund Murney, Hastings MLA, Belleville lawyer and magistrate

Mrs Simpson's Tavern, from a painting by an unknown nineteenth-century artist. John and Margaret Simpson opened one of the first taverns in the district in 1789. After John's death his wife continued the business, replacing the original log house in 1827 by the frame building shown here. It stood at the corner of Front and Dundas streets in Belleville until 1973, when it was demolished for road-widening.

Belleville in the early 1830s, from a drawing by Thomas Burrowes, surveyor

Battle of the Windmill

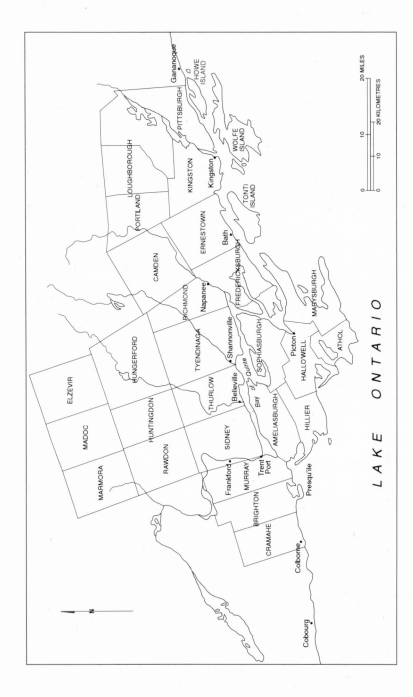

Hastings County and the surrounding area

The Rebels of Hastings

Introduction

This is an account of the Rebellion of 1837 as it involved people in the eastern part of Upper Canada, especially around the Bay of Quinte and with particular attention to Hastings County. It was prompted by reading the claims submitted by residents of the county in 1845 to a commission appointed under the Rebellion Losses Bill. These documents raised an obvious question: how could people in Hastings County have any claim for compensation arising out of a rebellion that took place in Toronto – at that time distant at least two days journey – when they were living in an area generally believed to have been unaffected by the rebellion or the Patriot incursions which followed it? *The Rebels of Hastings* is the result of research made over a number of years in order to answer that question, research that has provided a few surprises.

Although the Rebellion of 1837 is one of the most exciting occurrences of the nineteenth century in Upper Canada, now Ontario, even those residents whose schooldays were spent in the province often know very little about it. This is not because there is any lack of information. Books and articles have been written about the rebellion ever since it took place, and those who study Canadian history at any advanced level are acquainted with a wide range of literature on the subject. Other people, however, get their ideas about historical events from more condensed sources, from school books, newspapers and magazines, and from casual references. The points that are generally remembered are these: that the rebellion was led by William Lyon Mackenzie; that he had published a newspaper in which he criticized the ruling clique in Toronto, the Family Compact; that he provoked this group until some of their young relatives wrecked his press and dumped his types into Toronto Bay; that later on he gathered rebels at Montgomery's Tavern just north of the city; and that the rebels, most of them armed only with pikes and hayforks, were quickly defeated and set on the run. Altogether it is usually seen as a rather puny attempt at revolution, not to be taken very seriously.

It is true there are elements of farce in the story. Mackenzie himself can be portrayed as a figure of fun. He was a small man with a large bald head, which he covered with a flaming red wig. During the crucial days at the beginning of December 1837 he wrapped himself in seven layers of coats and shawls, stamped about like a minor Napoleon trying to rally his troops, and is said to have personally held up the mail coach. Then there was the governor, Sir Francis Bond Head, so self-satisfied he could not be persuaded that anyone would follow the hothead Mackenzie to rebel against him. Convinced only when the rebels had established their camp two or three miles away, he excitedly rushed his family onto steamboats in Toronto harbour and finally allowed the militia to be armed. There was the occasion two days before the rebellion when the high sheriff of York and a score of picked men hid in the bushes by the side of Yonge Street to wait for the rebels' advance on Toronto. When the rebels appeared, the sheriff's men fired on them, the fire was returned, and this sudden engagement frightened both parties so much they ran from each other as fast as their heels would carry them. Chiefly, however, what makes the rebellion seem ridiculous is that when the confrontation came on 7 December 1837, after Mackenzie's frenetic efforts to round up his followers and the furore in Toronto to protect the city from fire and destruction, with messengers sent across the province calling on all loyal men to come to the defence of the government, the rebellion collapsed in about half an hour. It has become the fashion for writers to describe it as 'comic opera.'

But men died. Several died within three or four days around the rebel camp. Rebel leaders Samuel Lount and Peter Matthews were hanged, and twenty others followed them to the gallows during the next year. Hundreds suffered arrest and imprisonment. Scores were transported to the prison colony of Tasmania, then so remote it seemed a living death. Thousands left the country, and thousands who stayed had their lives disrupted, some by petty persecution or loss of property, others by militia duty which was often irksome and sometimes dangerous. Plainly the rebellion did not end on the seventh of December on Yonge Street. It was the aftermath of that battle that caused most of the turmoil around the province, including in Hastings County.

Mackenzie escaped to the United States, and about him gathered the so-called Patriot Army. This was made up of some Canadian fugitives and a large number of Americans, with support from the still greater membership of the Hunters Lodges. The result was what is known in the northern states as the Patriot War, which often had semi-official support from state politicians and militia. There were raids across the border, most of them into the western half of the province, but the biggest engagement of the rebellion years in Upper Canada took place near Prescott at what is known as the Battle of the Windmill.

Those who have written about the year that followed the Yonge Street rising have usually focused on the western half of the province, that is, from Toronto to Windsor. It has been said that 'the whole eastern half of the province was tranquilly loyal,' a statement that would have astonished the people of Hastings at the time.[1] After December 1837 the whole province was so rocked by the Patriot outrages that only someone living deep in the backwoods could have been unaffected by the warlike atmosphere, and Hastings County was as much disturbed as other places along the front. There were more men imprisoned in the Midland District, made up of Hastings, Lennox and Addington, and Frontenac counties, than in all the rest of Upper Canada east of Toronto, and many of them lived in Hastings. The people of Hastings were anything but tranquil; they were in a state of anxious excitement, a state induced by the fears of some about the disloyalty of others.

It has also often been assumed that the district was unaffected by the rebellion because the inhabitants were descended from United Empire Loyalists and therefore gave complete support to the government. This is far from the whole truth. The United Empire Loyalist settlement had been established about fifty years before the rebellion, and immigrants from the United States as well as from a changing Britain had come into the area since that time. It is also true that while very few descendants of the United Empire Loyalists took any part in the rebellion, they were by no means all supporters of the government. For several reasons many were Reformers and, as will be seen, differences between political groups were often deep and sometimes violent. It seems these differences may account for some of the arrests and charges of treason that followed the rebellion. It was easy, and perhaps natural, to accuse Reformers of being responsible for the rebellion, although it had been led by a comparatively small group of radicals.

The United Empire Loyalists earned their name by loyalty to Great Britain, that is, to the Crown, during the American Revolution. Almost without exception they and their descendants retained this loyalty for generations. At the same time they had, by definition, lived in the Thirteen

Colonies; they were American and had absorbed certain American ideas. They were people of the frontier, self-reliant by necessity, more inclined to be ruled by their own good sense and conscience than by the edicts of someone appointed to office. They were not the best subjects for the elitist state that was imposed on them in the constitution of 1791 by which Upper Canada came into being. At that time no doubt many of them were in favour of it, and quite a few continued to support it because they benefited in some way. This might be by appointment to the legislative or executive councils. No Hastings man received this honour, but several in Kingston did. There were many other office holders, local magistrates being the most important, but even minor posts were treasured because they were marks of distinction as well as sources of income. Militia appointments were also made by the government to reward, and secure, loyalty from those receiving them.[2] Those to whom the government made large land grants were likely to support it, and so were all those who continued to believe that it protected their interests in any way, or who saw the government at York as it liked to represent itself, an extension of the British Crown.

This is not to say that Reformers were distinguished by being disloyal to the Crown, but they were people who, for various reasons, wanted some change in the rules by which government was carried on. It might be that they were opposed to the arbitrary way in which land was given out or appointments were made. They might be discontented about the painfully slow development of a potentially rich country when no one could ignore the bustling activity south of the border. It seemed to some Reformers that ordinary people could get things done better and faster if control of expenditures were to be handed over to their elected assembly. Under the constitution most of the power was held by the appointed legislative and executive councils, the 'Family Compact' as they came to be known. This represented for the most part the well-to-do, the lawyers, and the land developers of their day. There is a strong element of class conflict in the growing tension between groups before the rebellion.

Religion was another subject for dissension, one of the most important in Hastings County. In the beginning the Church of England had been uniquely favoured with certain privileges as well as the proceeds from a seventh of all granted land, a gift that brought an immediate and long-lasting protest from all the other sects. The Presbyterian Church, which was the established church of Scotland, and the Roman Catholic Church, which was established in Lower Canada, wanted to share in the advantages. It brought just as loud opposition from those churches which held there should be no such thing as established, or government-sponsored, churches at all. Chief among these was the Methodist Church, whose congregations by the time of the rebellion made it the most numerous denomination in Hastings County. When these people also divided among themselves over internal problems, created by politics as much as religion, another reason was added for wrangling and bitterness.

Originally, in examining the rebellion losses claims, it seemed unlikely that Hastings County harboured any rebels or dangerous conspirators during 1837 and 1838. Research at first revealed nothing that would have justified the magistrates in arresting their fellow citizens and charging them with serious crimes, some of which carried the death penalty. Of those who were sent down to the district jail at Kingston or to Fort Henry most were never tried, and not enough evidence was brought against any of the rest to convict them. It was hard to believe, for instance, in the guilt of the eight men, solid citizens all, whom the magistrates seized as soon as they got news that Mackenzie's men had gathered at Montgomery's Tavern. It seemed as if they and all the later Hastings prisoners were guilty of nothing more than of belonging to the opposition political party, and that the magistrates acted vindictively, or merely out of panic, in charging them.

In fact, all the activity by the local authorities that followed the first alarm – the arrests, the calling out of the militia, bringing the arms from Fort Henry for all the militia regiments in Northumberland, Prince Edward, Lennox and Addington, and Hastings, and placing a guard of 240 men in Belleville – all of it seems a tremendous overreaction to a danger that was already past by the time they were ready to meet it. The local authorities were too fearful; they were battling shadows. Only after reading a great many documents concerning the rebellion, Hastings County, and the people who lived there at the time, do events take on a different colour, and it is a darker hue than at first appeared. Even though none of the Hastings men was convicted of treason, it is no longer possible to say with any confidence that they were all as innocent as they claimed. Treachery appears to have existed even if it was never identified beyond reasonable doubt. Clifton McCollom had been a Belleville magistrate before he was sent into exile in 1837, and his letters to William Lyon Mackenzie are real enough. So were the sleighs full of armed men at Shannonville and on the back roads of Hastings on the eve of the Patriots' intended attack on Kingston, as were the large quantities of ammunition found afterwards abandoned in the woods near Napanee. The accounts of Richard Bonnycastle and of Mackenzie corroborate each other about the conspiracy in preparing that attack.[3] Donald McLeod, the Canadian Patriot general, wrote about the Hastings men who were responsible for burning the *Sir*

Robert Peel. The latter were at the time out of the country, but the depositions against farmer Cornelius Parks suggest that at least one cell of Hunters was operating in Thurlow Township. It is not always true that where there is smoke there must be fire, but when smoke is drifting up from so many sources it does seem there are probably at least a few flames licking through the underbrush.

The times made for distrust and suspicion. Any of us would feel decidedly uneasy to be living among neighbours who might prove to be rebels or in collusion with rebels, particularly when there was frequent bad news, and worse rumour, of piracy, brigandage, and invasion. Even today a report of an incursion by several hundred armed men at Niagara or Windsor or Prescott would be enough to alarm the whole province, and today there are police and a professional army to protect the country. In 1837–9 the people around the Bay of Quinte, like others in the colony, had for the most part to rely on themselves to protect their homes and communities against an elusive enemy who could hide behind the American border, gathering a small army wherever he chose. In February 1838 this enemy, and Mackenzie had a share in the plan, chose the area around Oswego and prepared to strike a major blow at Kingston. The mild winter delayed the attack, the plan became known on the Canadian side, and in the absence of the British regulars the militia regiments were called out. These were made up of men more accustomed to farming than to soldiering, but what the militiamen lacked in discipline and experience they made up in numbers. They came from Hastings and from all around the Bay, and from as far down the St. Lawrence as Brockville. By his elaborate preparations Richard Bonnycastle did not win a famous victory, but he did ensure the safety of Fort Henry and the Bay of Quinte.

It is true some of the militiamen contributed to the lawlessness of those years. There were startling events, not always a credit to the County of Hastings, but they do at least make this a colourful period in its history. Any sketch of it is enhanced by the arrival in Belleville in 1838 of Captain George, Baron De Rottenburg, and by his nuptials there the following year. John Wedderburn Dunbar Moodie, husband of Susanna, came about the same time as paymaster for the militia the baron commanded, and some description of different factions in Hastings and of life in the militia at that time is to be found in his letters to his wife.[4]

In the end, what did it all accomplish? It has been said that the only result was suffering and the evils of a minor war. It has also been said that, although painful at the time, it was the cause of responsible government being granted to Upper Canada. It is not possible to ignore the destructive nature of the hostilities, the loss of life, of livelihood, of property. At the same time the rebellion brought Lord Durham's commission, the Durham Report, and a recommendation for the union of the two Canadas and the granting of responsible government. This endorsement encouraged Robert Baldwin and his Reform party, so that they renewed their efforts and did not give up pressing the governors and the Colonial Office until responsible government was a reality. After three years of the union the governor-general wrote, no doubt despondently, that the principle had already been conceded, [5] although it was to be another five years before the new relationship was firmly established.

The rebels had broken with the rest of their party. When they were frustrated in their efforts to get control of government into the hands of elected representatives, they set a new goal: independence. Most Reformers did not join them either in taking up arms or in seeking a republic. When the Reformers of Hastings met at Hayden's Tavern in 1837, they declared their determination to secure the reforms Mackenzie was advocating across the province.[6] The rebellion did not win any of them. The great underlying principle in which they believed, however, was that the executive, or cabinet, must be responsible to the majority in the legislature. The British government and its representatives, the governors, had opposed granting this for various reasons. Partly it was to keep control of colonial trade in British hands, but also they felt a disgust for the kind of party politics that must follow and, as they saw it, the inevitable strife and corruption that went with such politics. Not everyone would say they were wrong. On the other hand, neither strife nor corruption had been eliminated by the constitution the British parliament had drafted in 1791.

They had in the end to give way. Several factors brought about the transformation of government in the Canadas, and the rebellion was one of them. After that upheaval the moderates came into their own and, in due course, brought about fundamental change. For better or for worse, the Reformers of Hastings, and of the rest of the country, were finally triumphant. Fortunately the loyalists were also successful in defeating invaders and those who would have weakened the country in its infancy by cutting it loose from Britain and therefore adrift in the powerful magnetic field of the United States.

It is never easy to uncover the history of events that took place at least 150 years ago. Apart from any difficulty in finding the material, much of it is handwritten. Any official letter was written by a secretary who qualified for the position by his penmanship, and there are others like Billa Flint, a merchant in Belleville, and John Macaulay, a lawyer of Kingston, whose letters are as easy to read as the printed page. But there is writing that ranges from difficult to unreadable. The original spelling often gives added colour to these documents and has been interrupted by '[sic]' as little as possible. Old newspapers can also cause some eyestrain. However important the local event, it seldom found its way onto the front page but was buried in a long column of print somewhere inside. Since there is not always a heading, it is necessary to look over every item. To give the old-time printer his due, he made fewer spelling and typographical errors than are to be found in later newspapers, but unfortunately he had poorer types to use, some of them very small, some worn and uneven. The *Intelligencer* of Belleville has been published since 1834, but a fire in January 1863 destroyed almost all the files, a great loss to research in Belleville and Hastings.[7] Considerable use has been made here of Kingston newspapers, particularly the *Chronicle and Gazette*. Finally, there is the difficulty that most of this material is on microfilm which is usually imperfect and well used. The work of burrowing into all these archives, however, is in the service of understanding a rebellion that involved thousands of people and resulted in far-reaching changes. It is justified if it helps to explain why the rebellion occurred, what happened during those years, and a little of the outcome.

In all of this the people of Hastings County played an important part, a part that has been largely buried and forgotten, but which seems well worth the effort of bringing again into the light.

GUNPOWDER

1 In the Beginning

The Rebellion of 1837 in Upper Canada was led by William Lyon Mackenzie, a fiery newspaper publisher in Toronto, and those who took part in it lived in the city or in the townships around it. For years, however, Mackenzie had been raising a clamour all around the province, and in the months before the rebels gathered at John Montgomery's Tavern on Yonge Street, he had been drumming up support for political unions. Such societies had been formed several times in the past, usually to influence a single election. This campaign had a larger purpose for Mackenzie hoped that by its size it would persuade the government to reform the whole political system of the colony. Outside the Toronto area he fostered independent unions by correspondence. Contrary to much that has been written, Reform sentiment was strong in Hastings County. Shortly before the rebellion there was a meeting at Hayden's Tavern in Thurlow Township for the apparent purpose of organizing a political union, and it attracted a number of prominent residents.[1] None of the Hastings men joined in the rebellion, but when news of it burst upon the district the local authorities and other members of the government party, the Tories, were afraid Reformers had been plotting with Mackenzie, and all who were known to have attended the Thurlow meeting were treated as conspirators. There is evidence that some Hastings men were at least in sympathy with the rebellion, but suspicion fell on everyone in the Reform party, and in the excitement of the times the magistrates' response was to arrest many of the leaders and clap them in jail. The result, not unnaturally, was to drive the two sides even further apart and raise their quarrel to a new level of acrimony.

Among people in any community there will arise differences of opinion.

For several reasons the people of Hastings County seem to have held their different opinions more fiercely than did most of their neighbours. It is not possible to discover everything that led up to this state of affairs, but a brief look at the life and growth of the county from its beginning fifty years before will help to explain the predicament in which its people found themselves during the rebellion years of 1837 to 1839.

Geography was the primary factor in the early settlement of Hastings County. Before Lake Ontario narrows into the St Lawrence River at Kingston, its northern shore is broken for about seventy miles by a scattering of islands and projections that are almost islands. The most westerly of these, in fact, is called Presqu'ile, a small finger of land that is today a provincial park. Next to it there is the larger area of Prince Edward County, joined to the mainland at The Carrying Place, in times past an important portage between the lake and the Bay of Quinte.[2] With its ragged shoreline, cut by inlets and reaches, this county almost encloses the Bay, whose waters are bordered on the north by Hastings County. The southwest corner of Hastings is marked by Trenton, formerly Trent Port, at the base of the Trent waterway, and the southeast corner, by the town of Deseronto. Between them, at the mouth of the Moira River, is Belleville, the largest city and the centre of administration. All this land was originally part of the extensive hunting grounds of the Mississauga Indians, who conceded it, except for four hundred acres around the mouth of the Moira, in 1783.[3]

After the American Revolution there was an exodus from the United States of about sixty thousand people who remained loyal to Great Britain. Some chose not to live in the new and raucous republic, but most were driven out, sometimes with physical abuse, their property confiscated or stolen. As reward for their loyalty, the British government granted them land in the colonies. Probably as many as forty thousand moved north, the greater number to the colony of New Brunswick, created for them in upper Nova Scotia. Others sought refuge in the old province of Quebec, which at that time comprised all the land west of New Brunswick as far as the Hudson's Bay Company territories. In 1783 British ships brought about six thousand from New York to be settled along the upper St Lawrence and the Bay of Quinte. One group stayed in the Eastern Townships. Some went to Newark, now Niagara-on-the-Lake, under the protection of Fort George. About half of the Mohawks, faithful allies of the British throughout the fighting, went to land set aside for them along the Grand River, the rest to a tract at Deseronto. As far as possible people were settled according to the military units in which the men had fought, such as the Glengarry Highland Regiment, whose members were sent to the county that bears the regiment's name. Other companies were placed along the shore as far west as Marysburgh in Prince Edward County.[4] The disposition of all these veterans in their units was made partly to help the newcomers, isolated as they were in the forest wilderness, so that they should at least not be among strangers. It was also a defence measure to provide a shield against American aggression. Michael Grass and Peter Van Alstine each led a company of somewhat different composition, one to Cataraqui, the other to Kingston. These were called Associated Loyalist Companies because they were made up of an assortment of civilians and military veterans.[5] They were mostly small farmers and tradesmen, and they were the source of Kingston's growth and importance as it became, and for decades remained, the largest town in Upper Canada.

The settlement of Hastings County came a little later. It was not needed for the first influx of settlers in 1784, so that surveying was not begun for another three years, and then it proceeded slowly. In the front townships of Sidney and Thurlow it was not completed until after 1795. From the beginning, however, there were people who moved onto the land, especially near the mouth of the Moira, content to be squatters until they could apply for deeds. The Mississaugas retained ownership of this land around the Moira until 1815, when it was finally surveyed as a town plot.[6]

Because of the long delay in opening up this desirable area, a number of people, beginning in the early 1780s, had made their own arrangements with the Indians. The first were traders who dealt in goods for which the Indians exchanged furs, as well as in items needed by pioneer families. They were joined by a variety of enterprising settlers.[7] The 1816 plan shows that in the centre of what is now Belleville there were two blacksmiths, two distilleries, a brewery, a hatter's shop, and mills belonging to John W. Meyers and Thomas Coleman on the east side of the river. The survey caused acute anxiety to most of the residents since they had no deeds to the land on which they had put up their houses and buildings, some of which lay across the new road allowances. Their lots were now open for sale, and they anxiously pressed their member of the legislature, James McNabb, to represent their prior claim to the ground on which they had built. Happily he was, for the most part, successful.

Without exaggerating its significance, it is possible to see in this first unauthorized settlement by Bellevillians and some others in the front of Hastings an indication of a certain independence of spirit among the founders of the county, later reflected in the large number of Reformers in the area. On the other hand, there was a strong conservative sentiment among them, particularly on any question that related to the British connection, so that before long there were two groups, fairly well balanced, with opposite views on a variety of subjects. It would be some time before there were any parties, Tory or Reform, but no time at all before people held great differences of opinion. Yet they had a good deal in common. There was the American experience which marked all of them to some degree. All shared the difficulty of establishing a family in a strange and uncompromising landscape. The British government gave them help in the first years, but for everyone there were still many trials.

All those people who had supported the British during the American Revolution, mercenaries, militiamen, or civilians, had proved their loyalty and had earned the title of United Empire Loyalist (UEL). A grant of two hundred acres of land was made to each family, and the same to each child, to the boys when they reached twenty-one and to the girls when they married. Officers were given additional grants according to their rank. All land in the colony of Quebec, however, was held in seigneurial fiefs, and to this the Loyalists strongly objected, as they did to finding themselves subject to French civil law. They petitioned the British government to repay their loyalty and all they had sacrificed for it by giving them their own laws, particularly the right to own land in freehold. The British government acceded to their request by passing the Constitutional Act, often called the Canada Act, in 1791. By this act Quebec was divided by a line that met the St Lawrence just below the present city of Cornwall to create Upper and Lower Canada. The next year Governor John Graves Simcoe was sent out to proclaim the act, to call together the first parliament of the new upper province, and to guide its members in enacting the first laws.

This constitution of 1791 requires some explanation since it not only provided the framework for the province of Upper Canada but in time gave rise to a level of controversy that threatened to shake it apart. It was written by a British government that wanted to be sure above all that the Canadas did not follow the United States out of the British Empire. British parliamentarians believed that disaster had occurred because the inhabitants had been allowed to develop too much independence and too little respect for authority. They took care to put in all possible safeguards against any repetition of these evils, and the result was an act that attempted to make Upper Canada into a little England.

The king was to be represented by a governor sent from England.[8] He would appoint leading citizens to a legislative council, similar to the House of Lords. Appointments were for life, and it was intended that, in time, members would be given hereditary titles. Fortunately there was always something absurd about backwoods peerages, so that the colony was saved from having a Robinson, Duke of Toronto, or a Baron Hagerman of Kingston, or Hastings.[9] The governor was also to appoint an executive council to advise him and to carry on the business of government, in the same manner as the British cabinet. There was to be an elected assembly or parliament with limited powers. With the hope of one day making the Church of England the established church, one seventh of all land granted was to be set aside to support 'a Protestant clergy,' a phrase that in England at the time meant only clergy of the Church of England, but in Canada was bound to be interpreted differently by members of various Protestant denominations.

The trouble with this constitution was that it had been manufactured in Europe and was not suited to the very different conditions of North America. It was also drawn up late in the eighteenth century just as the nineteenth was about to bring profound social change, to North America as to Europe. As time went on, people looked for change and improvement, and rumbles of discontent were heard when improvement was disappointingly slow to come about. The voters sent their local members to the assembly to effect the changes they wanted, but while the legislative assembly could pass any bill at all, none could become law unless approved by the legislative council, and the appointed council members were extremely reluctant to pass any law that was likely to hurt their own interests.

The government very soon came to be dominated by a small group of people, some of whom sat on both the legislative and the executive councils. It is true that the population was not large and the number of men who had the education and the resources to take such positions was limited. This may also be the explanation for their tendency to appoint their relatives to government posts, so that in time they became known as the Family Compact.[10] Whether or not the title was justified there is no denying that a small group of people combined to wield a great deal of influence. Their power came not only from their function as legislators, but also from the thousands of acres of public land they had in their gift, and from their use of patronage. As the population grew, so did the number of functionaries. Senior positions were filled from England, but there were many lesser ones to be awarded by the government at the little capital of York.

The principal way in which the council members exercised control and promoted their own views was by the appointment of magistrates. In the absence of municipal government the magistrates had authority over almost all local affairs. They were the peace officers. They sat together in the courts of quarter session, where they decided such things as the location of roads, the granting of licences, and the levy of local taxes. They formed a court of first instance and had judicial power in all minor cases, both civil and criminal. They affected the average citizen more immediately and importantly than did any other arm of government, and the members of the Family Compact did their best to appoint only those men whose politics agreed with their own. Two or three magistrates could sit as a court of requests, not unlike the modern small claims court. These courts did a great deal of useful work over the years, but this of course depended on the presence of capable magistrates. From Ameliasburgh forty-seven 'dutiful and loyal Inhabitants' wrote to complain that 'From the absence of one of our Justices of the Peace and the premature old age of the other with its concomitant infirmities, delinquents escape punishment and our Courts of Requests are neglected and disgraced by intemperance.'[11] These courts were frequently held in taverns, a circumstance not likely to contribute to their sobriety.

Another form of patronage that forged the bonds of loyalty between the government and individuals was the use of militia commissions. Because of recent experience defence was very much on the minds of these frontier people, and of their British protectors. By law all male citizens between the ages of sixteen and sixty were required to enrol for militia service. One of the earliest groups organized in Upper Canada was the Hastings militia. Governor Simcoe had named John Ferguson to the old English office of Lieutenant of the County of Hastings. On 29 November 1798 Ferguson, a merchant at that time in Kingston, wrote to William Bell of Sidney, his friend and protégé,[12] that he had recommended him for a commission as captain of a company and adjutant of a battalion of militia. At the same time he gave Bell detailed instructions for notifying the men of Sidney, Rawdon, and 'up the Creek' to attend the first meeting, at the home of William Sherrar in the fifth concession of Sidney on 5 December.[13] Ferguson signed Bell's commission but warned him to go at once to York to have the governor confirm it before anyone found out about it. There were, after all, men with at least as good a claim as Bell to the appointment, and there may well have been some jealousy because Ferguson had bestowed it upon his friend. A commission gave a man responsibilities, but it also carried considerable social prestige. Whether he went secretly to York or not, Bell's commission was confirmed. He proved to be a dedicated officer. From reading his correspondence over the next twenty-five years, it is hard to believe anyone could have done more.

During the War of 1812–14 the militia gained experience. In addition to the infantry and cavalry there was a Provincial Marine Service for volunteer navy men, and Kingston was one of the principal naval stations. Other units fought alongside the British regiments. One of these was a troop of Provincial Dragoons raised by Captain Thomas Coleman of Belleville. It is uncertain how long they were active, but by official report they were 'present at St David's, at the Capture made at Fort Stoper and Black Rock Sandwich' on 31 August 1813.[14] With peace restored, however, the old fervour subsided, in Hastings County as in the rest of the province, where, apart from a few volunteer companies, men turned out once a year as required by law, sometimes to be drilled, sometimes to do no more than sign their names. Hastings did have a volunteer company which is said to have met every two weeks, to drill in a field at the corner of Front and Dundas streets in good weather, or nearby in Mrs Simpson's Tavern in bad.

The British government, through the Colonial Office, appointed not only the governor but other officials of some importance. In 1808 David McGregor Rogers, the Hastings-Northumberland member of the assembly and a United Empire Loyalist, complained about appointments made in England, the giving of offices to favourites there, while 'Americans' were ignored.[15] All government appointments were eagerly sought. The clerk of the court died one morning in Picton at six o'clock, and that same day John McCuaig sent off a letter asking to be appointed in his place. He hoped for a favourable reply as 'he was anxious to recoup the losses to which a protracted illness had subjected him.'[16] Another application came from Edward Beeston, the collector of customs at Hallowell, who thought he should have the job because he had taken in just over two pounds in the past two months, not enough to support his family.[17] Letters asking for appointments seldom mentioned any qualification for the post, only the applicant's need and, whenever possible, military service. There was no independent civil service, then or for a very long time to come. The qualification wanted was loyalty, to the Crown, and above all to the government. Besides military service, being a member of a United Empire Loyalist family was one recommendation, and belonging to the Church of England was also helpful.

Although from the inception of Upper Canada counties had been drawn on the map, these at first represented only great tracts of forest with few inhabitants. For the purpose of administration they were grouped into districts, four in the beginning, but as the population grew these were divided, usually along county lines, until by 1837 there were thirteen. The county served as the unit for the election of members to the legislature and for the organization of the militia. Hastings was part of the Midland District, which extended from Gananoque to the Trent River and included the counties of Frontenac, Lennox and Addington, and Prince Edward. The last named county became Prince Edward District in 1831.

Evidence of the independent spirit among settlers of Hastings County can be seen in the archives of Sidney Township, where it is recorded that a town meeting was held as early as 1790. Such meetings were not authorized until September 1792, and even then some members of the government thought them dangerously republican. The minutes of the 1790 meeting record that a number of the inhabitants met at the home of Aron Rose 'to Act upon Town Business.' John W. Meyers was elected moderator, a position he held until the end of 1793. There were also a town clerk, a constable, path-masters, and fence viewers. There was no tax collector, but at the 1792 meeting the town clerk was authorized to charge sixpence for entering each person's cattle mark in the record.[18]

The population of Hastings county grew slowly, as did that of the whole province. Governor Simcoe believed many loyal people remained in the States, held back from leaving the county only by circumstances. He therefore held out to them the same offer of land grants that had been given to the United Empire Loyalists, with good results. After a few years, however, the United Empire Loyalists became resentful of these johnny-come-late-lys, accusing them of coming to Canada not from convictions of loyalty but only to get free land, and the offer had to be withdrawn in 1798. In the meantime, however, it had added many useful citizens to Upper Canada, since everyone agreed that Americans made the best immigrants. They were accustomed to the life and able to cope with the demands of a pioneer homestead in a way European settlers were seldom able to do. Even without the inducement of free land they continued to enter the country and many settled in Hastings County. No doubt Hastings County attracted more settlers than the rest of the Midland District because it had more available agricultural land. The Canadian Shield dominates the landscape north of the lower two tiers of townships and then angles down towards Kingston. This leaves Frontenac with little productive hinterland, and Prince Edward County was early taken up by United Empire Loyalist families. Lennox and Addington shares many of the same characteristics as Hastings, and therefore much of the same history, pattern of immigration, and social tensions. Another group who added to the population of both these counties was made up of children of United Empire Loyalist families. As the young people came of age, most of them looked for fertile land on which to farm, and many found it here. There was also some immigration from Great Britain, which included Ireland, although this did not account for any large number until the 1820s, and more especially the 1830s. It became a complaint often heard that, in contrast to the United States, where immigrants poured in by the hundred thousands, Upper Canada grew and developed at a snail's pace. Many people came into the Canadas, but more often than not they moved on south.

At first the settlers were fully occupied in clearing some land, getting shelter, raising food, and cutting firewood to keep them through the winters, too busy to think of much that lay beyond their own homesteads. Catherine Chrysler was the daughter of a United Empire Loyalist family who settled in Sidney, and years later she recalled: 'We never thought of these privations ... no unsettled minds, no political strife about church, government, or squabbling municipal councils. We left everything to our faithful Governor. I have often heard my father and mother say that they had no cause for complaint in any shape, and were always thankful to the Government for their kind assistance in hour of need.'[19]

It may be that Catherine Chrysler reflected a rosier light on those early days than they enjoyed at the time, but it is true that the pioneers seldom had time for more than their own life and work, their families and immediate neighbours. As time went on, however, horizons broadened and they began to look for improvements that failed to materialize. And always, just across the border, they had a view of phenomenal growth and development to sharpen the edge of their discontent. Grievances began to accumulate, most of them centred on the subjects of land, religion, arbitrary government, and a general dissatisfaction with the backwardness of the colony.

Perhaps the chief complaint was about the handling of land grants. In the beginning the only wealth of the colony was land, and everything depended on its distribution and use. The objective should have to establish settlers. Instead, by 1838, fifty-four years after the beginning of the colony, and when of the 17,000,000 surveyed acres all but 1,600,000 had been given out,[20] the population was still under 500,000.[21] The Family Compact, not the assembly, controlled the granting of land through the executive council, and their management proved to be erratic, inefficient, and self-serving. Not only was every seventh lot given to clergy reserves,[22] but another seventh was reserved as Crown land, of which the council designated large tracts to support road building, education, or anything the council wanted to legislate but for which it had no funds. In addition, grants were often unreasonably large. In 1795 Edward Carscallen wrote to the executive council 'praying for 1400 Acres in the Midland District in part of the 2000 to which he is entitled as a reduced Lieut.'[23] At first whole townships were given out to men who promised to settle fifteen loyal families in them within four years. One day in 1792 thirty townships were given out in this way, among them Huntingdon, Rawdon, Loughborough, and Murray. The condition was not met in these four, and in May 1796 they were opened up for individual settlement.[24] Even the two-hundred-acre lots were more than a man could clear in a lifetime, and by their size they separated neighbours and discouraged community.

With so much land held for speculation, prices remained low. The two hundred acres granted to daughters of United Empire Loyalist families were often sold, and it was said 'the general price of these grants was from a gallon of rum up to perhaps six pounds.'[25] In 1815 Richard Cartwright of Kingston left in his will 28,632 acres, of which 5,292 were in the Midland District.[26] From time to time the legislative assembly passed bills to increase the trifling tax on 'wild lands,' which would not only encourage their sale and development but would add much needed funds to the provincial treasury. The legislative council, however, always refused to approve such bills, all the members being large landowners. By 1838 five legislative councillors and their families held among them fifty thousand acres of land.[27] On the other hand, bona fide settlers often met with several obstacles. They might be sent to a location that was not where they wanted to go, or onto poor agricultural land. The rules and fees for obtaining a patent were different in different places, might change at any time, and were not always easy to discover. During the 1830s in Hastings County the agent came to Belleville just one day a month to do business with those wanting to obtain land. And many would-be owners met with another difficulty. For the eleven years from 1834 to 1845 the deputy registrars, Robert Smith and Robert McLean, pocketed fees for registering the deeds of land purchasers, and at the end of that time it was found they had failed to register any of them, preferring to pass their time in local taverns. The resulting confusion in titles throughout the county required an act of parliament to set things right, at least so far as that was possible.[28] The whole system, it seems, was poorly supervised and controlled. Peter Robinson, brother of John Beverley, was successful in settling many Irish immigrants, including some in the back townships of Hastings County, and he was the founder of Peterborough. When a new system of land sales was introduced in 1825,[29] he was made commissioner of crown lands with overall responsibility for the distribution of land, either by sale or by grant to those who were still entitled to free land. When he suffered a stroke in 1836, an acting surveyor general took over his office and discovered that his accounts were short by £11,000.[30] This is said to have been the result more of poor book-keeping than of any dishonest intent, but the province suffered from both.

Religion was an integral part of the lives of most Upper Canadians and certainly played a large part in the life and history of Hastings County. By the 1830s churches were being built in many parts of the county, but in or out of church most people were conscious of the presence of Divine Providence.[31] The United Empire Loyalists belonged to a variety of sects and were generally tolerant of all; most also shared a belief in the separation of church and state. The intention to make the Church of England the established church of Upper Canada was therefore in direct conflict with their religious convictions and a potent source of trouble, causing more unchristian wrangling than anything else in the colony. They resented not only the land given to support the Church of England, whose membership was smaller than that of several other denominations, but also the privilege enjoyed by the clergy of that church alone to conduct marriages and other sacraments. This seemed an unnecessary hardship when travel was difficult and there was a shortage of priests, even though in some circumstances magistrates could substitute for clergymen. It was not until 1836 that there were five clergymen in the Midland District, so that the magistrates' right to conduct marriages was withdrawn. This right had been extended in 1798 to Lutheran and Church of Scotland ministers, but Methodist clergy were not included until 1831, and even then they were required to take an oath of allegiance before they were given a certificate.

Members of the Church of England around the Bay of Quinte had just one priest, the Reverend John Stuart of Kingston, until 1820. Then a congregation, led by John W. Meyers and Thomas Coleman, built St Thomas Church in Belleville and obtained the ministry of a resident priest.[32] In Kingston the largest congregation was Presbyterian. A group of that denomination in Belleville first applied in 1822 for land on which to erect a church, which was completed in 1831. The Baptists were most numerous around Foxboro. In 1789 about fifty members of that sect had moved from Prince Edward County up to Thurlow, where they settled along the Moira River.[33] There were members of the other denominations, including Roman Catholics and Quakers but the largest group were the Methodists. They may or may not have been in a majority among the United Empire Loyalists, but they were by far the most successful in attracting new members.[34]

There were several reasons why Methodism was particularly suited to a frontier society, and also why it ran into trouble with the government. One was that it brought religion to the people, and spoke to them in ways they understood and appreciated. Early saddlebag preachers came up from the Genesee Conference of New York State and travelled about the Bay of Quinte, calling at homesteads and preaching 'wherever two or three are gathered together.' John Wesley had begun his work in England to bring religion to simple, uneducated people, and in its American form Methodism was well suited to the settler in the backwoods. Camp meetings and revivals, with their hymn singing and emotional services, had a wonderful appeal to men and women whose lives were often monotonous and lonely. There was a dramatic element even in the sermons that blistered many a pulpit and seared the conscience of the sinner, although it should be added these were not limited to any one denomination.

While the established churches had to depend on clergy coming (often reluctantly) from universities abroad, the Methodists were readily served from the nearby United States, and very soon by a home-grown clergy as local men began to enter the ministry. Laymen were inducted as elders, exhorters, deacons, and preachers. They were pious and determined but seldom had much education, which earned them the scorn of some other sects. More than a religion, Methodism was a social movement, and this, combined with its American roots, made it a danger in the eyes of the ruling party. Simcoe had believed that 'without a Bishop to inculcate a religious and industrious spirit, the settlers will be the fittest Instruments for the mischief making Enthusiasm of the Sectaries to work upon ... the Aim of the Sectaries is undoubtedly to destroy the national establishment.'[35] At that time the only bishop was Bishop Mountain in Montreal, and he was even more blunt: the Methodist preachers were 'ignorant enthusiasts whose preaching is calculated only to perplex the understanding, & corrupt the morals; to relax the nerves of industry, & dissolve the bonds of society.'[36]

After the War of 1812–14 it seemed expedient to the Methodists to separate the Canadian Church from its American parent. The first Canadian Conference was held in Hallowell, now Picton, in 1824. In 1828 the Methodist Church of Upper Canada became completely independent. Methodism remained suspect, however, because it had American origins and because many of its members were politically Reformers.

Most itinerant preachers were Methodist, but there were some others. One was the Reverend Robert MacDowell, a Presbyterian, who for many years travelled the whole Bay of Quinte district. Catherine Chrysler wrote of him that he was 'a kind, warm-hearted man, who came on horseback through the woods from Kingston, and where he saw smoke from a house he always made up to the residence ... all who were inclined to marry he spliced, with many a kind word to the young folks.'[37]

Governor Simcoe had said that 'such education as may be necessary for people in the lower degrees of life ... may at present be provided for by their Connections and relations.' What the colony needed were schools for the education of the upper classes, or else 'the cheapness of education in the United States ... will invite the Gentlemen of Upper Canada to send their children thither,' a choice which he feared would pervert their British principles.[38] This division of the population into gentlefolk and common people was perpetuated by the Family Compact. In 1807 the first public schools were authorized, and they were grammar schools, intended to prepare gentlemen's sons for professional life. One was set up in each district, the school for the Midland District being in Kingston. This prompted inhabitants of the Midland District to complain to the government that 'by reason of the place of instruction being established at one end of the District, and the sum demanded for tuition in addition to the annual compensation received from the public, most of the people are unable to avail themselves of the advantage contemplated by the Institution. A few wealthy inhabitants, and those of the Town of Kingston reap exclusively the benefit of it in this District. The Institution, instead of aiding the middling and poorer classes of His Majesty's subjects, casts money into the lap of the rich, who are sufficiently able, without public assistance, to support a school in every respect equal to the one established by law.'[39]

In 1816 a Common School Bill was passed to enable communities to establish primary schools. In the years before the rebellion there were not many of these in proportion to the population, and those that existed were not of a very high standard. Considering how little money was spent on them, this is scarcely surprising. The same session of the legislature that voted £6,000 for all elementary schools in the province voted to spend £3,000 on a silver service to be presented to the departing governor.[40] Public education did not have a high priority on the government's agenda. In 1820 the grant was reduced to £2,500.[41]

The obstacles to all progress were lack of settlers and lack of money. The government at York had few sources of revenue. There was little outside investment and the British government, concerned about the cost of maintaining its growing empire, several times reduced imperial grants. The result was a perpetual shortage of capital for public works. Roads were essential both for getting settlers into the country and getting their products out to market, yet roads were one of the amenities most notably lacking. Another hindrance to commercial activity was the constant shortage of any means of exchange, either sound paper or coin. The low level of commercial activity neither brought in much money nor encouraged its circulation. An immigrant wrote in 1832, 'The greatest falt I have to the cuntrie is cash being so scarce ... They do a great deal in barter but where there is cash the best bargan is to be had.'[42] Banking, too, was slow to begin. A group of merchants in Kingston petitioned in 1817 for a bank charter, but royal assent was delayed and they had to introduce a new bill in 1819. The legislative council reworded this bill, substituting Family Compact members' names for those of the Kingston merchants, and changed the location for the proposed bank from Kingston to 'the seat of government.' In 1821 they got their charter. Many members of the government executive were also directors of this Bank of Upper Canada. The government bought shares in it, and when the amount of capital specified in the charter could not be raised, it was a simple matter to pass another bill reducing the legal reserve. In 1830 a bill asking for a Kingston bank charter was introduced. At first the board of the Bank of Upper Canada tried to block this, proposing instead to open a branch in Kingston, but in 1831 they gave way and the bill passed, creating the Commercial Bank of the Midland District.[43] Soon afterwards a branch was opened in Belleville.

Over the years these and other irritants, minor as well as major, gave rise to considerable disagreement among local groups. This was sometimes increased by individuals with strong personalities. Two such men were Thomas Coleman and James McNabb. Both were mill owners with adjoining properties on the east bank of the Moira River. McNabb was a member of the legislature and a strong supporter of the government, Coleman became interested in reform, and the two carried on a noisy feud which received wide publicity. On one occasion McNabb's brother, Simon, arranged to have them meet, hoping to bring about a reconciliation. Coleman conceded afterwards that it might have been as well if they had not met in a tavern, for he could not remember saying that those who voted £3,000 to buy Governor Gore a silver service were 'a damned set of perjured villains.' McNabb charged him with seditious slander. Coleman said, 'The malignant disposition of James McNabb has pursued me with more than ordinary rancour,' and he called McNabb 'a mean malignant man.' In reply McNabb said Coleman was 'a scurrilous and most turbulent person.'[44]

'Turbulent' no doubt described Coleman. When in 1819 he and Captain Meyers were named trustees to arrange for the construction of the church in Belleville, he donated the plan and in return was given the honour of naming the church. He named it St Thomas.[45] Two months later, the board 'resolved unanimously that Mr. Thomas Coleman having refused to act in accord with the other Trustees, and opposing the adoption of the last resolution, be hereafter no longer considered as a Trustee of the said Church and that the Secretary do erase his name out of the list of Trustees – and that another be appointed in his place.' The resolution to which

Coleman objected called on the trustees to make up any difference between subscriptions collected and the £800 the building was to cost. If he felt unable to take on such a financial obligation, it would have been normal simply to resign, but there must have been some hard words, for minutes from a later meeting mention Coleman's 'expulsion.'[46] No doubt both parties had their supporters who enlarged the quarrel.

While this was a minor affair, it was one more rift among local residents, who shared in all the differences that had arisen among the larger community of Upper Canada. Any basic change in the government would have to come, of course, from the British parliament. Occasionally groups sent petitions there, bypassing their own government, but this made for an irate legislative council and brought little satisfaction from London. Both sides complained about the remoteness of the secretary of state for colonial affairs, and what seemed like his indifference. There was, in fact, no consistent British policy for Upper Canada. Frequent changes in the Colonial Office – as many as four colonial secretaries in three years – made it impossible to develop one.[47] This in turn led to considerable uncertainty in Canada and impeded its progress.[48]

The province that began so hopefully in 1784 was continuing to grow, but never as fast as the inhabitants wanted. In 1819 Midland District residents brought some of their concerns to the attention of the lieutenant-governor. A farmer who lived just north of Kingston wrote that he had been unable to get his potatoes to market because of 'the badness of the Roads ... and the poor devils in the rear can only get to town three months out of twelve, which is shocking encouragement for actual settlement.'[49] Agriculture early became well established, and so did the timber trade both for export and for domestic building. There were some infant industries and a framework of institutions. The foundation of the province had been laid, but it incorporated some serious faults and weaknesses. These were creating problems whose solution was not proving easy to apply. Some people were becoming more and more determined to correct the faults; some, more and more alarmed that such renovations might bring the whole house tumbling down. Out of these two schools of thought grew the Reform and the Tory parties.

2 The Lines Are Drawn

The Family Compact was always opposed to immigration from the United States, afraid that American democratic ideas would stir up unrest, but in fact several Britons probably did most to arouse interest in change. One of these was Robert Gourlay, a Scot who had studied agriculture and who came to Upper Canada in 1817 hoping to found a settlement of farmers from Great Britain. For this purpose he asked to be given a grant of 1,200 acres. It was just the kind of scheme the government encouraged, and Gourlay got a sympathetic hearing from such an impressive list of officials it is hard to understand why the grant was not promptly made, especially since other grants were given to men who seemed less qualified.[1] Perhaps someone should have told him to call first on the rector of York, John Strachan. According to an editorial in the Kingston *Gazette*, no grant was forthcoming because of 'the jealousy and prejudices of one man, whose illiberality is becoming proverbial, and who seems to have it in his power, as well as his disposition, to counteract the most useful undertaking if not originated by himself.[2]

While he waited for a decision, Gourlay began to compile statistics on the colony as a help in attracting immigrants. For this he wrote to every township, asking residents to meet and answer questions about the soil, weather conditions, population, number of mills, and so on. The last item on his questionnaire asked what most hampered improvement and what would best contribute to it. This was a question that made some members of the government very uneasy. From the general population, however, there was a good response. Meetings were held in most townships, including those around the Bay of Quinte, and many leading citizens took part.

The Thurlow meeting was held in Belleville at Mrs Simpson's Tavern, attended by residents who included James and Simon McNabb, John W. Meyers, Robert and Thomas Smith, John Hubbard, John Canniff, and Thomas Coleman. The Sidney meeting was at the home of John Ketcheson, and Captain Jacob W. Meyers, John Row, Elkanah Fairman, Ezekiel Lawrence, Alexander Chisholm, and Moses Moses [3] were present. In Rawdon the questionnaire was considered by those who gathered at Lewis Rosebush's house. At a meeting in Adolphustown the questionnaire was presented by Daniel Hagerman, and those present were favourably impressed, saying that a statistical account of the country would be a great benefit. The annual town meeting in Ernestown appointed a committee that included Sheldon and Davis Hawley and Daniel Perry. Among other meetings held were those in Sophiaburgh and in Hallowell, where Daniel Washburn, a lawyer well known throughout the Midland District, chaired the committee.[4] Having attracted so many people of local prominence, Gourlay's project seemed to be set fair.

He had, however, made a powerful enemy. Dr Strachan visited some committees and persuaded them not to send in their reports to Gourlay. No doubt influenced by Strachan, Daniel Hagerman's attitude to the questionnaire underwent a change, and when the Ernestown report was mailed to Kingston to await Gourlay's arrival there, he asked John Macaulay, the postmaster, to give it to him instead, and Macaulay complied.[5] When Gourlay reached Kingston and discovered this, he confronted Hagerman over taking his mail illegally, but the only reply was a threat of physical violence. A few days later Daniel's brother, Christopher, met Gourlay on the street in Kingston and lashed out at him with a horsewhip.[6] In spite of such opposition the meetings continued. In Adolphustown the committee charged with preparing the report gave in to pressure and decided not to write it, but when Peter Perry learned this he convened a second meeting and made sure a report was delivered.[7] Colonel Joel Stone, a leading resident of Gananoque, got possession of the report prepared there and destroyed it. There was considerable furore in other places, too, as opponents took it upon themselves to prevent their neighbours from answering the questionnaire.

At a second round of meetings representatives were chosen for a convention in Kingston, and, later, from these men some were elected to attend a province-wide convention in York.[8] For the latter the Midland District delegates were Daniel Washburn of Picton, Jacob W. Meyers of Sidney, Davis Hawley from Ernestown, Paul Peterson of Fredericksburgh, and Thomas Coleman of Belleville.[9] After all the fear displayed by members of the ruling party, this convention turned out to be a quiet affair. One observer wrote of Gourlay,'I cannot think he is so dangerous a character as the men in power would have people believe. He is very free in giving his opinion concerning the character of the Governors, and I suspect his greatest fault is in speaking too many truths.'[10] A friend wrote to William Bell of Sidney that 'times are exceeding dull at little York – no such thing as cash to be seen – We expect ... Mr. Gourlay is doing all he can to put our Land Granting Gentry and big Wigs through their pacings and all I can say for him is God Speed the Plough.'[11] These contemporary comments help to explain the reaction Gourlay provoked from the government, and the treatment he received. It was not only that the leaders saw any suggestion of change as criticism of them; it was the fact that he had organized people to ask for change that made the Family Compact nervous.

It must be said that Gourlay was quick to find fault, and less than diplomatic in his speeches and writing. Strachan was particularly stung by Gourlay's criticism. He had Gourlay arrested twice, and although Gourlay was twice acquitted, Strachan would not give up. Spies were instructed to follow the man around to gather evidence on which he could be charged.[12] The third time he was arrested he was put in solitary confinement for about eight months, so that when he was brought to trial without legal counsel he was disoriented and unable to defend himself. The court ordered him exiled under the penalty of death if he returned, a strange and probably unconstitutional sentence on a Briton.

A petty revenge was taken on anyone who had been active in Gourlay's meetings and convention. Men lost government appointments or militia commissions. Thomas Coleman, in spite of the troop of cavalry he had raised during the War of 1812–14, lost his commission and had to make a formal apology to the government before he got it back again. But the Family Compact had won a pyrrhic victory. A biography of Gourlay correctly labelled him a gadfly; in getting rid of one gadfly the government raised up a swarm of others. Gourlay's treatment roused so much indignation against his persecutors, it drew even more attention to the man and his mission than they might otherwise have received. It was no longer possible to ignore the questions he had raised nor the lines of organization he had laid. Reformers began to coalesce, not yet into a party, but into a loose grouping that would in time become a party.

The patriarch of Reformers was William Warren Baldwin, teacher, doctor, lawyer, architect. He emigrated with his family from Ireland in 1824, and shortly afterwards settled in York. William's son Robert, a lawyer, was later responsible for suggesting the general plan of responsible government that appeared in Lord Durham's Report and which was eventually adopted in the Canadas.[13] The Baldwin family of Toronto was well acquainted with Belleville and Bellevillians. William Warren's brother Henry had settled in the village, where he had begun a steamboat service to Prescott and Kingston. Uncle Henry's relationship with the family does not seem to have been as warm, however, as that of Aunt Mary Breakenridge, William's widowed sister, who came to Belleville around 1828. There were family visits back and forth between Belleville and Toronto, and local friendships were formed. At Robert's wedding the surveyor James Hunter Samson of Belleville was best man. The Baldwin and Murney families were friends, and Edmund Murney married Robert's cousin Maria Breakenridge. Unfortunately, the two men became personal as well as political enemies. They later contested two local elections for the union assembly, the second a notoriously violent affair for which the troops had to be sent out from Kingston.

The brothers George, John, and Egerton Ryerson at first made an effective trio in the Reform movement. When the Methodist Church decided in 1829 to publish a weekly newspaper, the *Christian Guardian*, young Egerton was made the editor. It was the beginning of a long and influential career in the church, in politics, and in education. He wrote often and at length in defence of the Methodist Church against the charges of Strachan and others that it was led by ignorant religionists who were subject to the rules of the American Church, and he wrote just as strongly against the clergy reserves. It is questionable, however, to what extent he was a Reformer except on the question of the clergy reserves. He was not an advocate of responsible government, believing it would 'open the door wide to party strife with results of the most serious nature for the internal peace of the colony and for the connection with the mother country.'[14] This opinion was shared by a number of moderate-minded people who hoped for change but at the same time were fearful of what might happen if there were any basic shift in the form of government.

Living in Lennox and Addington were three Reformers of renown. In 1810 Barnabas Bidwell had been the attorney general for the State of Massachusetts after several years in Congress as the representative of Thomas Jefferson's executive. He was being considered for the Supreme Court when a discrepancy was found in his accounts as treasurer of Berkshire County. He claimed innocence, placed the blame on his political enemies, but did not stay to fight the charge.[15] He moved to Bath and for a time taught school; later he settled in Kingston, where he was manager of a law firm. In 1821 he was elected to the Upper Canada assembly. His formidable experience and republican background being well known, his election brought an immediate reaction from the Family Compact, already worried by the number of Americans in the country. There had been very little immigration in the years immediately after the War of 1812–14, but by 1820 there was again a steady flow.[16] The legislative council drafted an act to expel Bidwell on the grounds of his allegiance to a foreign country. After much debate the assembly voted to exclude him but, to the chagrin of the Compact, on the basis of a charge that he had misappropriated public funds, not because he was an alien. Since the majority of people in the province were American-born, a decision to exclude all of them from public office would have had drastic results. In the next two or three years several such laws were introduced with a view not only to reduce American immigration, but also to keep the Bidwells out of the legislature.[17] Eligibility to vote and to hold office went along with the ownership of land, and in the end none of these bills passed because it proved impossible to separate a citizen's political rights from the right to own land. However it was worded, no law could protect the ownership of land which was held by those born in the States, or which had ever been held by such persons, and at the same time disenfranchise the American-born, or even prevent them from being eligible for election to the legislature. This became a burning question throughout the province as every introduction of an alien bill made a great many people anxious about their property. Some of those who had come, or whose families had come, from the United States had lived in the country a good many years; some had held public office, and some had fought with the militia to protect their new homeland during the 1812–14 war. It is easy to understand their anger at having their citizenship put in question. The extent of the problem in Hastings County can be surmised from a document dating from 1813. Of the thirty-five legible entries on the roster of those who were in Thomas Coleman's troop of dragoons in the War of 1812–14, thirteen gave their country of origin as Canada, nineteen were from the States, and one each from England, Scotland, and Ireland.[18] Some of those who were born in the United States may have been UELs, but they too were alarmed since the proposed laws threatened the security of their ownership. Although it proved impossible to get rid of the Bidwells in this way, the introduction of such bills was not only an irritant to American immigrants already in the country; to those contemplating immigration it was also a discouraging sign that there was no welcome mat waiting for them. As well, it gave a common cause to those under attack, by this time a sizeable portion of the population.[19] It was a victory for the Reformers, and a humiliating blow to the Family Compact, when the Colonial Office finally recognized the need to accommodate these immigrants and instructed the government to pass a law which effectively removed all obstacles that kept them from acquiring citizenship, though this law was not passed until 1827. The prolonged agitation had given strong impetus to reform, as well as to anti-American sentiment.

When Barnabas was unable to take his seat in the assembly, his son, Marshall Spring Bidwell, ran for election and despite various opposition tactics won a seat in 1824. Five years later he became speaker of the house, a position much like that of the modern house leader. He was undoubtedly a man of great ability and charm, the brightest star among the Reform group. In 1837 he would have been the rebels' first choice to be their leader if he had been willing, but he was not. He fought on his own battlefields, the assembly and the courts, and in both he was outstanding. At the time the rebels marched on Toronto, the Colonial Office had endorsed the recommendation for his appointment to the bench, and it was Sir Francis Bond Head's refusal to carry out these instructions that led to his recall.

The third Reform leader from Lennox and Addington was Peter Perry, also a member of the legislature. He had none of the polish of a Bidwell, but some rated him 'the ablest stump orator of his time.'[20] It was said that he 'could not read, write, nor spell correctly a sentence in his own or any other language,' but this did not seem to deter his constituents. Many of them could not read or write at all. Sir Francis called him 'the most powerful, as well as the leading speaker of the Republicans,' the name Sir Francis gave haphazardly to any Reformer.[21] At the time of the outbreak of rebellion he had just moved away to a location near Whitby, where he continued his participation in public affairs.

There were other men in the assembly who made a name for themselves as Reformers. Dr Charles Duncombe had great influence in the London District, where he led his own rising a week after Mackenzie's. Dr John Rolph from the Talbot Settlement was clever, eloquent, and cautious. He was one of the small radical circle around Mackenzie. There are many unanswered questions about the part he played in the rebellion, but if it had succeeded he would have been head of a provisional government. Mackenzie was accused by his enemies of swollen ambition, but he never laid claim to a future presidency.

In fact it is hard to think of William Lyon Mackenzie as anything but leader of the opposition. He emigrated from Scotland in 1820, and four years later began to publish a newspaper, the *Colonial Advocate*. As he subsequently wrote, 'I had long seen the country in the hands of a few shrewd, crafty, covetous men, under whose management one of the most lovely and desirable sections of America remained a comparative desert.'[22] He became obsessed with trying to loosen their grip. His attacks on the Family Compact were so frequent, and on one occasion so scurrilous, that a few young members of leading families sought revenge by wrecking his press and throwing the types into Toronto Bay. It was an ill-advised attack. Not only did compensation set him up in a secure printing business, but public reaction ran strongly in his favour. Two years later he won a seat in the legislature, so that he had the two best platforms on which to air his views, particularly on the deficiencies of the constitution and the abuse of power by those who held sway under it. To his opponents Mackenzie was just a rabble-rouser, but to others he must have seemed like a champion sent to fight on their behalf for justice, and perhaps a little vengeance as well.

Mackenzie was elected to office over and over again, with large majorities. In 1834 the Town of York became the City of Toronto, and he had the honour of being chosen its first major. He had just been expelled from the legislature, not for the first time.[23] That he could inspire bedrock loyalty, as well as intense hatred, is shown by his escape after his defeat on Yonge Street on 7 December 1837. He met very few who would have stopped him, in spite of the £1,000 offered for his capture. It is surprising how many instead put themselves at risk in order to give him refuge and help him to safety, so that his flight to Buffalo reads like a *Boy's Own* adventure story.

His rebellion was not as totally rash as it has been represented. Had all the rebels gathered on the seventh as Mackenzie intended, the element of surprise might well have won them victory in Toronto, at least for a time. Mackenzie was not the only one who thought such an initial victory would bring in thousands who sympathized with his aims but were not willing to declare themselves until there was some assurance of success. The letters of Sir George Arthur, who succeeded Sir Francis Bond Head as lieutenant-governor, show that he believed the same thing during 1838 and 1839, and so did many others. Arthur's often-expressed fear was that, if the rebels ever managed to gain a toe-hold on the Canadian shore, there would be a general rising. Ironically it was hot-headed 'little Mack' who would have captured the Toronto store of arms in October when they could have been taken with little effort, and the reasonable business and professional men in his radical council who balked, and lost the opportunity. Similarly it was the wily, cool-headed doctor and lawyer John Rolph who ruined the plan for the march on Toronto. First, he jumped to the conclusion, on very little evidence, that the militia was being called out days before there appears to have been any chance of that happening; and, second, he told the rebels, and only a part of them, to gather at Montgomery's Tavern three days early, thereby setting in motion a chain of events that resulted in fiasco. The rebellion would not necessarily have succeeded without Rolph's extreme caution, but he almost guaranteed its failure. It may be that the country owes a debt of gratitude to this inadvertent spoiler.

The Family Compact led those who opposed reform.[24] Although privately its members often railed against the British government for its ignorance of the colony it ruled from afar, they were completely loyal to the British connection, distrusted most things American, and had a vested interest in keeping the constitution intact. They saw themselves as defenders of the country against republicanism and moral decay. They disagreed among themselves on many points, but they shared a view of society that bound them together. It is not easy to be fair to the men of the Family Compact today when democracy is almost a moral determinant. It was not so in their day. As 'Old Subscriber in Ernest Town' wrote to the *Chronicle and Gazette* of Kingston, 'What we have to fear is the downward progress of the American people from the vices inherent in their democratic form of Government, and the debasing effect of universal suffrage, and the inversion of the first law of society, by placing the will of the mob of illiterate, vicious and needy over that of the educated, sober, and wealthy conservative portion of society.'[25]

This was not just the opinion of one eccentric. It was shared to a greater or lesser extent by many others, including the retired British officers who arrived to take up their free land, quite a few of the middle class, and even some in humble circumstances, immigrants as well as native born, who found security in a tiered society. Because the United Empire Loyalists usually arrived in groups in which all members had suffered losses and trials, and then faced the same difficult years of survival, it is tempting to see them all as equals, sharing everything in a democratic and classless society. As the old couplet goes, 'When Adam delved and Eve span, / Who was then the gentleman?'[26] The flaw in this picture is that even in the beginning some Adams and Eves were able to pay others to dig and spin for them. In Hastings, Captain John Meyers, for instance, brought resources that enabled him to build a mill almost as soon as he arrived. Some, like the Meyers, Wallbridge, Leavens, and Finkle families, brought their slaves with them.[27] Most had been in the army, and all who held commissions kept their rank and also enjoyed the gift of extra land in accordance with that rank. And those who had been accustomed to give orders, like those who had obeyed them, tended to continue in the same way. Since the arrival of the Loyalists, many more people had come into the country, some bringing an American disregard for social distinctions, some from Britain expecting to enjoy equality in the freer atmosphere of Canadian society,[28] like the Scotch immigrant who, on approaching land, jubilantly told his companions, 'We'll a' be lairds here.'[29] Others, however, saw this trend towards class levelling as an aberration in a new, underdeveloped country and a threat to any stable society, and they did their best to correct it.

Chief among the educated, sober, and conservative who expected to be at the apex of society was John Strachan, a man who had a lasting effect on Upper Canadian education and religion. He came out from Scotland in 1799, first teaching in the home of Richard Cartwright of Kingston, then in 1802 opening his own academy in Cornwall. There he taught the sons of many prominent families, boys who grew up to become the elite of government and the professions. For the rest of their lives his pupils seem to have regarded him as their mentor, and to this and to his indomitable will he owed his powerful influence. He was a man of courage and boundless ambition. Finding little chance of advancement in the Presbyterian Church, to which he belonged, he took orders in the Church of England.[30] He served with all the zeal of a convert, becoming Archdeacon of York and, finally, Bishop of Toronto. It is unfortunate that the impact of his unyielding disposition overshadows the legacy of high standards in education which he helped to establish in the province.

Of all John Strachan's pupils, John Beverley Robinson could be called the prefect. With a brilliant mind, astute, strong-willed, trained in the law, he wielded as much power as any man in Canada. He took part in the War of 1812–14, and at the age of twenty-two acted as attorney general at the Ancaster treason trials, where he secured the conviction of fifteen accused, of whom eight were hanged.[31] Such early advancement no doubt contributed to his arrogance. He was made solicitor general in 1815 and attorney general from 1821 until he was appointed to the bench in 1829. He is one of those who set an admirable standard of decorum in the somewhat primitive courts of Upper Canada. He was a devoted public servant, an effective prosecutor, and a distinguished judge. On the other hand, at times he manipulated the law in order to protect those he considered to belong to his own class, and against some who did not. The most aristocratic of all the Family Compact in manner and outlook, Robinson fought every advance of democracy and every advocate of it. He believed 'a body of nobility' was the only buffer that could protect 'the rights of both Crown and People.'[32]

It was natural that conservative Kingston, a garrison town and administrative centre of the Midland District, should be the home of a number of members of the Compact. There was the Cartwright family, whose founder was Richard Cartwright. As former secretary to Colonel Butler of the Queen's Rangers during the Revolutionary War, he had easy access to the military when he came to Canada in 1786. He began supplying the garrison at Kingston after he moved there in 1789 and branched out into various kinds of trade until he became one of the wealthiest men in the colony. As a member of the first legislative council in 1792, he criticized Governor Simcoe for his plan to bring in more people from the United States. Simcoe believed many there were still loyal to Britain and would be valuable settlers. Cartwright thought, probably rightly, that most who came were interested only in getting free land, and he spoke his mind on the subject, saying he had been appointed because of his knowledge of the country and 'not merely to show my Compliance to the person at the head of the Government.' Although a member of the Church of England, he was opposed to the exclusive privileges given that church by the Marriage Act.[33] His son, John Solomon Cartwright, became a district court judge in 1834 and a member of the assembly from 1836 to 1844. His influence was for the most part local, although he did give his support to the Family Compact.[34]

Thomas Markland, second only to Richard Cartwright in wealth and business success, was also a member of the first legislative council. He was active in affairs of St George's Church, which later became the cathedral, but he also contributed to the building of the Presbyterian church and the Wesleyan chapel in Kingston. He became a justice of the peace in 1792 and a militia captain in 1812; he was a trustee of the abortive Kingston Bank of Upper Canada, sometimes called the pretended bank, and in 1832 was a director of the Commercial Bank of the Midland District.[35] After him, his son George Herkimer Markland became a legislative councillor in 1820 and a member of the executive council in 1822. Until 1836 he was one of the most influential members of the Family Compact, working closely with John Strachan on the latter's favourite project, King's College, which was intended to be the future university. He was also involved with founding Upper Canada College, and was later accused of using government university funds for the college. His career came to a sudden end when scandal erupted 1836 over his alleged homosexuality.[36]

Members of the Macaulay family were all staunch supporters of the government, and were rewarded with various government jobs. John Macaulay was appointed postmaster in Kingston in 1815 and was later in charge of the Port of Kingston. He moved to Toronto when he was appointed surveyor general in 1836, then private secretary to the lieutenant-governor in 1838.[37] The next year he was made a legislative councillor, perhaps as consolation for not receiving the paid government position he expected with the country about to be reorganized in the new union. His brother William was a Church of England clergyman who served as rector at Picton.

The brothers Daniel and Christopher Hagerman belonged to another Tory family. Both were elected to the assembly in 1820, and Christopher continued as a member until 1840. In 1837 he was appointed attorney general, but the colonial secretary did not confirm the appointment. He was seen to be totally committed to the Crown and the Church of England, but he was too careless of offending those who disagreed with him, sometimes doing more harm than good. In 1840 he became a provincial judge.[38] Although Anna Jameson found him 'somewhat coarse and overbearing,' he could also be genial and good-natured, and there is no doubt he was both intelligent and capable.[39]

Even by 1837 there were no formal political parties, certainly none organized as they are today. Men still advertised themselves as 'independent' when they campaigned for election, 'party' being often associated with republicanism and the kind of venial party warfare that was being constantly reported from the United States. There are therefore no well-defined names for the political groups that existed in those years, and the labels that are used should be loosely attached. The ruling group which controlled the legislative and executive councils, along with their adherents and supporters, came to be called Tories because of similarities to the British Tory party. They called themselves Constitutionalists, defenders of the constitution as it stood, or more often loyalists, written here with a small *l* to avoid confusion with United Empire Loyalists. The name of Whig, the other large British party, was occasionally used to denote those who were opposed to the Tories, but in general they were called Reformers. It was a small number of these who eventually separated from the rest of the Reformers to pursue more radical aims, ending in rebellion. Fortunately there were many moderates, and the opinion of the voting public was usually formed more by the situation in which individuals found themselves at the time of any election, and no doubt by their reaction to the personality of leaders, than by any question of the constitution.

It is often taken for granted that all United Empire Loyalists and their descendants were small *l* loyalists. This has led some to believe that the eastern part of the province was unaffected by the rebellion because of its original settlement. This is, first, to ignore all the new arrivals since 1784 and, just as mistakenly, to assume that every twig on a United Empire Loyalist tree was a Tory. Peter Perry was the scion of a United Empire Loyalist family just as Christopher Hagerman was, and so were many of those around the Bay of Quinte who voted for Bidwell, Perry, Roblin, and other Reform candidates. Their desire for changes in the government did not affect their loyalty to the Crown, even though this was the frequent accusation of their political foes.

The British government failed to recognize the growing conflict, at least, the governors sent to Upper Canada did nothing to resolve differences between the factions. The social circle around them was dominated by the Family Compact. Sir John Colborne arrived in 1828, the latest of the generals left unemployed after the long Napoleonic Wars and sent to Canada as governors. He proved unpopular with a considerable portion of the Upper Canadian population, and by 1832 petitions were being sent to London to ask for his recall. One from Hastings bore 1,100 signatures.[40] One Kingston petition was accidentally burned, but John Vincent, who had charge of it as secretary of the meeting where it was prepared, wrote to say that it had been signed by at least 1,000 people.[41] Several lengthy petitions were worded exactly the same, possibly composed by Mackenzie, who carried a number of them to England and delivered them to the Colonial Office. One of these came from Lennox and Addington, and it read in part:

> We feel the most sincere regret in being obliged to state to your Majesty that the hopes which we in common with our fellow subjects generally throughout the Province, formed on the arrival of our present Lieutenant Governor, have not been realized, that he has pursued the same system of policy, and been manifestly and unhappily under the influence of the same advisers, as his predecessor ... that instead of an impartial protector of all classes of your Majesty's subjects committed to his government, he has exhibited himself as the partial friend and advocate of a sectarian party, few in number compared with the whole, although arrogant and exclusive in their pretensions, that he has treated with unprovoked and unmerited indignity a respectable denomination, that notwithstanding his military experience and qualifications he is not well fitted to administer satisfactorily this important colony.[42]

The petitioners asked for no radical change, only for 'the benefits of their constitution which to this day have been denied them.'

Not everyone joined in seeking Colborne's removal. There were at the same time petitions or loyal addresses which expressed 'approbation of the general manner of Your Excellency's Administration,' including one from Lennox and Addington, another from Kingston bearing 1,410 signatures, and one signed by 600 Bay of Quinte Mohawks. From Georgina Township north-east of Toronto, which later provided a number of rebels, an address deplored 'the impertinence and folly of the disaffected since your Excellency's government has given general satisfaction to all *those whose opinion is worth having.*' Eighty-nine satisfied inhabitants signed this document. Port Hope residents pledged their support, but asked for 'the investigation of all real abuses so as to secure the loyalty of the inhabitants.'

The British parliament took notice of all these Upper Canadians demanding attention for their real or imagined grievances. At the end of 1835 the Colonial Office moved Sir John Colborne down to Quebec to be the military commander of both Canadas. To replace him they sent Sir Francis Bond Head to Toronto. For Upper Canada this turned out to be a case of 'out of the frying-pan into the fire.'

3 A Slow Fuse

By 1836 there were about ten thousand people living in Hastings County.[1] Most of them were in the front townships of Sidney and Thurlow, although Rawdon, Huntingdon, and Hungerford Townships were also beginning to be settled. Part of the Indian reserve had been taken in 1820 to form Tyendinaga Township, where Irish immigrants had moved in, Roman Catholics around Marysville and Protestants around Shannonville. Each of these was still just a cluster of houses, and there were similar hamlets dotted about the county, usually growing up around a mill on one of the streams or rivers. One of the larger settlements was Rawdon, later named Stirling, which possessed a grist mill, two sawmills, and a distillery. In 1834 Sheldon Hawley 'and others residing at or near the mouth of the Trent' had petitioned to have forty acres surveyed and laid out in town lots.[2] They also asked that land be set apart for a market-place 'to hold weekly markets and quarterly or annual fairs' since this 'invariably stimulates the industry of the poorer class of Agricultural Settler – at the same time that it affords great convenience and facilities in the disposal of their goods to the Merchant, the Storekeeper and the Mechanic.' There were around four hundred people in the immediate area. In the beginning, some of them seemed little inclined to obey the law and for a time gave the place a bad reputation, according to the *Chronicle and Gazette*, which reported that ruffians had inflicted such frequent damage that Jacob Ford, a tavern owner, was forced to give up his business and move out of his house.[3] By 1836, when the first town lots of Trent Port went on sale, things had apparently settled down. There were mills in or near the village as well as stores and several craftsmen's shops, such as a blacksmith's, a shoemaker's, and so on;[4] a covered bridge had been built across the Trent River, and work had begun on the Trent Canal.

Agriculture was the occupation of most people and mixed farming the rule. This was true of Hastings County and of the province as a whole. A by-product of land clearing was potash, which was made from wood ashes, and there was a ready export market for it. Lumbering had also become an important source of employment. Every spring the rivermen drove the logs down when the rivers were in flood and formed their great rafts on the bay.[5]

Hastings County not only had fertile land for crops and livestock, as well as forest – boundless forest as it seemed at the time – but at Marmora it also possessed an extensive deposit of iron ore. As early as 1820 a road had been built from Crowe Lake to the Trent River in order to bring out the ore and take in supplies. Because of rapids on the Trent and the poor state of road building, however, transportation remained one of the worst obstacles to those who worked the mine and mill, and its difficulty cut down the profits. Nevertheless the mine was productive, and besides the ore it exported there was a good local trade in useful items such as kettles, stoves, and mill irons. The several hundred men who worked at the mine created a good market for the farmers and tradesmen round about.[6] At nearby Madoc an American, Henry Pendergast, together with a partner was building a modern iron foundry, where they hoped soon to employ another hundred men, but plans were curtailed when it was discovered that Pendergast had misappropriated some of the funds and departed for the United States, where he would later cause further mischief for Canadians.[7]

Belleville by 1836 had about 1,800 residents. In addition to the original saw and grist mills down by the harbour, a new modern lumber mill operated by steam was expected to be in production the following year.[8] The owner was Billa Flint, an energetic young man who came to town in 1829 from Brockville and who was destined to play a leading part in the life of the county.[9] There was also a paper and a cloth mill,[10] distilleries, and a number of artisans' workshops. In Belleville a man could buy almost anything he needed, to eat, to wear, or to use about his house and farm. Certainly he need never go thirsty anywhere in the Midland District, for the magistrates in quarter sessions that year granted 155 licences for the sale of spirits, either in taverns or grocery shops. Belleville also had several doctors and at least two drug stores.

The Commercial Bank of the Midland District had had a rocky beginning but seemed to have achieved stability, and the Belleville branch was open.[11] Most banking, however, was still in the hands of the merchants, who extended credit usually against the harvest, when the farmer received the only cash he was likely to see all year. In general, daily transactions continued to be carried on by barter. A few men had enough capital to act as bankers, although they might be better described as money-lenders than as what we think of today as bankers. Their business practices were informal. In 1838 young William Wallbridge moved into his Uncle Turnbull's house. At that time Turnbull was the chief banker in the town. William wrote to his sister, 'Here I am in what Turnbull calls his counting house for he keeps a branch of the bank here, but what I call our bedroom for we use it as such.'[12]

Communication was another community requirement which was not well met. Of necessity the mail was as slow as the travellers who carried it, and it was also expensive since the post office was run, not as a service, but as a source of revenue. Newspapers regularly published lists of names of those who had letters waiting for them. The lists in the Kingston papers are long, some names appearing over and over. This is not always because the addressee received more than one letter, or because he or she had moved away, but sometimes because of the postage due. The poor immigrant might have even poorer family at home, so that the sender did not always pay the postage, or pay it in full, and the amount due was often equal to a day's pay or more. Anna Jameson, who was in Toronto in 1837, painted a pathetic picture of immigrants turned away, unable to redeem letters from home because they could not afford to pay the postage.[13] The postmaster general is said to have grown rich, especially from the high rate charged for mailing newspapers.[14] This was one of Mackenzie's constant grievances.

There were schools around the county, most of them small and private, varying greatly in the level and quality of teaching. The public secondary school at Kingston still had to serve the whole District, and it could not have had many students since by 1841 total provincial attendance at these schools was just 311.[15] Only a small fraction of the children attended any school at all. William Hutton, an Irish immigrant who opened a school in Belleville in 1835, found his pupils 'a shrewd, clever race so far as abilities are concerned,' but their minds were 'wildernesses as uncultivated as those woods around us.'[16] The 'common' schools were the publicly supported elementary schools, 'providing for the education of the inferior classes,' as James Macaulay described them.[17] Canniff Haight, a resident of Prince Edward County who was at this time enrolled in a common school near Hay Bay, later wrote that they were few and bad. One teacher of whom he had painful memories 'evidently believed the only way to get anything into a boy's head was to pound it in with a stick through his back.'[18] Schools were the responsibility of the province and community together, but neither was yet able or willing to spend enough money to provide good education. The editor of a Cobourg newspaper in 1838 facetiously wrote, 'We understand that an order has been passed by the Board of Education, which provides that Teachers of Common Schools must be able to *read* and *write their own certificates*.'[19] It may be that dissatisfaction with public education was increased in Hastings because of the energy of the local churches. In 1822 members of the Congregational, Presbyterian, and Methodist churches began a union Sunday school in Belleville. Within a few years this had a membership of two hundred. Soon the Methodist conference voted funds for library books wherever a Sunday school was established, and no doubt the other churches contributed as well. Having people read the Bible and religious tracts was an important part of the church's mission, so that the missionary often placed 'evangelical emphasis on literacy.'[20] There is little evidence of the effectiveness of a once-a-week school, but it must have been the only schooling many children had, while even those who attended week-day classes often received little education.

While no doubt some good teachers came along, the pay was not enough to attract very many. In 1835 John Holmes, teacher of the common school in Belleville, wrote to the Hastings member, Henry Yager, who was attending a session of the legislature in Toronto: 'I am in hopes there will be some measures taken respecting school business for as things are I have hard rowing, how ever I am determined to stay here a little longer if the lord will. Times are very hard here I can hardly get enough money to rub along with ... if it was not for hope the heart would break. As to my school I get along very well I get more schollars [sic] than money.'[21]

Teaching was so badly paid it was too often undertaken by those whose only qualification was that they could find no other employment. This was likely to be true of newcomers to the province. A report on the state of the province written in 1838 described education as the writer saw it: 'In many parts of the province the teachers are American, the books they use are all American, filled with inflated accounts of American independence and the glorious wars with England. The boy gains a smattering of geography out of an American compilation in which the state of Rhode Island occupies as much detail as the eastern hemisphere and in which England appears a pitiful little island filled with tyrannical landlords and fat clergymen and a great number of tenants and labourers. Ireland is a joyless land of bogs, pigs, and Catholics, and Scotland an out of the way place in which the mountains and the men have a national prejudice against decent covering.'[22]

Lack of money continued to hamper the development of the country. There were no railroads, and transportation overland was inadequate to open up the country back of the front townships. Where there were roads, they were corduroy, and travel over these must have been a kind of punishment. Accidents were frequent. Horses were lamed, coaches upset, goods – and people – were damaged. When the Moodie family moved to their new home in Lakefield, the wagon overturned and all the dishes were broken.[23] But there were improvements, in Hastings as elsewhere. The first bridge across the Trent at Trent Port had been built in 1834, greatly speeding the journey between Hastings and Toronto. The stage coach made the trip almost every weekday, taking two days each way. It was a rough, jolting ride, and in spring breakup and during fall rains the road was sometimes impassable. Steamboats called in at Belleville going to Kingston or Toronto, and they provided comfortable travel as long as there was open water.[24] Belleville harbour was a busy one, with freighters loading and unloading at its five wharves.[25] As 1836 began there seemed substantial reasons why Hastings County should look forward to a year of continued progress and a considerable degree of material prosperity.

Hastings County society, however, was divided in several ways, and relations between the groups were not harmonious. Politics was one reason. By 1824 the population of Hastings County qualified it to elect two members to the assembly. Campaigns were, at the very least, enthusiastic. Large crowds turned out for political meetings and often broke up the proceedings.[26] The two sides were well enough balanced that the county often returned one Reform and one Tory member. In 1836 these were Henry Yager and James Samson.

Hastings County had been petitioning the executive council for some time, asking to be made a separate district. The population warranted the county's independence, which would require the establishment of a courthouse and jail in Belleville. The trouble and expense of litigants, witnesses, jurymen, and magistrates travelling to Kingston or Adolphustown to attend court were often formidable, and sometimes justice was subverted because some failed to appear. Residents signed a petition again in 1835, but it was given to Samson, the Tory member, who failed to present it to the council.[27] Stephen Benson, a magistrate, circulated another and sent it to the Reform member, Henry Yager, asking that he take it to the lieutenant-governor without delay. Benson said he had recently attended a meeting of magistrates to consider a vacancy on their bench. Thomas

Parker presided, and he ruled that they could not forward any names at all because, as Benson commented sarcastically, it would be unconstitutional, and might even be un-British. Benson was sure this was simply a ploy to prevent the recommendation of any Reformer, while Parker intended secretly to submit the names of Henry Baldwin, William McAnnany, William Hutton, 'or others of the same kidney' – all Tories. Apparently if the governor first accepted the petition for separation, Benson thought this would thwart such a manoeuvre.[28] It is obvious that, years before there were organized political parties, there were well-defined political factions. In another letter Benson noted that a meeting was being held in Belleville 'to form a Branch of the Toronto Constitutional Society – another prop to their Faltering Cause attended only by Tories – poor fellows.'[29]

Conflicts and intrigues about politics are not uncommon, but in small communities they tend to become personal quarrels. This is even more true of disagreements over religion. There were the same disputes in Hastings as elsewhere about the clergy reserves, 'the perpetual spring of discord, strife, and hatred.'[30] Another source of conflict was created within the Methodist Church when a merger of Canadian Episcopalian and English Wesleyan Methodists was arranged in 1833. To many of the Episcopalians it was a shot-gun wedding in which they were the unwilling partner. Like other sects which did not enjoy official approval, Canadian Methodists had for years taken issue with the government over the privileges of the Church of England, including Strachan's plans for a publicly supported university which would be a Church of England institution.[31] The *Christian Guardian* carried a banner proclaiming 'Equality and Equal Rights.' The Wesleyans, on the other hand, taught obedience to authority and deference to one's superiors, and the new Union Church was Wesleyan in nature. This suited the government very well; in fact, both the lieutenant-governor, Sir John Colborne, and the Colonial Office had invited the Wesleyans over in order to combat the 'American' Methodists, as they insisted on calling the Canadian congregation. The Wesleyans were offered grants and other advantages; and while the Church of England was beginning to reap a profit from the clergy reserves, the Episcopalians, in spite of their growing numbers, were falling increasingly into debt. Their leaders felt powerless, seeing no hope of success against the open opposition of the government and two comparatively wealthy church organizations: union of the two Methodist groups seemed to offer the only way out.

Egerton Ryerson, as an acknowledged Methodist leader, has often been blamed for the decision to end the independence of the Episcopalian Methodists in Canada, but at the time he had very little choice. With the blessing of the Colonial Office and after constant consultation with Colborne, the Wesleyans accepted a merger with their Canadian co-religionists. They were in a position to set all the terms. The Episcopalians had to agree that they would take no part in politics, nor make any further protest against the clergy reserves.[32] It was a serious blow to Reformers when the *Christian Guardian* failed to support them before the election of 1836, but this may have had as much to do with Ryerson's own political stance as with any agreement made with the Wesleyans.[33] Equally serious to many Methodists was the fact that the new Union Church accepted grants from the government. This was a betrayal of one of their basic principles: the complete separation of church and state. They were also angered by the substitution of a president with wide powers of discipline in place of a conference-selected bishop. Many Methodists, in Hastings probably a majority, refused to accept the union. John Ryerson was the presiding elder of the Bay of Quinte District, and he wrote to his brother Egerton, 'The work of Schism has been purty extensive on some parts of this District. There have left or been expelled on the Waterloo Circuit 150,[34] on the Bay of Quinte 40, in Belleville 47, Sidney 50, on Cobourg 32.'[35] These Bay of Quinte Methodists decided to continue as they were, and they elected John Reynolds, an itinerant preacher who lived in Belleville, as their bishop. Others in the congregation were more amenable to the new order and agreed to join the Union Church. Then the question arose, Who owned the church building and property on Pinnacle Street?

The Unionists, led by Billa Flint, John P. Morden, William Ross, Jonas Canniff, Asa Yeomans, Benjamin Ketcheson, and their pastor Henry Wilkinson, occupied the chapel, and an action was brought against them by John Reynolds, P.G. Seldon, James Bickford, and Aaron Dawe, with the support of Thaddeus Lewis of the fourth concession of Sidney, Albert Taylor of the third, and Nathan Parks. The case, which attracted wide publicity, was heard at Kingston assizes on 11 October 1837.[36] The continuing Episcopalians won their case, but it was immediately appealed. As it happened, the appeal was not heard until 1840 because the rebellion intervened, tying up all the courts, but until the outbreak of revolt there was almost feverish activity among Methodists as the two sides prepared for the second round of their fight.[37] On 27 November Egerton Ryerson wrote that he had travelled almost five hundred miles that week as he worked 'to secure our Church property from the grasp of an insignificant & worthless party.'[38] Such an uncharitable attitude on the part of a leader of the church gives some indication of the rancour that must have existed among Hastings County's Methodists.

The year 1836 was one of elections in Belleville and Hastings. While Hastings did not achieve the status of a separate district for another three years, Belleville did become a police village. This required the election of a police board which would have the authority to pass laws for the good order of the community. There followed a hot contest for places on the board. C.O. Benson wrote to his brother John in Napanee that the campaign divided the whole town into 'the Flints and the anti Flints.'[39] But although Billa Flint waged a vigorous campaign, he lost out by two votes to Henry Yager. Because of the system of constituting the board, however, this was not the end of the matter. The four elected members then chose Flint as the fifth member and president of the board. What Henry Yager and the Reformers thought of this outcome is not recorded.

The death of James Samson, MLA, in early 1836 made a by-election necessary, and the campaign was as vigorous as the parties could make it. The poll opened in Belleville with the nomination of James McNabb by Ruliff Purdy, and of Nelson Reynolds by Joseph Lockwood.[40] Voting went on all week. Reynolds was slightly ahead until the last day, but the *Chronicle and Gazette* reported on 4 May, 'The Radicals Defeated and Totally Vanquished by the Glorious Re-Action at Hastings – It is with infinite satisfaction we announce the glorious result of the contest for the County of Hastings.' It had been gained in spite of the endeavours of Peter Perry, 'the *Radical Doyen* of the Upper Canada Assembly, and Mr Roblin, M.P.P. his Jackall.' Perry and Roblin had spent the week at the polling station, 'and from what we have heard of the impudence of the one, (sometimes repressed by palpable hits at the gentleman,) and the sly endeavours of the other, it speaks favorably of this part of the country that the lynching system of our neighbours was not resorted to.' This seems to condone violence – at least the 'palpable hits,' if not the actual lynching of political opponents.[41] James McNabb, the Constitutional candidate, was elected by a majority of eleven votes. He was the son of James McNabb, the Belleville mill owner mentioned before, who had also been a member of the assembly. The son had no chance to enjoy his success, however, because of the parliamentary crisis which was taking place and the general election that followed.

When it was announced early in 1836 that Sir Francis Bond Head was to succeed Sir John Colborne as governor, there was a general impression that he was a reform-minded gentleman. The Family Compact was distrustful, the Reformers hopeful. His first move seemed to bear out his reputation, for he added three members to the executive council, the Reformers Robert Baldwin and John Rolph, and the non-partisan receiver-general,

John H. Dunn. They soon found, however, that Sir Francis rarely consulted them and failed to follow their advice when he did. They resigned and, rather surprisingly, so did the rest of the council. The assembly appointed Peter Perry to chair a committee to investigate this turn of events. The committee's report, delivered in the assembly by Speaker Bidwell, severely criticized the lieutenant-governor's treatment of his council.[42] In the course of their investigation, the committee had also discovered that before he left, and unknown to the assembly, Colborne's last act had been to endow fifty-seven rectories of the Church of England with twenty-two thousand acres of land. This was a disclosure bound to cause anger among members of all other churches, as even the Scotch Presbyterian and the Roman Catholic clergy were excluded, although theirs were also established churches. The committee reported that the government was operating on arbitrary principles and recommended that supply be stopped.[43] Sir Francis went one better. He refused assent to money bills already passed, which meant no money could go out to pay employees or government contractors. He then dissolved the House, and the parties squared off for an election.

In April the inhabitants of Hastings were called to a county meeting 'to discuss the question at issue between his Excellency and his late Executive Council.'[44] The meeting elected Peter O'Reilly as chairman and Nelson Reynolds as secretary.[45] Joseph Canniff had prepared a resolution which censured the governor and approved the conduct of the executive council. Thomas Parker introduced an amendment that would have changed this to support for the lieutenant-governor and regret that the executive council had resigned. This was seconded by Edmund Murney. These men then asked for a discussion, but it was 'decided by noise and confusion that there should be no discussion.' According to the report, about 250 left and assembled in the street, where they elected Thomas Appleby chairman and Anthony Marshall secretary. They adopted an address which declared they had read with pleasure 'your Excellency's determined, talented, and firm arguments,' which received nearly 220 signatures. The only question about this report concerns the numbers. If, as it says, there were 300 in the courtroom and 250 disagreed with what was going on, one would wonder how 50 were able to keep control of the room while 250 had to continue in the street. Of course, it may have happened just as it appeared in the newspaper, but these reports were so biased, the numbers must always be suspect. Around the county no doubt there were more meetings, but the only other of which there is any account was a Constitutional Meeting at River Trent, a small community north of Trent Port, called by Robert Wilkins, the senior magistrate. With William Robertson in the chair, a Mr

Henderson as secretary, and helped by Adam H. Meyers and J.B. Crowe, those present gave three cheers for the constitution and thanks to his Excellency for his 'wisdom, firmness, and integrity.'[46] While his treatment of his executive council had roused a storm of controversy, evidently Sir Francis could count on quite a lot of support when he took to the campaign trail in person. 'When therefore Sir Francis Head threw himself with great energy into the electoral arena, when he bade the foes of the Empire 'come if they dare!' when he called upon the 'United Empire Loyalists' – men, who in 1770 had thrown away their all, rather than accept an alien rule – when he traversed the length and breadth of the land, making himself at home in the farm-houses, & calling on fathers & sons & husbands to stand up for their hearths, & their old traditions of honour & fealty to the Crown, it wd have been strange indeed had he failed.'[47]

He did not fail. In the Tory landslide even Mackenzie lost his seat. In Hastings two Tories were elected for the first time. The candidates had been Nelson Reynolds, Edmund Murney, Henry Yager, and Anthony Manahan, a resident of Kingston who was managing the Marmora Iron Works.[48] There seems to be no explanation for McNabb's failure, when his party was riding a wave of popularity, to stand for the assembly to which he had so recently been elected. The winners were Murney and Manahan. Dr Duncombe carried out an investigation of the election and took to the Colonial Office a mass of evidence showing widespread irregularities, particularly in the property qualification of voters, and in other ways as well.[49] For instance, the King's Printer had been commissioned by the government to print a thousand copies of a sheet entitled 'Peter Perry Picked to Pieces,' which had then been distributed to voters in Lennox and Addington.[50] Perry and Bidwell were both defeated by Tory candidates.

The election had been made more acrimonious by the Orange Order, a secret society which had been introduced into Canada by immigrant Irish Protestants. Since 1798 it had grown in Ireland during civil strife when some lodges became militia units and acted like private armies.[51] The Order loudly proclaimed its allegiance to Protestantism, the Crown, and the constitution and did not hesitate to use violence in their service. It is not immediately apparent why Orangeism succeeded in this country as it did, since the Canadian situation in no way resembled that of Ireland. Roman Catholics were in a minority and posed no threat. In any event Ogle Gowan, a driving force in organizing the lodges in Upper Canada, struck up an alliance with the Roman Catholic Bishop Macdonnell in order to bolster his claim that the Order was non-sectarian.[52] Since the Order had been founded for militant defence against Roman Catholics, if they were not to be the enemy the society might seem to have lost much of its purpose. Ironically, in the short term, the Reformers provided another. They were dedicated to changing the constitution which the Order was pledged to defend. In Upper Canada it was a very different constitution from the one that protected their interests in Ireland, but this did not affect the slogans. In spite of his overtures to the bishop, Gowan did little to promote good relations between the Order and the Roman Catholic population. The rank and file were and remained anti-Catholic, but in the meantime they were equally anti-Reform.

Hastings was soon a hotbed of Orangeism, warrant number 3 being issued to a lodge in Lonsdale in 1830. By 1837 others had been issued to Hungerford, Tyendinaga, Rawdon, Thomasburg, Trent Port, and two each to Stirling, Roslin, and Latta's Mills, and in 1838 Frankford and Shannonville were added.[53] Formation of lodges around Belleville was no doubt encouraged by George Benjamin, publisher of the *Intelligencer*, who soon became prominent, second only to Gowan, in the provincial organization. The Order provoked so much violence that governors and legislators frequently declared their determination to put an end to it as soon as the rebellion was over, but by then it was too late. The government had made use of the organization against their enemies, and it grew too strong for them. Many people came into the country during the 1830s, leaving family and friends, for a strange and often lonely existence in Upper Canada. There were few organizations, and most of them were exclusive in some way, by trade, religious sect, or social position. The Order welcomed every Protestant, whether Irish or not, and offered the humblest immigrant a place in the lodge. To simple people it supplied simple slogans about true blue loyalty. It gave them a sense of worth, which in the beginning was no bad thing. Unhappily it also encouraged them to become bigots.

Local society seems not to have been divided in at least one of the ways which is said to have caused trouble around Toronto. Although towns were still very small and most of the population was engaged in farming, there was already some division of interest between town and country. Sir Francis in a speech to the assembly said that 'if the Yeomanry and Farmers ... are not yet sufficiently tired of agitation – if they do not yet see what a curse it has been to them ... it will be out of my power to assist them.'[54] It has been said that there was 'antipathy between farmers, who ... produced most of the country's wealth, and the merchants and government officials,' who seemed 'parasites growing fat on the fruits of their labour.'[55] The rebellion is sometimes unfairly called the farmers' rebellion. As far as can be determined, however, around the Bay of Quinte there does not seem to have been a clear division between the two groups. There were merchants and government officials, but they often farmed as well. Whatever the conflicts, and they were many, they do not seem to have been along these lines. Agriculture being the mainstay of the economy, it is natural that most of the men later accused of being rebels were farmers, but some were merchants and some were mill owners. Perhaps Hastings was still too rural to be seriously split in that particular way.

Immigration continued to create new stresses among the population. The native born did not always welcome those settlers who came from outside the country. If these were Americans, they were sometimes distrusted as disloyal and responsible for the spread of republican ideas. Those who came from Britain, including Ireland, fell into two groups, the half-pay officers and others who arrived with some capital, and the poor. The poor were a burden on the community, one that seemed all the heavier because these people were strangers. The half-pay officers frequently assumed a superiority local people were not prepared to acknowledge. On the other hand, families who were long established in the country displayed too often a condescending manner that was resented by their newer neighbours of any origin. To the differences among the religious groups were now added the division among Methodists and the Protestant-Catholic confrontation engendered by the Orange lodges. While there were all these various conflicts among the residents, one issue had come to dominate, and, although they were not formally organized, two groups were emerging on either side of it. One was made up of those who, whatever their opinion on any particular issue, could be relied upon to support the status quo because they valued stability above all. This group included those who held any public office or expected any benefit from government, as well as those who believed in a hierarchical society. To the other group the most important question was one of self-government, an overriding wish for democratic control of the administration, since they were convinced that the improvements they wanted could be gained in no other way. Within this general division people took different sides on any number of questions, but the broad issue was control of government by an appointed elite or by the elected representatives of the people.

This was not a question that could be resolved by Upper Canadians without the blessing of the Colonial Office. Unfortunately, in the guidance of Canadian affairs, the British parliament had good intentions but little understanding of Canada or Canadians, nor were all the men who held the office of colonial secretary equally capable. Although he was not as incompetent as his critics claimed, when Lord Glenelg resigned the post,

John Beverley Robinson wrote to the lieutenant-governor that Glenelg had been 'worse than useless – all unite in saying that in regard to the colonies he appeared to know nothing – to do nothing – and to care nothing.'[56]

A greater anxiety than the politics of the day was soon facing many families. The harvest of 1836 was almost a complete failure. Many were left without enough feed for their cattle, some without food for their families. To add to the problem, an international economic depression was developing which affected both Europe and North America. In the United States it soon became apparent that however fast new settlers rushed into the Midwest, they were not going to overtake the speculators. A spate of bank failures there signalled a financial collapse, which soon had repercussions in Upper Canada. Calling in of credit by Montreal wholesalers from local dealers and merchants, who in turn tried to collect from farmers and other customers, resulted in numerous bankruptcies and mortgage foreclosures.

There is no doubt that even some prosperous residents of the area were in trouble, but it was much worse for those who were not yet established or who were looking to be hired as labourers. This was especially the case for recent immigrants, many of whom arrived with little or no money. At the quarter sessions of April 1837 in Ernestown, the magistrates recorded 'the need to put a Stop to the Evils of Street begging and idle pauperism' by establishing a house of industry. This was the hated work house, which the Kingston *Chronicle and Gazette* also advocated in numerous editorials.[57] Just before the rebellion the Kingston *Spectator* reported, 'There are hundreds of distressed people mostly strangers about Kingston, nearly destitute and without employment. What is to be done with them during the winter we cannot say. Many had been working on the Waterloo Road, and at the Government works on the Point, but were discharged.'[58]

The harvest of 1837 was only adequate. It provided the farmer with enough to maintain him, but not enough to help him recover from the failure of the year before, to pay off debts, or to buy back cattle he had sacrificed. The Commercial Bank of the Midland District suspended payment, although it was allowed to keep its charter. Surviving American banks had already stopped payment and did not resume until April or May 1839. Canadian banks waited until August of that year before again paying in specie.

As the year 1837 went on, the conditions that foster political unrest increased steadily, and in Toronto a bitter Mackenzie was prodding and agitating the discontented into open revolt. If his opponents had been wise, they would have realized Mackenzie was safer in the assembly than ousted from it; he was now plotting their downfall in secret, instead of making speeches about it openly in parliament. And a capable administrator would not have ignored the growing danger but would have taken steps to ameliorate some of the provincial grievances. Unfortunately the man at the head of Upper Canada's administration was Sir Francis Bond Head, who seemed deaf to the storm warnings that rumbled all around him. Anna Jameson had an unusual opportunity to observe the social scene in 1837; although she wrote about Toronto, her words applied equally to the rest of the colony when she said regretfully, 'there reigns here a hateful factious spirit.'[59]

4 Explosion

When Mackenzie was no longer able to speak out in the assembly, he turned his attention to other means of battling his political foes. His current newspaper, the *Constitution*, kept up a barrage of criticism, but he became convinced that something more forceful was needed. During the summer of 1837 he instituted political unions around the province, and through his writing, as well as by speaking at numerous meetings – some of which turned violent – he enrolled a large membership in them. Included were many residents of Hastings County. The next year one of these supporters claimed 482 local men had signed up, ready to do or die in Mackenzie's cause, but there is no independent evidence for either their number or the obligations of their membership. Billa Flint later said he had seen 'one of their constitutions.' While he found it radical and even revolutionary, he quoted nothing that went beyond the usual platform of the Reformers during the past election. Within a few months membership lists had become dangerous, and the local one was destroyed.[1] The Hastings County union may have been organized earlier, but the only known meeting took place at Dr Hayden's Tavern in Thurlow late in November. No doubt it was well publicized and well attended by prominent Reformers. Unfortunately for them, news of the rebellion followed soon afterwards, and the magistrates did not hesitate to identify as a rebel or fomenter of rebellion anyone who had been present, so that there were a number of immediate arrests.

In the autumn Mackenzie made plans to bring to Toronto union delegates from across the province. They were to meet in a convention to draw up a new constitution for Upper Canada.[2] But when it seemed numbers alone would not be enough to persuade the government to adopt such a constitution, he began to encourage men to drill and to hold shooting practice. Some thought the drilling and the shooting were to make the marchers impressive enough that the government would take them seriously, but talk at the meetings had a more and more revolutionary sound. Until this time Mackenzie had never publicly questioned Upper Canada's status as a colony in the British Empire. Now he decided that independence from Britain was the only way to break the hold of the governing clique and, as a consequence, that a republican style of government like that of the United States was the model Canada should adopt. This was a drastic change of course along which many Reformers could not follow him.

Meantime in Lower Canada there was also a strong Reform movement. While there was a considerable number of English-speaking residents among the Reformers, most of the conflict had grown up between the original settlers, the French, to whom land and agriculture were all-important, and the later arrivals from the United States and Britain, the 'English,' with whom mercantile interests took precedence. There were about six times as many French as English, but most government offices were awarded to the English. Speculators bought up land that was needed for the natural increase of farm families, forcing young people to take small acreages or, very often, move to the United States. The Land Tenures Act was passed in England to change the seigneurial system for the benefit of the English, who wanted land in freehold for easier buying and selling. Union between Upper and Lower Canada was being actively promoted in order to swamp French votes in a combined legislature.[3] The French felt threatened on all sides. They formed a large majority in the assembly, where they were led by Louis Joseph Papineau, the speaker, but since the legislative council had to approve all bills they suffered the same frustration as Reform assemblies in Upper Canada. In 1836 they stopped supply, and the colonial secretary brought on a crisis when he rejected outright the assembly's grievances, the 'Ninety-two Resolutions,' and ordered accounts to be paid without the assembly's consent. More and more the *patriotes* looked for a radical solution, spurred on by several years of crop failure and economic distress. On hundreds of farms there was little to eat but potatoes, and only parish relief kept some families from starving.[4] In this desperate situation many lost confidence in British administration and in 1837 raised the banner of republicanism and independence. This scared off the moderate Reformers, including the clergy, who had for the most part been sympathetic. That the rebellion in Lower Canada failed as it did was partly due to the influence of the church, which ordered its members to submit to their temporal rulers. The priests threatened with excommunication anyone who took up arms, and many a man who would have joined the rebels stayed home. The church could not prevent the rebellion, but it could ensure its defeat.

During the autumn there were public meetings around Montreal in which thousands took part. Sir John Colborne in Quebec became alarmed and in October asked Sir Francis to send down some of the British regulars stationed in Upper Canada. Supremely confident in the popularity of his own rule, Sir Francis sent them all.[5] Nothing could have given greater encouragement to open rebellion in the upper province. When he heard about it, Mackenzie, could he have persuaded the other radical leaders, would have marched on the Toronto city hall, where four thousand stand of arms had a single guard, and he would have started the rebellion there and then. But the rest were more cautious, and the opportunity passed. From then on, however, the thought of those arms burned like a beacon in Mackenzie's mind.

Not everyone saw the folly of Sir Francis's action. In Belleville George Benjamin wrote an editorial in the *Intelligencer* in praise of Sir Francis's wisdom, rejoicing that the defence of the colony was now in the hands of its loyal militia.[6] Daniel Perry, captain of the newly formed Belleville Cavalry Militia, offered their services anywhere in British North America and said he intended to call them out to start drilling 'as soon as the mud is frozen up.'[7] In Kingston the largest public meeting ever held up to that time, according to the *Chronicle and Gazette*, discussed the uncertain situation in Lower Canada and passed a number of loyal resolutions.[8] In Brockville a retired officer wrote that he had called a meeting and was organizing a group of local men to march on Montreal. In fact, during October and November of 1837 Upper Canadians seemed to be blind to all that was happening at home. Their eyes were focused almost continuously on Lower Canada. Later, Samuel Strickland wrote that he had read the newspapers and had therefore been aware of 'the inflammatory speeches of William Lyon Mackenzie and his coadjutors. Little danger, however, was apprehended from them or their writings, especially by the loyal inhabitants of Northumberland and Peterborough, who were actually taken by surprise on hearing that a body of rebels ... were actually in arms and on their march to invest Toronto.'[9]

Strickland had been living in Peterborough at the time. His sister Susanna Moodie in nearby Lakefield wrote of 'the astonishment with which the news has been received by all the settlers in the bush.'[10] They were in the backwoods, remote from the events they read about, but others who lived near centres of rebellion were just as unprepared. Mrs Merritt of St

Catharines wrote on 8 December, the day after the rebellion, that 'all last week, the papers were filled with accounts of the Proceedings in L. Canada, not to the advantage of Papino's party, the People never dreaming of any disturbance in this Province, the Governor had let all the Troops go from Toronto.'[11]

Perhaps part of the reason for such lack of concern, even after alarming reports of mass meetings and threatening speeches, was that people were accustomed to the political meetings of the time and the rowdyism which was part of them, always increased by the amount of liquor that flowed on all such social occasions. Whatever the reason, those who might have taken action to prevent open revolt did nothing. Sir Francis continued to regard Mackenzie as beneath contempt, a sputtering firecracker making a lot of noise but unlikely to do much damage. Later on he said the rebellion broke out 'in a time of profound peace,' and he may have believed it.[12] Inaction remained the official attitude in spite of warnings, such as the resolutions proposed at a large meeting of Markham and Pickering men. These were reported in many newspapers, including those in Kingston. One was 'that this meeting approves the conduct and proceedings of the Hon Louis J. Papineau and his brother Canadians of Lower Canada, for the manly and bold stand they have taken against the British Ministry, whom this meeting, and, we believe, a very large majority of the people of Upper Canada, repose not one jot of confidence in, as they will always be for plundering and oppressing the people to keep up the old and the rising aristocracy.' A man with the ominous name of John Brown moved: 'That every man in this Township who has not got a good rifle do forthwith prepare him with one, as we do intend to maintain our political rights inviolate, let consequences be what they will. We know our cause is a great and honest one, and we will have one who is stronger than man to go with us; therefore, brother reformers, be encouraged, be true to each other, as union is strength.'[13]

In late November fighting broke out in Lower Canada south of Montreal. Within two weeks, after several bloody and costly battles, the rebels were defeated, but they repulsed the first attack made on them by British regulars. On receiving this news, Mackenzie decided the hour had struck. He travelled through the townships around the city distributing handbills headed 'Independence!' which urged, 'Up, then, brave Canadians! Get ready your rifles, and make short work of it.'[14]

There are no reliable figures for the number who responded to this call. Mackenzie no doubt exaggerated when he claimed that over two thousand made their way to Montgomery's Tavern, the gathering place north of Toronto. Whatever the number, so many plans went wrong that those who came, even by Mackenzie's account, were never all present at the same time. As some arrived, others left because of the lack of organization and leadership at the camp, and in the end there were probably no more than four hundred who stayed. It is generally believed others were on their way to take part on the rebel side when they discovered they were too late and quickly joined the militia. It is an open question how many had come prepared to fight, and how many believed there was to be a peaceful march. The first group must have been disappointed to learn there was no supply of arms; the second group, to find they were expected to bear arms at all.

The militiamen in Toronto were no better organized than the rebels. Colonel James Fitzgibbon, a hero of the War of 1812–14, was the man in charge of them. He was one who had been alert to the growing menace and for weeks had been pressing Sir Francis to let him arm the militia. In vain. Even when reports were circulating of a rebel camp north of the city, Fitzgibbon found it impossible to convince the governor. Only after two men had been fatally shot on 4 December would that supremely confident man believe what was happening. Then in great excitement he bundled his family onto a steamboat in Toronto harbour and began handing out arms to all who asked for them. The Kingston *Chronicle and Gazette* reported that the next day a visitor to Government House found Sir Francis 'wearing a fuzee or light musket across his chest, two horse pistols in his pockets, a double barrelled gun in his hand.'[15] The result must have been striking, Sir Francis being a very small man.

Fitzgibbon was at first in despair. He did not have enough men, and for a time it seemed impossible to get those he had into any sort of order.[16] The outlook began to change when in a day or two several groups came in from Scarborough, Hamilton, and a few other townships near Toronto. On Thursday, 7 December, Fitzgibbon succeeded in forming his amateur troops into three lines. Then, led by military bands, they marched up Yonge Street. When the rebels heard them coming, they scrambled out to meet the attack. The fighting lasted about half an hour. The few assorted firearms of the rebels, their pikes, and other makeshift weapons were no match for the muskets of the militia, whose superior organization would probably have won the day in any event. Mackenzie was one of the last to leave the battlefield, and riding west, then south, he escaped to Buffalo. A few men were killed, others wounded; hundreds were captured and imprisoned; and hundreds more followed Mackenzie into exile.

TREASON

5   The Gallant Militia

In October 1837, when George Benjamin rejoiced that the defence of Upper Canada was placed completely in the hands of its loyal citizens, it was easy to agree with him. As long as the only source of trouble appeared to be around Montreal, anyone might feel confident that the militia could replace the regiments of regulars. Even when the Mackenzie rebellion did break out, this confidence seemed to be well placed. Militia officers assumed responsibility promptly, even eagerly, and in the Midland District when the first muster was ordered the enlisted men responded well. Many of them served over the next year and a half as often as they were called out, although with decreasing enthusiasm as danger receded. The men were never as interested as the officers in militia parades unless they saw a need for them. In October 1837 Colonel Coleman had given the required eight days notice for the Belleville company of the First Hastings Regiment to parade, and he was surprised and disappointed to have just 25 of the 120 men turn out. He blamed Anthony Marshall, a Belleville doctor and magistrate, who had stated publicly that there was no legal way of exacting a fine from any man who failed to attend. For most of the men this had apparently removed any reason for going to the drill. Some of the officers seem to have neglected their duties too, since Coleman also complained about Captain James McNabb, who had in four or five years seldom put in an appearance or called a meeting of his company.[1]

In theory the militia gave the province a fighting force of overwhelming strength since it included every able-bodied male citizen except for those, like the Quakers, who were excused because of their religion. In practice it meant instead a great untrained mass. Militia commissions, being awarded for political loyalty, were often held by men with little military knowledge, and since most of the regiments met together only once a year even experienced officers could not be expected to turn out well-drilled troops. In the summer of 1837 Anna Jameson visited a family whose sons, Charles and James, were about to take part in the annual parade day. One was 'in the pretty green uniform of a rifleman, the other all covered with embroidery as a captain of Lancers.' The whole family turned out to watch the three or four hundred men assembled in a nearby field:

[A] few men, well mounted and dressed as Lancers, in uniforms which were, however, anything but uniform, flourished backwards on the green sward, to the manifest peril of the spectators, themselves and their horses equally wild, disorderly, spirited, undisciplined, but this was perfection compared with the infantry ... Here there was no uniformity of dress, of appearance, of movement; a few had coats, others jackets; a great number had neither coats nor jackets, but appeared in their shirt-sleeves, white or checked or clean or dirty, in edifying variety! Some wore hats, others caps, others had their own shaggy heads of hair. Some had firelocks; some had old swords, suspended in belts, or stuck in their waist-bands; but the greater number shouldered sticks or umbrellas. Mrs. M ... told us that on a former parade day she had heard the word of command given thus – 'Gentlemen with the umbrellas, take ground to the right! Gentlemen with the walking sticks, take ground to the left!' Now they ran after each other, elbowed and kicked each other, straddled, stooped, chattered; and if the commanding officer turned his back for a moment, very coolly sat down on the bank to rest ... Charles M. made himself hoarse with shouting out orders which no one obeyed, except, perhaps, two or three in the front; and James, with his horsemen, flourished their lances, and galloped, and curvetted to admiration ... The parade day ended in a drunken bout and a riot, in which, as I was afterwards informed, the colonel was knocked down, and one or two serious and even fatal accidents had occurred.[2]

This seems a wildly exaggerated account, yet there are other descriptions of drill days not very different from this.[3] It is easy to understand why Upper Canadians were not well prepared for the threat they were to face during the rebellion years. The navy that had played such a large part in winning victory during the War of 1812–14 had almost disappeared from the lakes. When Captain Sandom of the Royal Navy needed vessels in 1838, he had to mount guns on passenger steamboats. After Sir Charles

Grey, a British officer and brother-in-law of Lord Durham, visited Kingston during the summer of that year, he wrote that the dockyard there was in 'a terribly ruinous condition' and that Sandom's pennant was hoisted on a vessel 'still only in frame (!) as she has been for the last 20 years and probably may be 20 more.'[4] The fort at Niagara had become almost derelict. To quote Mrs Jameson again, the force there 'consists of three privates and a corporal, with adequate arms and ammunition, that is rusty fire-locks and damaged guns. The fortress itself I took for a dilapidated brewery.[5] It was only Fort Henry at Kingston, store of most of the arms and ammunition for the defence of Upper Canada, that was in any way ready to meet the emergency of December 1837, and even Fort Henry was in the process of being rehabilitated after years of neglect.[6] Nevertheless it was to prove adequate, and adequately protected by the militia until the regulars returned. Richard Bonnycastle, who was acting commander at the time news of the outbreak came to Kingston, was able to supply arms to regiments in the Midland, Prince Edward, and Northumberland districts. He later wrote of the manner in which he learned about the emergency: the news came to him by land and by sea.

Edmund Murney was an ambitious young man from Kingston, where he had studied law. In 1834 he moved to Belleville and set up a practice. The next year he was made a magistrate and a militia captain. On the first weekend of December 1837 he was in Toronto, where he heard the news, as well as the wild rumours, about the rebel camp just outside the city. He went to someone in authority and got a signed order for the commander at Kingston to give out arms.[7] Then, uncertain of the hazards of the journey, he had the order sewn to the inside of his coat sleeve and, with another man, set out for home. Mackenzie had by this time stationed guards at the bridge over the Don River, and they stopped and searched the travellers. For some reason they made the other man a prisoner, but they failed to find Murney's message and they let him go. He rode on to Kingston, where he gave the order to Colonel Bonnycastle.[8] It is interesting to note that news of the rebellion reached Kingston, and no doubt Belleville on the way, the day before it took place.[9]

Murney had acted bravely, but his mission ended in something of an anti-climax. The same message had already arrived at Fort Henry by steamboat. As Bonnycastle later described it:

I was sitting very quietly at home in Kingston one evening at the beginning of December ... when I was surprised by a person running into my room and telling me that the steamboat, the *Traveller*, had arrived from Toronto with Sir Francis and all who had been able to escape from the city, which had been taken by Mackenzie and burnt. I buckled on my armour to go down to the Artillery Barracks and I had just got out, when a second breathless messenger came in, for the hall door was open to my neighbours, who, alarmed beyond measure, were crowding in to hear the news. This gentleman informed me that the steamboat had brought nothing from Toronto, but some serious outbreak had occurred there.[10]

The ship had, in fact, brought a letter for Bonnycastle instructing him to send certain arms back to Toronto and to distribute others 'to all loyal men.' Soon the *Traveller* turned about with arms and ammunition under a guard of volunteers from Kingston and sailed back to Toronto. Bonnycastle gave out arms locally and sent them to nearby militia units, those for Hastings and Northumberland being entrusted to Anthony Manahan, the colonel of the Second Hastings Regiment. He saw the arms loaded onto another steamboat, the *Kingston*, and sailed for Belleville on the night of 8 December. If the dispatches he sent back to the newspaper and to the adjutant general seem to turn this simple undertaking into a major military operation, it must be remembered that the countryside was in a state of great excitement. News of what was happening was scarce, and mixed with the wildest rumour. No one could be sure what was lurking around the corner. As a result, fear expanded with uncertainty and heightened the sense of importance these men felt in their mission.

The first thing they had to contend with was the weather. The long rainy spell that had kept the harbours open and allowed the steamboats to ply the lakes so late in the season broke that night, and rapidly forming ice forced the *Kingston* to put in at Culbertson's Wharf at Deseronto, where John Culbertson had a tavern. There they ate a very early breakfast and warmed themselves with a quantity of liquor before tackling the rest of the journey.[11] The Mohawks of Tyendinaga offered to take the arms on to Belleville, but instead

> fourteen waggons were in almost immediate attendance and the whole were put into the waggons and by two o'clock we proceeded on our march to this place accompanied by an additional guard of Thirty of the Indians of the Mohawk Tribe who were sensibly anxious to give us every assistance we required. We halted at Shannonville for the night induced to this by the intelligence I received on my way that an attack was meditated in a pine thicket that outskirts that Village by the Rebels

of whom there are several in the second third and fourth concessions of Thurlow along the front of which Township we had to pass – having used due precaution in guarding the waggons for the night in which I was ably assisted by the Magistrates of the place Messrs. Appleby, Blacker, Murchison, and Lazier.[12]

If there really was any danger of attack, it was faced by the Mohawks, to each of whom Manahan gave a musket and ten rounds of ammunition, and they cleared the woods throughout the line of march.[13] Captains Benson and Bonter had accompanied the arms train, and at Shannonville they were joined by Captain McNabb with a contingent of volunteers from Belleville, 'all armed and bravely determined to defend the armament with their lives.' On they went until, in Belleville, 'a multitude of the inhabitants of this populous Town' turned out to greet them. As R.V.C. wrote to the *Upper Canada Herald*: 'In such times of alarm it is gratifying to witness the spirit of loyal devotion, shown throughout the country by the Faithful Militia. On Sunday week it was a stirring sight to behold a long train of waggons with a strong guard coming into Town with arms and ammunitions of war for the different Regiments – Nor was it the least cheering, to find our brethren of the Mohawk Tribe of Indians, with their Flags waving, accompanied by their Chief, leading on the whole as the advance escort.'[14]

For the time being Manahan kept a guard of Indians and asked permission to form them into a rifle company, 'as they had requested, under their chief John Culbertson.'[15] Manahan wanted to set up an arms depot at Rawdon, which he did for a time, and thought they would 'form the most efficient and least expensive guard for that place.' The army leaders, however, were always reluctant to call on the Indians since they were afraid they could not control them, although the Indians seem to have acted with restraint whenever they were in action. Manahan had no fear of the Indians, but he did not trust the other inhabitants of the district. He wrote that in Belleville 'there is as far as I can learn but a small proportion disaffected. I must not, however, conceal the fact that there are in the Rear of Sidney and Thurlow very many of the Inhabitants who have attended seditious meetings and signed Articles of association in direct opposition to the laws of the Country and the Queen's authority.'[16]

Powder for blasting was stored at Chisholm's Rapids on the Trent, and Manahan feared it would be taken by the rebels, 'hundreds of disaffected persons residing in the neighbourhood.' His solution was simple: 'My advice to the Magistrates is: make Prisoners of the Ring Leaders – commit without bail – Search their papers & take Arms from all that are disaffected.'

Further evidence of disloyalty in Hastings was given when Murney wrote to the lieutenant-governor on 12 December:

> Our Magistrates are very active and have made arrangements for two Companies from the first one from the second and one from the third regiments of Hastings to be on duty in Belleville for the protection of the Town and Country – Many of our Farmers and Townsmen have refused to take the oath of allegiance which through my suggestion is tendered to every militia-man & they the farmers have organized societies through every part of the Country the ostensible object of which are not to take up arms on *Either* side – These societies are very strong, they commenced no doubt through Mackenzie, but he has rebelled too soon for them, public opinion was not sufficiently ripe for him in these parts & they condemn him not for his rebellion but for his rashness – I have seen many of their resolutions, but they are so vaguely expressed that without having their watchwords it is impossible to make treason of them.[17]

The last sentence reveals as much about Murney's bias as about the real nature of the resolutions he had read. In Manahan's letter to the *Chronicle and Gazette*, describing the transportation of arms to Belleville, he said, 'In this part of the country there have as yet been no meetings – two it is said are intended for Tuesday next [19 December] – one constitutional, and another to *declare a neutrality* – singular enough.'[18]

In the counties adjoining Hastings there seemed to be little fear of disloyalty. Manahan's wagons had brought to the Belleville magistrates 1,000 stand of arms, 150 pistols, 50 rifles, and 200 marine sabres, with 10,000 rounds of cartridges for muskets and 1,000 for pistols. As soon as these were distributed to the three Hastings regiments and the Third Northumberland, the men were notified to parade, and the colonels of these regiments reported with some pride on the turnout.

The colonel of the Third Northumberland was Henry Ruttan, sheriff of the Newcastle District, who lived at Colborne. In his regimental order for the Third Northumberland he thanked his men 'for their prompt answer to the call of their country, to rally round its constitution, and protect it from the unhallowed and polluted touch of a band of Traitors, secretly organized under the name of *Reform*.'[19] To Fitzgibbon he wrote, 'You may rely on this District for 3,000 effective men in any case of Emergency.' He had sentries posted on every road by which the rebels might try to leave the country, as well as two companies, each consisting of sixty men, stationed in

Colborne and at Trent Port.[20] He did complain that there were some skulkers who should have turned out for militia duty and did not, but said that if there were any rebels in the Newcastle District they had not shown themselves, although 'how far this state may be the effect of the prompt answer of the Loyalists to their Country's call is still uncertain.' Ruttan was a keen officer, writing three reports to Fitzgibbon and delivering an address to the troops, which he also published in the newspaper, all within the six days when he was assembling his men and placing his guards and sentries. In each report he stressed the need to keep an eye on the neighbouring County of Hastings, which 'I am informed has a few refractory spirits who require Keeping in order.'[21] In another report he said, 'I understood there were some slightly traitorous Symptoms among a few individuals in Hastings but my Regiment lies next to them and should it be necessary I will teach them a lesson never fear.'[22]

On the other side of Hastings in Lennox and Addington the Second Regiment paraded, and 'upwards of one hundred and fifty men volunteered for immediate service in any part of Upper or Lower Canada.'[23] In Picton Colonel John McCuaig assembled the Second Prince Edward Regiment and read out to them documents 'Emanating from His Excellency regarding the disturbed state of the province,' with gratifying results:

[T]he whole body of the people, there being no less in the Judgement of good Judges than one Thousand present, manifested great indignation at the proceedings of the rebels, and at the Close of Each paper three loud and long cheers were given for Queen and Constitution and our gallant Sir Francis Bond Head, with tremendous cries of 'where are the detested rebels, where are they, we shall put them down we shall hunt them like blood hounds.' Then Mr Wilkins addressed them as a Magistrate ... that his Excellency had shown them an Example worthy of their imitation that he had led the Civil Authorities from the City of Toronto. Met the rebel faction and dispersed them, with considerable loss, on the rebel side! – Tremendous cheering.[24]

There is no doubt about the enthusiasm and patriotic fervour of many of the inhabitants in the whole area around the Bay. According to the *Chronicle and Gazette* there was even a muster in the little village of Milford, which is about ten miles from Picton in the Township of Marysburgh, where, it was reported, several hundred men turned out.[25] In spite of the 'none too loyal' people in Hastings, Colonel Coleman was able to report on 11 December that the First Regiment of Hastings had assembled one-thousand strong in Belleville. He was gratified that 'several of the Magistrates and other respectable individuals having joined the Ranks, with an offer of their Services, in case of emergency, they made a most formidable appearance.'[26]

One community whose loyalty was never in doubt was the Mohawk settlement. Bonnycastle recalled, 'The Indians harnessed their little wagons and leaving only the women and children, the feeble and the aged of their tribe, drove into Kingston, ninety in number, with the old Union Jack floating proudly over them, to offer their services to me.' They were put into barracks and given daily rations. When it was all over, they were, he said, amply repaid by a few yards of cotton, a few handkerchiefs, a good rifle or two for the chiefs, some tobacco, and a few pipes.[27] The Indians were not part of the militia, but were allies and independent. Even so, their reward does not seem overly generous.

Anyone privileged to have an overview of Hastings County in December 1837 would have seen a sudden quickening of activity as soon as messengers brought news of the rebellion. It must have been a little like the Shakespearian stage when the urgent cry goes out, 'To horse, to horse!' Some went to join their cavalry units, but others rode away in haste, heading for the border. These were men who had agreed too publicly with Mackenzie and his aims, and were now afraid of the consequences. Others saddled up their horses in order to carry the news to their neighbours, and there must have been many excited and anxious gatherings around the county. Then the magistrates ordered militia officers to effect a number of arrests, and bring the suspects in to a hearing at Belleville. Immediately after that, those who did not satisfy the justices of the peace were taken to Kingston to the district jail or to Fort Henry, and for this purpose teams of horses were harnessed to wagons, or to sleighs when there was enough snow. The open winter made the roads even worse than usual, so that it must have been an incredibly rough ride for those who were taken in farm wagons without springs on a journey that required two days. And it was not only prisoners who were carted about, for many of the claims that were later presented were for conveying militia to and from various parts of the county, or even farther afield.

Quite often, too, men went long distances on foot. The men who arrested Henry Alicumbrack at his home in the second concession of Huntingdon seem to have walked, for in his claim he said they 'marched' him down to Belleville. James Whiteman went on foot with other volunteers from Shannonville to Hayden's Corners to arrest Anson Hayden. They could not find him, but they went on to Joseph Canniff's, took him prisoner, and brought him to the magistrates in Belleville.[28] Perhaps in an economy drive, in November 1838 an order was issued stating that the militiamen had been riding too much and the wagons were in future to be used only by the sick or for the heavy baggage of a regiment or detachment.[29] If the order was obeyed, the men must have walked many weary miles. In a book published in 1841 the author mentions a settlement near Kingston, placing it at a distance of sixteen miles by road, but 'when we say 16 miles, we mean in winter, for in summertime the depth of the mud holes has to be added to the length of the way, which will bring it to 18 miles, the usually estimated distance.'[30] Marching over such roads, the militiaman's lot could not have been a happy one.

At the time of Mackenzie's rebellion Sir Francis sent messengers far and wide, alerting everyone to the danger and asking them to come to Toronto to protect the government. Many in the eastern part of the province responded, from at least as far north as Peterborough and as far east as Prince Edward County and Hastings.[31] John Macaulay's mother wrote to her daughter-in-law to say how proud she was that 'we sent a gallant Company of "Picton Volunteers" to the "Seat of War" last week and ... they were joined by another Company at the Carrying Place.'[32] From Hastings County a claim was later submitted for teaming arms to Cobourg, and another for sending supplies there at the time of the rebellion. About two thousand men gathered at Cobourg and Port Hope, where they were told the insurrection had been put down and they should go home again. Despite this, many went on to Toronto to see for themselves what was happening.[33]

It would be spring before the regular troops came back to Fort Henry, and meantime it was left to the militia to protect Kingston and the fort. From the surrounding country they quickly flocked in. The Frontenac County men were soon joined by others. On 13 December the *Chronicle and Gazette* reported three additional units had come to town, a troop of dragoons from Camden East under Captain Clarke, another from Ernest-own led by Captain Fralick, and militia from Bath led by Captain McKay,[34] so that, in Bonnycastle's picturesque description, 'the usually quiet streets of Kingston now echoed day and night, either to the tread of marching men [or] to the neighing of the eager steed.'[35] The men of the First and Second Frontenac and the Lennox and Addington regiments wore the standard uniform in two shades of gray with red shirts and fur caps.[36] The Queen's Marine Artillery were in blue knee-length frocks with white anchors embroidered on the sleeves. The dandies were the Frontenac Light Dragoons in uniforms of blue faced with buff, topped by tall bearskin helmets. Occasionally there was an eye-catching addition, the newly formed Loyal Scotch Volunteer Independent Light Infantry Company. They wore Highland bonnets, trews of Royal Stuart tartan, and blue jackets. Two of the young men in the company were Oliver Mowat and John Alexander Macdonald.[37]

On 27 December the 'loyal and patriotic ladies' of Kingston met to plan for a set of colours for the Frontenac regiment.[38] The equally loyal and patriotic ladies of Belleville had stolen a march on them; they already had a flag for the Second Hastings Regiment. On New Year's Day 1838

Major Parker, the officer commanding in the absence of Colonel Mana-han, marched the Voluntary Company of the Regiment at present doing duty at this place under Captain Mackenzie, escorted by the Corps of Riflemen lately formed under Captain W. [Wellington] Mur-ney, with the band of the Regiment, to Mr Samson's residence. The two companies having been drawn up, Mrs Samson came forward, supported by the Reverend Mr Cochran and Dr Ridley, bearing the flag, tastefully inscribed with the name of our Queen, 'Victoria,' and '2d Hastings,' and delivered the following address:

Officers and men of the 2d Hastings Militia, – I have much pleasure in presenting you with this Flag, inscribed with the name of our youthful and gracious Queen. In placing it in your hands I well know I am giving it to some of Her Majesty's most true and gallant defenders. Ever will it wave victorious in the battlefield.[39]

When the Kingston colours were delivered in June, the newspaper report, in the style of the day, stated that Mrs Major Smith and Mrs Captain Harper ceremoniously presented them to the 'brave defenders of our insulted country,' otherwise the First Frontenac Regiment.[40]

As it turned out, there was not to be any battlefield in the Midland District to engage all these volunteers. Even so, life in the militia was not without its hazards. Before the end of December two local men met their deaths while on service. The *Chronicle and Gazette* reported: 'We regret to learn that Mr. William Church, of Shannonville, on Thursday evening last came to his death in the following melancholy manner – He and another man (both being dragoons) had escorted the mail through the Indian woods, and stopping at a tavern in Shannonville, the comrade of Mr. Church, in loosening his cloak, let his pistol fall, which coming in contact with the stove, discharged, when Mr. Church received the contents just as he was stooping to sit down, and died instantly.'[41]

The other fatal accident took place a few days later in Belleville. It involved James McNabb, the man who had been elected to the assembly the year before and who was serving as captain of the First Hastings. The report read, 'We regret to hear that J. McNabb, Esquire, of Belleville, has suddenly met his death in the most heartrending manner. An alarm of fire being given, Mr. McNabb was hurrying through the dark passage of an Inn, where a number of the armed militia were quartered, when he ran upon the fixed bayonet of one of the men, which pierced his abdomen. He died within twenty-four hours.'[42]

On 19 December George Benjamin, as clerk of the bench of magistrates of Hastings County, wrote to the adjutant general's office about the 240 men on guard in Belleville: 'Out of this number 120 are from the Back Townships, and away from home, it is necessary that they should be supplied with food and other necessaries, and to this end the Magistrates have appointed Billa Flint to furnish the needful. But it is found impossible to continue this, unless a small sum say from £100 to £150, be placed at the disposal of the Magistrates, for the purchase of such provisions and other necessaries that cannot be provided without the cash.'[43]

It is unlikely this 'small sum' was forthcoming. One of the most common complaints was the difficulty of getting money or supplies from the commissary department. In October 1838 Captain De Rottenburg, a British officer then in charge of the local militia, wrote to the assistant commissary general 'upon the unsettled claims of the Inhabitants of Belleville & its vicinity. & I am directed by His Excellency to convey to you his peremptory orders that you take immediate steps to settle the same provided that no error exists in the accounts.'[44] Even a peremptory order may not have had effect. Billa Flint was one of those who had to put in a claim in 1845 for supplies furnished to the militia in 1838. Lack of funds put an end to such a large body of men being kept as a guard for Belleville, but now that there appeared to be a real threat to the country there was no lack of defenders. In April 1838 William Wallbridge wrote of 'the astonishing eagerness of the men to serve in the militia,' so that the Belleville magistrates had to keep sending them home again.[45] There was probably more than one reason for this. Economic conditions were still depressed, and early in the year unemployment was extensive, particularly for those not long in the country. Those who were established, however, with farms or regular occupations, soon wanted to get back to them. Everyone engaged in agriculture, the principal industry, needed to get onto the land by springtime, so that the situation was changing even at the time Wallbridge was writing.

Military duty also interfered at times with other work. Nicol Hugh

Baird was the engineer in charge of canal construction on the Trent, and some of the men working there appealed to him about the orders they received. Both Colonel Manahan of North Hastings and Colonel Henry Ruttan of Colborne claimed the command of these men, since they were working on the boundary between the counties of Hastings and Northumberland. The men protested because on more than one occasion they had been called away from their work and had to make their way through several miles of bush to some place where they were told they would be drilled. On one occasion they reached the spot where they were to assemble, only to find the order had been cancelled and they had to walk back again. They asked Baird what they should do because, as they put it, 'we have military men enough among us but we will be ruled by none but you.'[46]

In spite of all the official reports and the public show, there were many internal quarrels and jealousies within the militia. The adjutant general's correspondence during the rebellion years contains many letters from officers in the militia complaining that they, or their sons or their friends, did not get promotion; protesting that those who got promotion were unqualified in ability or character; or accusing fellow officers of misdeeds and asking that they be court-martialled. There is even a complaint against the adjutant general of militia himself, Colonel Richard Bullock. This is in the file in the form of a copy of a letter the Belleville magistrates were sending to the lieutenant-governor, Sir George Arthur, telling him of the 'harsh and uncourteous language' used by Bullock when he refused one of the several requests the magistrates made for a guard of one hundred men to be stationed in Belleville.

A letter from Colonel William Murchison of Shannonville states that Captain John Blacker was insubordinate and had disrupted a parade; Murchison wanted Bullock to take some action against him, preferably by court martial. What appears to have happened is that Murchison called the men out and, until the hour of assembly, passed the time in a nearby tavern. Blacker and the men assembled, waited for a while, and then, being cold, sent for Murchison to come out, or at least give orders to the officers. Murchison failed to appear and, after a second summons, said the men should just go home again. Thinking this an 'injustice' to the men, Blacker addressed them in the usual form, urging them to remain loyal and ready to defend home and country. Meantime Murchison came out of the tavern and indicated that he wanted to speak, 'but it seemed he could not speak much although he was not interrupted.' That, at any rate, was the somewhat indignant explanation Blacker wrote in reply to the charge.[47] In Lennox and Addington Cornet William Fairfield sent on to Colonel Isaac Fraser so many complaints alleging that Lieutenant Fralick had 'kept in his own hands' the pay the men of the First Troop of Cavalry had earned in the winter of 1837–9, that Fraser felt obliged to ask the adjutant general to order an investigation.[48] Fairfield had insisted on 'a genuine court martial,' but these were expensive and Bullock was not sympathetic to the appeal, although he may have ordered an investigation.[49]

One of the worst cases was in Belleville, where Colonel Thomas Coleman accused his officers of mutiny. He wrote to Captain McNabb that he had heard of a secret meeting of his officers, who had so far forgotten their duty as to impeach their colonel, and reproached McNabb for 'combining' with them.[50] In fact, it was Benjamin Ketcheson who had chaired a meeting of officers of the First Hastings and had drawn up a list of charges, among them that Coleman had called a muster on 13 January and then had failed to show up. On the 9 January 'Ensign Grass went to Coleman's house on Militia Business, he lay drunk and could get no Satisfaction from him.' The following day Captain Elijah Ketcheson went 'but could not see him he being still intoxicated,' and 'while the different Companies of Militia were on duty in this place, during the late disturbed state of affairs, he was taken up by the guard as a disturber of the public peace, and conduct[ed] home, he being too intoxicated to go home by himself.' He had also failed to appear at a militia meeting he called on 28 December, 'even after having been sent for twice (and I believe perfectly sober at the time),' added Captain Ketcheson.[51] The officers wanted to be rid of a superior who could not be said to command any respect 'for his drunkenness and gross acts of impropriety, which will be substantiated by almost every officer in the Regt, as well as by many of the Magistrates of the County of Hastings.' And they got their wish, for Coleman resigned. The adjutant general, however, was always in favour of avoiding courts martial and scandal. He accepted Coleman's 'explanation' and reinstated him, suggesting that the officers 'as gentlemen' should apologize to Coleman for the accusations they had made against him. Morale in the First Regiment could scarcely have been good during, and after, this affair.

The lack of response from the adjutant general must have galled those who took their militia responsibility seriously, as undoubtedly many officers and men did, and if the officers were enjoying their temporary importance, that was only natural. To those accustomed to soldiers who were well trained and officers who were professional, these amateurs in uniform were a poor substitute. Sir George Arthur in numerous letters regretted the absence of the regiments, and John Langton, who had settled near Fenelon, wrote to an English friend about the contemporary scene:

As yet the military mania has not reached us, though on the front everybody is mad. In the streets of Toronto every third man is a soldier, and at least every fifth an officer. Captains and colonels are as thick as blackberries, and the cavalry (lancers no less) are galloping about to the imminent risk of the lives of passers-by – and their own. Military tailors not being plentiful here, the variety in the uniforms is amusing and their cut as absurd as that of their wearers. But the article in greatest demand is a sword; anything with a hilt will sell for £5, if it also has a point it will fetch £10.[52]

However others might make fun of them, the officers took it all very seriously, and from them the community expected no less. When Daniel Bowen of Frankford was made a lieutenant in the militia late in 1838, he wrote to his brother William, a magistrate in Frankford. In reply he got some brotherly advice: 'Now my Dear Brother you are on military duty you must pay strict attention to your business in that line [–] do not think of any other business but your duty – be punctual in all your transactions and let the world see that you are a man of strict honor and loyalty [–] be sprightly [–] walk a little more straight like a soldier and look out for number one.'[53]

6 Pirates and Brigands

Two days before Mackenzie's rebellion there was a public meeting in the frontier town of Buffalo, New York, 'to express sympathy with the Canadian revolution.' When Mackenzie arrived there four days after his defeat, he was among friends. He addressed a crowd said to have numbered three thousand. By this time he was a thoroughgoing republican, eager to break all connection with England and resolved to 'throw off the yoke of oppression.' To his American listeners the tyranny of Great Britain was already an article of faith, and their response was wildly enthusiastic. They offered arms, money, and men for the liberation of Canada, and seem to have taken control of further plans. Soon Rensselaer Van Rensselaer was in charge of operations, although it is hard to know what qualification he had for the job apart from the fact that his father had been a militia general during the War of 1812–14. He and the committee at once disagreed with Mackenzie, who wanted them to go to Fort Erie to aid Dr Duncombe, who, Mackenzie believed, had a large force ready to march on Toronto. Instead, the committee decided to establish a camp on Navy Island, a Canadian island in the Niagara River. There Mackenzie set up a provisional government and issued a manifesto, promising three hundred acres of prime land and $100 in silver to each volunteer, payable after the liberation of Canada. He later claimed that over the next month around six hundred recruits joined his island republic.[1]

Those who flocked to his standard were an assorted lot with little discipline and less aptitude for military life. Not a few were boys and youths who saw an opportunity for adventure. The economic slump had left thousands of men out of work, and this offered employment of a kind. There seemed little danger since the leaders always represented Canadians to be waiting with open arms for their liberators. No doubt all these people hoped to get Canadian land as a reward for their efforts, but they justified this in the noble cause of bringing freedom to an oppressed people. Mackenzie insisted that Canadians needed only a little help in order to achieve an American-style revolution, and he clung to this belief long after events proved it false. The name these men took was that of 'Patriots.' Many Canadians joined the Patriot army, but the name was misleading. By far the greater number of recruits were American, and even among the Canadians the majority were no doubt of American origin. In Canada they were often called by less flattering names, such as 'pirates' and 'brigands.'

The United States was at peace with Britain and Canada, and this army threatened that peace, yet the American government did little to stop it. Part of the reason was the degree of independence enjoyed by the individual states, each of which controlled its own militia, and, as in Canada, the militia was the principal defence of the country. The United States Army numbered just over 7,800, and most of this force was engaged in fighting Indians in Florida. The policy avowed in Washington was to maintain neutrality in Canadian affairs, although it is questionable how firm that policy was. In any case the federal government was not in a strong position to enforce it. Most Americans agreed with the aims of the Patriots, and if the result of their activities was American acquisition of Canadian territory, they would not be displeased. The British ambassador in Washington, Henry Stephen Fox, wrote that American neutrality would end at once if any weakness were shown on the Canadian side: 'Whatever may be the wish of the president & the more respectable statesmen the torrent of popular will would be too strong. All Americans have been born & brought up in the expectation, that the Canadas were necessarily destined to belong, sooner or later, to them.'[2]

On 29 December Allan MacNab, the flamboyant militia leader from Hamilton, almost precipitated both sides into a war no one wanted.[3] A small steamboat, the *Caroline*, had begun the day before to ferry supplies to Navy Island from the American side. At that time the Patriots numbered perhaps two hundred. Instead of attacking them on their Canadian island, MacNab ordered a raid at night on the little steamboat tied up on the American shore. His men cut it adrift and set fire to it. At least one man died, an American on board the steamboat.[4] The *Caroline* affair meant that American territory had been invaded, which enraged both state and federal governments, making it dangerously difficult to keep the peace. In fact for months afterwards war seemed to many to be unavoidable. A letter of William Wallbridge's written at this time confidently predicted that war would begin within weeks, and if the United States had been in a stronger position this might well have been the result. Fortunately the sabre-rattling died down after a while, and meantime supplies, which had been coming to Navy Island before the *Caroline* began its run, continued to do so afterwards. Apart from desultory firing, little else was done to harry the rebel republic.

Professional military men were critical that those in charge had made no attempt to capture 'an accessible Island, garrisoned *at most*, by 500 Ragamuffins!! It is an eternal disgrace to Colonel McNab and Sir F. Head.'[5] That was the opinion of Sir Charles Grey, brother-in-law of Lord Durham, who arrived in Canada with his regiment in the summer of 1838. Many Upper Canadians, however, were delighted, acclaiming the *Caroline* affair as a heroic naval action. Samuel Strickland rejoiced to think of the glorious sight it must have been as the flaming ship swept over the falls.[6] The same vision inspired a number of artists who painted it variously and imaginatively. The facts were more prosaic than the pictures. The *Caroline* sank well before it reached the falls, and for years its rusting engine could be seen above water near Goat Island. However, if the militia were unable to dislodge the Patriots, the Patriots were equally unable to launch an invasion of Canada from an island in the Niagara River. In the middle of January 1838 they left it and returned to the mainland.

While Mackenzie was making his escape to the border, Dr Duncombe was haranguing the men of the London District from St Thomas to Brantford to join in the rebellion. The result is known as the Duncombe Rising. Communication was so slow that almost a week after Mackenzie's defeat on Yonge Street, Duncombe was still unaware of it and still planning to join forces with him. Accordingly, by the time he had assembled his rebels, the countryside was on the alert and MacNab was leading a large number of militiamen against them. Confronted by this much stronger force there was nothing for the rebels to do but scatter and hide as quickly as possible. Many were arrested; many others, including Duncombe himself, made their escape to the United States, some to return and fight another day.[7]

From then on Mackenzie seems to have had little to do with the Patriots' military plans. There was no lack of leaders, however. The Illinois Army of the Northwest, which Mackenzie credited with seven hundred men, had four generals. There were other armies and other generals in Buffalo and farther east. There was even an admiral in the person of Bill Johnston, a highly successful smuggler normally based in the Thousand Islands. He had been recommended 'because he can greatly annoy the Kingstonians.'[8] A generous assignment of commissions at all levels was one of the attractions of service with the Patriots. Training was at best sketchy, and there was no agreed chain of command. Sometimes their plans failed through bungling, sometimes through cowardice, but throughout 1838 and even beyond, they kept Upper Canadians in a state of uncertainty and fear, amounting at times to panic. The western half of the province was particularly vulnerable because it was at a distance from the centres of command and supply, and moreover had been settled to a great extent by Americans, part of the wave that rolled into Michigan and the Midwest. It was natural that they should lend the most sympathetic ears to the cry of independence, and that those who had fled across the border should focus attention there in any attempt to capture Canadian territory.

Early in January it was known that four hundred rifles had been stolen from the Detroit jail, and on 8 January perhaps as many as seven hundred men boarded ship for Bois Blanc Island in the Detroit River, not far from Amherstburg on the Canadian side. One of the little ships ran aground, and the militiamen on shore were able to capture about thirty of the Patriots who were on board. The others were unable to land because of heavy firing and returned to the American shore.[9] The next attempted invasion came at Fighting Island in the Detroit River, where about 150 men were turned back by regular soldiers, two groups of which had now returned to Upper Canada.[10] A more serious raid came at the end of February when some hundreds of men crossed on the ice from Ohio to Pelee Island. After several days British regulars and some militia cavalry drove them back, at the cost to the Patriots of eleven dead, forty-five wounded, and eleven prisoners.[11] Five soldiers were killed or died later, and twenty-eight were wounded. It is easy to see why people throughout the province were fearful of Patriot attack, and quick to suspect others of being in collusion with the enemy. However, there could not have been as many would-be rebels as the authorities feared, even in the western part of the province. At no time did any large number of Upper Canadian residents anywhere come out in support of the Patriot raiding parties. Nevertheless there were parts of the country where no reliance was placed on the loyalty of the population, and one of these districts was Hastings County.

Writing some years later, Colonel Richard Bonnycastle described the population around the Bay of Quinte as he judged it: 'Belleville at the upper end of the Bay of Quinte and its vicinity, the township of Sidney, afforded many specimens of furious revolutionaries, and a road leading along the Bay through the townships of Thurlow, the Mohawk Settlement, Richmond, and near Camden and Portland in the counties of Hastings,

Lennox, and Addington and Frontenac, crossing the river at Napanee ... had long been celebrated as leading to the heart of the country to which Bidwell, Perry, and other Reformers always looked for their chief stronghold.'[12]

Among those who shared Bonnycastle's distrust was the Reverend A.F. Atkinson of Bath. In late December he wrote a letter to the lieutenant-governor and the Kingston *Chronicle and Gazette*, predicting that 'the disaffected who reside around this place will no doubt encourage the Americans to make a descent hereabouts.' He had thought all danger was past, but on looking over the American papers he was surprised at the number of meetings in support of the Patriots which were advertised in them.[13] Everyone who lived around the Bay of Quinte felt threatened by the enthusiasm for the Patriot cause in places like Watertown and Rochester, and they also believed some, perhaps many, of their neighbours were in league with the enemy. They did not hesitate to take strong measures.

As soon as word of the rebellion reached them, the magistrates of the Midland District acted swiftly to arrest anyone they suspected of sympathizing with it. Those they seized were all Reformers, but whether they were all radicals, let alone rebels or in league with rebels, is open to question. On 9 December 1837 the same issue of the *Chronicle and Gazette* that carried news of the rebels gathering outside Toronto also carried this report about a seller of tracts who was well known around the Kingston area:

We have learned from the most authoritative source that the case of John G. Parker of Hamilton is hopeless.[14] The immediate cause of his arrest has been the interception of three of his letters severally written to three immaculate characters: Henry Lasher of Bath, and John Vincent and Augustus Thibodo, both of Kingston. Let these gentlemen look out ... If they have written to John G., as he was usually called, we tell them for their comfort, that their letters stand a good chance of coming to light: for all his papers have been seized, after a prodigious struggle of the constables with Mrs. Parker who had committed them to the flames ... We are in great hopes that the seizure of this Correspondence will make known the names of many snakes that are now crawling in our grass, that we and the world may be rid of them forever.

On 16 December the Belleville magistrates must have congratulated themselves on having captured some important snakes in the Hastings County grass. On that day Anthony Manahan wrote 'that several Persons, suspected on strong, some on unequivocal grounds of treasonable acts and designs and seditious practices, have just been sent under an escort of forty men under arms to the District Gaol at Kingston.'[15] They were quite a catch. Gideon Turner was the clerk of Sidney Township. Joseph Caverley, Aaron Hearns, and Peter Davidson were substantial farmers. Joseph Canniff was the owner of a sawmill and a grist mill in Thurlow Township, where he held the office of assessor and tax collector. Reuben White of Sidney had come from New York State in 1805. At the time of his arrest he was about seventy years old. He was a merchant, the owner of a large mill and one of the most extensive estates in the township. In 1815 he served as clerk of Sidney, in 1836 as commissioner, and he represented Hastings in the legislature from 1820 to 1828 and again from 1830 to 1834.[16] When the first bridge was built over the Trent River at Trent Port, he was one of three men given the responsibility for overseeing its construction. Although he was himself a Quaker, he gave land on the Trent Road and cut the timber for a church, known for over a century as White's Church, for the use of a branch of Presbyterians, and when they proved too few to keep it up it was dedicated to a Methodist congregation.[17]

Reuben White and Joseph Lockwood were typical of quite a few Reformers who were leaders in their communities, prosperous and respected by the electors, yet never admitted into the local elite, as shown by the fact that they were never made magistrates, and the magistrates ordered their arrest and imprisonment as soon as news of the rebellion reached Hastings. Joseph Lockwood, a farmer and the owner of a distillery, was at the time moderator of Sidney Township, where he had been a warden in 1828, 1831, and 1836. From 1828 to 1830 he was a member of the legislative assembly. Like White, he was a long-time resident of the township, having settled there in 1800.

No one knows what evidence was brought against these men, but they seem unlikely conspirators. As for one accusation, that several had arms and ammunition in their possession, it must be remembered that hunting was for many people part of contemporary life, and sometimes necessary to put food on the table. Some of the prisoners, even if they had other occupations, were also in trade and normally carried guns and ammunition in stock. Whether they had them 'in unusual quantities' was not a question likely to be examined very objectively by the magistrates.

The eighth prisoner was a Belleville merchant and a member of the first board of police, Clifton McCollom. According to Manahan he was a man 'whose general conduct has had a tendency to republicanize his neighbours for several years – arrested upon a letter of his found in the papers of the Archrebel McKenzie – and who would be second to him only in attrocity [sic] of conduct had he but the opportunity of showing his real character – This man has Petitioned His Excellency to be allowed to leave the Province, a prayer which I hope will not be granted.'[18]

John Macaulay and John Cartwright, both Kingston magistrates, had arrested McCollom and left him under house arrest, guarded by a constable, while they waited for the result of McCollom's appeal to the lieutenant-governor.[19] They were not pleased to find that the Belleville magistrates had ignored this arrangement and had rearrested McCollom and sent him to the district jail in Kingston without, it seems, producing any additional evidence. Macaulay wrote a letter criticizing the Belleville magistrates' action 'for the satisfaction of Mr. Turnbull and Dr. Ridley in particular, & hope that your Worships are not in reality liable in this case to a charge of breaking faith, as alleged, in proceeding with needless hardships.'[20] According to the following letter from Dr George Ridley to Daniel Perry, it seems the Belleville magistrates had acted somewhat irregularly:

> I am afraid we are all in a scrape as regards the commital and arrest of those prisoners. Why did you not do it by warrant? I certainly thought it was to be so as I saw Mr. Bowen drawing a copy out however I understand they have sent up a remonstrance to His Excellency against the proceedings and stating that all their Bonds, papers and notes were taken forcibly from them. Will you therefore give His Excellency every explanation in your power. You must get us out of the business in the best manner you can your wits are sharp enough. Therefore make the best you can.[21]

Macaulay's letter seems to have caused a flutter among the Belleville magistrates. Ridley showed it to Thomas Parker, who wrote an angry letter to Anthony Manahan, member of the assembly, asking him to explain to His Excellency 'the circumstances as they took place for some of our "beautiful J.P.s" are frightened out of their minds – It may be that the arrests were not quite so legally done as they might have [been].' He trusted allowance would be made because of the necessity to arrest such people as Reuben White after information had been received that those who attended the Hayden meeting had made plans to capture Belleville. He asked if they should have waited for these rebels to march on the town, and protested that if they were to be treated in this manner 'their [sic] will not be found a Magistrate to act any more.'[22]

That White ever planned anything so violent is unlikely, but the intention of one member of the group is uncertain. Clifton McCollom may have been at the time as guilty as he was accused of being, or, like some others, he may have become a rebel only after he was arrested and jailed. That kind of treatment could provoke an extreme reaction from the most peaceable citizen – which, for all that is known, he may have been. McCollom was succesful in his appeal, and John Macaulay was soon reporting to the lieutenant-governor:

> On the 29th [of Dec.] I liberated C. McCollom from the Kingston gaol and gave him the option of departing the province or immediately repairing to Belleville and there abiding the decision of the Magistrates respecting the time that would be allowed him to settle his affairs. He desired to go as far as Bath, but I told him that in my opinion he should cross the St. Lawrence then or never. He took my advice and in a few hours was put by his gaoler into the ferry boat and proceeded to St. Vincent. – I hope it will not be forgotten to introduce a provision that none who now leave the province for political reasons shall return upon pain of death ... I enclose a memorandum from the prisoners sent to gaol. The Hastings magistrates submit nothing of the grounds of commitment, but I must regret the apparent harsh use of the proceeding whether they should prove innocent or guilty. You will find that such men as R. White whose friends are numerous in Sidney and the vicinity will make a great noise about the manner of their commitment without previous examination, and the carrying away of all their papers, notes, Bonds etc. from their Houses to be examined elsewhere. I would not care much about it if they could be convicted but I fear little evidence could be had against any of them.[23]

Macaulay was quite right. McCollom left the country on 20 December 1837, and the other seven were released on 2 January 1838. A true bill could not be obtained against any of them, and none of them was brought to trial.

McCollom, however, may have been the wrong man to send off to the United States. There he corresponded with Mackenzie, giving aid and comfort, if nothing more, to the Patriot cause. McCollom had been a merchant in Belleville, where he was a magistrate. When Belleville became a police village in 1836, he was elected one of the five members of the police board. He seems to have been a devious individual. According to Stephen Benson, another magistrate, he was at heart a Reformer who 'must have his own reasons' for siding with the Tories before 1837. At the time of the rebellion he was arrested because a letter of his was found among Mackenzie's papers in Toronto. He was married to a sister of Henry Lasher of Bath, and she soon joined him with their young children to take up residence in Oswego. Henry Lasher took charge of McCollom's affairs when he left the country and was able to keep in contact with him in spite of all the difficulties in getting letters across the border.

McCollom's first letter to Mackenzie after his exile was written on 28 January 1838. Its purpose was to 'enable you to look into the feelings of the Reformers of the County of Hastings & a little into those of the other Counties of the Midland District.' He gave the number of men in Hastings County who, he said, 'have pledged themselves upon oath to embark their lives and fortunes in the cause of Liberty,' claiming they had not only signed a manifesto, but were still ready to act in concert with Mackenzie:

Town of Belleville	41
Township of Thurlow	93
Township of Sidney	165
Township of Rawdon	86
Township of Tyendinaga	37
Townships of Huntingdon, Madoc, and Hungerford	60
Total	482

McCollom went on to say that no written documents were allowed to pass over to Canada without being opened by 'the Tory JPs of Kingston.' If Mackenzie wanted information, he should send someone he trusted, giving him numbered questions written on separate slips of paper, presumably so they could be more easily hidden, and the answers would be returned the same way. His messenger might pass openly at Kingston, but he could also go by back roads, cross to Bath, where he was less likely to be searched, and from there to Joseph Canniff of Canniff's Mills three miles north of Belleville on the east side of the river, 'and Canniff will see that the persons named in Hastings are forthcoming to his house.' McCollom particularly recommended three local men on whom Mackenzie could rely, Nelson Reynolds, Peter Robertson, and Henry Yager.[24] McCollom's statements, however confidently he spoke of these men, are evidence, not proof, of their rebel sympathies or activities. The name of Henry Yager in this connection is particularly surprising since no other indication has been found that he was suspected at home. He was a member of the assembly during 1834–6, was elected president of the Belleville board of police in

1837, and throughout the rebellion years kept his militia commission, being appointed acting quartermaster for 1837–8.[25] McCollom may have shared with Mackenzie the ability to believe what he hoped was true, yet Yager did correspond with the fugitive and even visited him in Oswego the following year. It is true that whatever information McCollom obtained from Yager may have been innocently given, yet it forms a curious footnote to the little that is known about Henry Yager.

Peter Robertson was another man the magistrates wanted to arrest. He had emigrated from Scotland and with his brother established a store in Belleville. He was an outspoken Reformer and, knowing he was likely to be arrested, he slipped away to Brockville with his wife in order to leave her safely with her family there. On 15 December Billa Flint sent the following letter to the magistrates of Brockville:

> Owing to certain events which have transpired Peter Robertson ... was to have been taken prisoner for Treasonable Expressions etc. this day, as a simultaneous move was to be made in several places on different persons. He left last night, and we suppose has gone to Brockville with his wife, and probably it will be well under the circumstances to have him caged until his case can be examined into agreeable to the Government orders. He was one, as information states, that signed the Political Union to stand by Mackenzie and swore secrecy. There are five persons from the gang now in custody, and expect hourly the arrival of three more.[26]

Being a justice of the peace at this time had become a demanding occupation. Still, it is hard to avoid the conclusion that Flint was enjoying some of the excitement of the hunt. Nor was he alone. About the same time, another Belleville magistrate, Thomas Parker, was dashing off a note to Manahan: 'I have barely time to say that a letter has this day been addressed to Mr. Joseph on the subject of money to support the people here on duty. Will you be kind enough to ask for a sight of it – that you may explain the necessity of complying with it. I have just issued a warrant & am on the eve of sending to Madoc for a notorious rebel.'[27]

The 'notorious rebel' is not named, so there is no way of knowing if he was caught, but the adjective seems a little over-enthusiastic. If he escaped, it was not for want of zeal on the part of his pursuers. In Brockville the magistrates called in Peter Robertson and questioned him. They asked him if he was a member of any reform society, or if he knew of any political society sworn to secrecy, but he refused to answer any questions. Then he was told, 'You are brought before the magistrates on suspicion of belonging to such a society, and from your refusal in answering the several questions, we infer that you a member of such a society.' To this Robertson's reply was, 'You may infer what you please, and you have good reason to draw such an inference.' At the end of the examination he protested 'that he did not see why he was selected as there were thousands of the same [mind] as him in Upper Canada although none he believed east of Kingston and he further stated that although he could not answer the questions as above he would fairly state what his Principles were which he said was a total disunion of Church and State, Universal Sufferage and vote by ballot.'[28]

The magistrates did not 'cage' Robertson as Flint had asked, but they required £1,000, a small fortune in 1837, as security that Robertson would return to Belleville and appear before the bench when summoned. Mrs Robertson's family posted the bond, and he appeared before the Belleville magistrates when summoned in February 1838. All the evidence indicates that he was a brash young man whose chief fault may have been to air his views in the wrong company. On at least one occasion he chose a dangerous subject for criticism, and that was Queen Victoria, who had come to the throne in 1837. After almost eighty years of the unfortunate George III and his regrettable male progeny, she was a complete contrast and a great relief. Britons at home and abroad welcomed this serious young woman as their new monarch. Everywhere she was praised as being courageous and just, noble and generous, virtuous and wise – every superior quality was attributed to her. She was, in fact, adored. When Robertson was brought before the magistrates in Belleville, one of them, Thomas Newton, was a witness against him. He stated that one day in Rufus Holden's drugstore, with a number of people present, Robertson had given as his opinion 'that the Government was not responsible to the people here but to the Downing Street four thousand miles away and said that the Tories spoke of the Queen in a disgusting manner, and by reading the Tory news papers they would make her out infalable [sic] as if she were some goddess, whereas she was only a redhaired wench of eighteen.'[29]

It is a wonder if no one offered to administer that most Victorian of punishments, a horse-whipping. 'Wench' was insulting, and at that time 'redhaired' was almost as bad. Robertson was sent to the district jail on 27 February. He was released on 16 May when the grand jury refused to indict him. Someone in Morristown wrote to Mackenzie about the case saying, 'He is a fine young fellow and if they do not imprison him he will join you soon. Kingston jail is full of patriots principally from Belleville.'[30] As far as is known, Robertson did not at any time join Mackenzie. According to

McCollom, Peter and his brother Charles were sympathizers who had a good store of arms, but whether they intended to use them for rebellion is another matter. Like most accusations at the time, this one was not backed up by proof.

Flint was afraid some suspected persons were treated too leniently. He complained to the lieutenant-governor's office that three persons were brought before the magistrates

> whose names were found signed to a constitution called the 'Reform Constitution,' which was a transcript as near as I can remember for the Constitution of the Central Committee at Toronto of which Mackenzie was chief. This was signed only last month when preparations were making for the Rebellion in L.C. – I cannot at present recollect the whole of this Constitution but in it was 'voting by ballot' '[re]modelling the Legislative Council' 'Purification of the Magistracy,' [']no church and state' & besides a great deal more that I cannot recollect. Just in my opinion the kind of constitution and meeting which led to our present difficulties. The persons arrested were the officers of this constitution – they were only held to bail for good behaviour.[31]

Some of the evidence against those put in prison was weak, and some may have been dishonest. One of those arrested was Hiram Baragan, a farmer in Thurlow. He was put into the district jail in Kingston on 29 December, while his neighbours were already preparing petitions on his behalf. The one below best describes the reason why they thought his arrest had little to do with the rebellion:

> The Petition of the undersigned Inhabitants of the Township of Thurlow respectfully sheweth, that Hiram Baragan of said Thurlow has been arrested, during the late excitement under a charge of Treason, upon the information of Thomas Rowan, that your petitioners are well acquainted with the said Hiram Baragan, and we believe him to be a loyal and respectable Inhabitant, and that we are also acquainted with the informant, and that we are also a little acquainted with the circumstances that led to the said Baragan's arrest, and we have every reason to believe it to be a conspiracy of one or two wreckless [sic] characters, to get away the property of Hiram Baragan, and injure and blast the reputation of said Baragan ... Your petitioners therefore humbly beg that Your Excellency will be pleased to allow said Baragan to be held to Bail, so that he may be allowed to return to his family, and honourably await his trial.[32]

This petition was signed by more than a score of residents, including several magistrates. It is dated 28 December, and the said Baragan was released on bail on 5 January 1838. He was never brought to trial.

Another prisoner was Anson Hayden of Hayden's Corners, now Corbyville. Like many men at the time, he had several occupations. He practised medicine; he was in business in Belleville; and he kept a tavern in Thurlow, where most political and other meetings were held. In November it had been the location for the large Reform meeting that was supposedly part of Mackenzie's political union and no doubt attended by many of those who were arrested. Hayden had also participated in local politics and had been nominated for the office of township clerk in 1836. He lost to George Benjamin in a closely contested election. Later that year Belleville was separated from the township and made a police village, so that Benjamin had to be replaced, and this time Hayden became the clerk of Thurlow Township. In his first minutes he noted that Benjamin had failed to turn over to him the township records, a circumstance which may show some animosity between them. Hayden was imprisoned from 19 December until 2 January. Soon after that he disappeared, no doubt across the border, and did not return. Oddly, the clerks of both Sidney and Thurlow were sent to prison. Gideon Turner of Sidney, arrested on 9 December, was also released on 2 January.

The circumstances of the time excited suspicion, and some people saw it as a civic duty to relay their suspicions to the magistrates. Information was laid against two militia officers of the area, and at least one schoolteacher. The latter was George Baxter, a schoolmaster of the district school in Kingston. At a meeting of the school board witnesses stated that, some time before the rebellion, Baxter had on one occasion said that Mackenzie was not wrong. Although when he heard of the rebellion he had also said 'that MKenzies [sic] taking up arms was very wrong and for which he ought to be punished,' in the opinion of the trustees his political opinions 'rendered him an unfit person to be entrusted with the education of Youth, under Her Majesty's Government.' They therefore dismissed him.[33]

Nelson Gilbert Reynolds was a natural target since he had been a conspicuous Reform candidate in 1836. At the time of the rebellion he was a lieutenant in the militia, recommended for promotion to captain. This brought a protest from some quarters. A petition opposing his promotion was sent to the adjutant general, describing him in these terms:

The undersigned inhabitants of the Town of Belleville ... beg leave to represent, that an individual named Nelson G. Reynolds, at present a Lieutenant, one of the late leaders & agitators in the Country, a man who has ever opposed the Government, and was a leader in Urging many individuals of this County, to petition for stopping the supplies, and as they are fully convinced, has done the utmost in his power to create discontent in the Country, and supported the late leaders of the rebel faction in this & the Lower Province.[34]

The petition was forwarded by the magistrates, and the clerk, George Benjamin, added his own opinion:

I know the circumstances under which the enclosed petition was gotten up – the person petitioned against is now under arrest for Treason – is & has been a leader of a party whose object has been subversion of the Govt & giving him Every allowance for good conduct he has suppressed information from the Govt. which every loyal man should have given – having been aware of p[ersons] holding seditious meetings – He never should have recd the appointment of Lieutenant & the men never will act under him as Captn.

The accusations are interesting. Reynolds, according to the petition, had been in opposition to the government and had supported the assembly in 'stopping the supplies.' For this he was charged with treason, a hanging offence. The magistrates were acting beyond the law, for at the most the charge might have been sedition, but in the poisoned air of rebellion it was not difficult to be named a traitor. According to George Benjamin's letter, Reynold's further offence was that he had not informed against other Hastings residents who had met together, for what purpose is not stated. This may have made him a rebel as the magistrates believed, but not everyone agreed. He was soon released on bail. Reynolds had had a more interesting career than most of his youthful contemporaries, and he seems to have been somewhat boastful. He claimed to have gained a commission in the lancers while he was in England and to have travelled as far as the Rockies in the service of the Hudson's Bay Company. He then returned to Belleville and stood as a Reformer in both elections in 1836, all by the time he was twenty. It seems a potential recipe for both admiration and envy. Added to this, he was the son of the Methodist Episcopal bishop, so that it was only natural the Tory magistrates would view him with suspicion.

Another complaint against a militia officer was sent in by J. Allen of Allen's Mills, Marysburgh, against Henry Dingman. Both were magistrates, but Dingman was also a Reformer who had made his political views known. Fortunately for him, he seems to have had enough influence with other magistrates to keep from being arrested, and to foil Allen in his efforts to take away his commission in the militia. Allen charged that Dingman 'has been considered a radical for several years past by the loyalists here' and that 'he has always refused to cheer our Governor Sir Francis Bond Head and stated that he was not worth cheering.'[35] In this time of conflict the loyalists took the position that those who were not 100 per cent with them were against them, but Dingman may have been like the editor of the *British Whig*, who called himself a 'disagreeable' because he disagreed with Mackenzie *and* with Sir Francis Head.[36]

One of the first of the Midland District prisoners was George R. Huffman of Frankford. He was a tanner by trade and he also kept a tavern. At the time of his arrest Anthony Manahan wrote to Fitzgibbon that 'Bowen the Magistrate Sent off a Prisoner from Cold Creek for Sedition and ... the prisoner's brother went before him to secure a rescue – I [am] despatching a Sleigh with Bowens brother and five Indians to follow – and before he is rescued – he will lose his head at the hands of the Indians.'[37] Manahan seems to have been more bloodthirsty than the Mohawks, but whether the parties met up or not, the prisoner was taken to Kingston. From the jail there he sent to the lieutenant-governor a petition which is a rare description of an arrest and examination:

May it please your Excellency to listen to the complaint of one of Her Majesty's dutiful and loyal subjects of the Province of Upper Canada and of the county of Hastings. On the morning of the ninth of December as I was taking my breakfast with my little family there came four constables and seized me and said they had orders to take me before W.H. Bowen Esq. but said they do not know what for. I told them it was almost impossible for me to attend until two o'clock in the afternoon for I was out of wood for my family and also out of hay for my cows but would give them any security for my appearance at two o'clock or in the Evening but they refused me and said they only wanted me for about two hours and then I might return and accordingly I went with them to Mr Bowen's house. Shortly after I entered it Mr Bowen came into the room and said he was sorry he was under the necessity of issuing a warrant against me for treason. I said I would like to know what I was brought for. He then read the affidavits of three persons who had sworn against me and when he was done I said I could prove my innocence in three or four minutes if he would call on three or four of the neighbours whose names I mentioned to him but he Refused me with a great oath and told me to take off my hat when before my betters. The most of us had our hats on. We immediately took them off and the Doors were locked and I was left in charge with two constables shut in one of his bedrooms and about three hours afterwards the Constable was handed a warrant for arresting me and taking me before Magistrate Bowen or any other of Her Majesty's Justices of the Peace in and for the Midland District. I wanted to be taken before Mr. Ketcheson or any other Magistrate in the District but he Refused me and about sunset Mr. Bowen asked if I wanted Squire Ketcheson sent for. I replied that if I could have an Examination or a trial I would like to have him sent for and accordingly my brother went for him a distance of about six miles.

Mr Ketcheson arrived there about eleven in the evening. The committee being called by Mr Bowen through the course of the day consulted together about thirty minutes and then signed it and gave it to the constables and ordered them to lodge me in Kingston gaol. In the meantime I had sent word to my neighbours and some of them were already there to prove my innocence, but I had not the opportunity to see those that had falsely sworn against me neither would they allow my witnesses to speak one word for nor against me but was ordered to proceed to gaol forthwith and since that time I have been confined here in the cells of this Prison.

I hope your Excellency will not think I am intruding on your time or patience when I tell your Excellency that William Bowen has been my sworn enemy for a little more than two years and During that time he has himself or through his influence had me before himself twice – before the Court of Requests twice and had me served with a writ to the Assizes at Kingston – but in all three I proved my innocence and acquitted honourably and during the same time he has started a tavern in this village in opposition to mine, and has frequently told me he would ruin me if he could and now has taken advantage of these critical times and cast me into prison without giving me a chance for Defence.

As for the witnesses that he has sworn against me, first his brother Daniel swore that I damn the Law. There is a young man present that will come forward and swear there was no such word mentioned by me. The second was John S. Larroy, a man that lives with another man's wife and is immediately under Mr Bowen. The third and last is Mr McGowan and he has taken a false oath on another occasion. Perhaps your Excellency will think I must be a bad character on account of being called before the Authorities so often but I mention this to show I was never called before them before only as a witness and also to show your Excellency that Mr Bowen is trying to put his threats into Execution ... With regard to my Former Character I will refer your Excellency to the Magistrates of the Townships of Ernest Town and Sophiasburgh, having spent most of my life in those two Townships. My Grand Fathers fought and bled in the American Revolution for the British Constitution and came to Canada in the first settlement of the Country and they have always supported the Government and the Constitutional Reform but not Revolt and I have followed in their footsteps so far and it is my Intention to Do so through life.

I have been brought near seventy miles from home from an affectionate and kind companion and her small children who depend on my labour for their support. My wife is far advanced in a state of pregnancy and expects to be confined in a few weeks.

All I have written here I can prove and I hope your Excellency when taking it into consideration will either appoint me a speedy trial or admit me on bail. If I have written anything in this letter unbecoming I hope you Excellency will not think it is done out of Disrespect but rather impute it to my inability, not being blest with a good Education.[38]

This remarkable letter was forwarded from Kingston on 28 December, and Huffman was freed on 4 January.

7 The Bloodless Battle

At the end of December 1837 it was feared there would be an attempt to invade Upper Canada near Niagara, where Mackenzie had his encampment. Men and arms were sent to the area, some supplies being taken from Belleville to Chippewa in January 1838 by a troop of militia commanded by Henry Yager.[1] The evacuation of Navy Island ended that threat, and the complete rout of the Patriots at Bois Blanc and Fighting Island discouraged the invaders for a time in the west; but, meanwhile, others in the east had been laying plans for their own campaign, assisted by Mackenzie after the Navy Island adventure.

Samuel Lennox was a resident of French Creek (now Clayton, NY), and he had two young daughters who were living with his brother Elijah in Thurlow. In late December 1837 he came over to visit them. On 25 December he made a deposition before Alexander Pringle of Kingston, and this was brought to the magistrates of Belleville. Some of the information in it was so important that George Benjamin, as clerk of the bench of magistrates, wrote to the office of the lieutenant-governor to inform him about it. The letter is a hodgepodge of statements about Lennox, his family, and people he knew on both sides of the border. Not all of it seems to be relevant; for instance, he was said to know both Dr James Hunter, who had fled from Whitby to the United States and was reputed to be a Patriot leader,[2] and Sheriff Henry Ruttan, the conscientious colonel of the Third Northumberland Regiment. Lennox appeared to suspect more than he knew; for instance, he 'knows Smith and Merrick. *Merrick receives letters frequently from Toronto*. Deponent could not ascertain from William Bass, the clerk of Merrick, the contents of a letter.' Apparently letters from Toronto placed the recipient under suspicion of being a conspirator; so wherever Smith and Merrick carried on business, it is to be hoped they appreciated the loyalty and discretion of their clerk. The importance of Lennox's statement, however, was in the last paragraph. About French Creek he said

> there is a great excitement there among the Inhabitants in favour of the Rebellious party in Upper Canada, that some of their leading men are favourable to that cause, that they have spies in communication with MacKenzie, that last Wednesday there was a meeting, and it was there stated by a person from Rochester that MacKenzie was there (at Rochester) on Monday last. That MacKenzie was in a position to organize a large party from Rochester, Oswego, and other places on the frontier, to meet at some place below Kingston, for the purpose of crossing to Kingston when the ice takes.[3]

This was the first warning the authorities received about the Patriot plan to capture Kingston, a plan which was being coordinated between Patriots in New York State and others in Hastings County and Lennox and Addington. The Patriots meant to cross on the ice to attack Kingston from the south, while local rebels overcame resistance from within the town. After the cold snap in December that had interrupted Manahan's convoy of arms to Belleville, the weather turned mild again, and it was not until mid-February that the St Lawrence River froze. The date finally set by the Patriots for the Kingston campaign was 22 February, Washington's birthday. By then Mackenzie and Van Rensselaer had fallen out. Mackenzie wrote that he 'could not sail in a boat to be piloted as he thinks fit'.[4] While Mackenzie could never sail in anyone's boat but his own, in this case he had good cause for Van Rensselaer was said to pour his courage out of a brandy bottle, no doubt one reason why all his voyages foundered. Mackenzie's part in the enterprise was limited to arranging by correspondence for the cooperation of sympathizers on the Canadian shore.

Both Sir George Arthur and the Patriots employed spies, and in any case the open border between the two countries made it impossible for either side to keep the other entirely in the dark. The day before the attack, the *Chronicle and Gazette* reported that it was expected, and that from six to eight hundred stand of arms had been stolen from the armouries in Watertown.[5] The Patriots did try to impose secrecy, and one traveller they detained at French Creek the day before the planned invasion was later able to describe the Patriot camp. He had been about to cross the river to the Canadian side when Bill Johnston told him he was 'a prisoner for the present as we are going to attack Gananoque this night.' He was then wined and dined, and apparently allowed to move freely about since he saw a great many men and sleighs there and on Hickory Island. But 'after all their efforts, by promises, flattery and threats, they could get but 110 to take up arms, most of them wanted to march straight on Kingston, but Van Rensselaer ... opposed it.' Next day the traveller was allowed to leave, both Johnston and Van Rensselaer shaking hands with him and wishing him safe passage.[6]

Colonel Richard Bonnycastle had made extensive preparations for the defence of the fort and of Kingston. When he knew men had gathered so far to the east of the town, he thought they must be a small force preparing a feint on Gananoque, while the main body marched directly from Watertown to Kingston just above the penitentiary. Fort Henry was garrisoned by civilians, and, as he learned, one of them who was 'accustomed to blacksmith work, was to spike the cannon ... and the outer magazine, full of Congreve rockets, was to be blown up. The town, also, in the melee, was to have been set on fire in various marked places.'[7] According to the account he later published, 'the rebels gathered in Kingston before the day set for the invasion ... sympathizers, under pretext of market or other business, were sent into the town, and took lodgings at different public and other houses, whilst one or two enlisted in the Militia. 'Bonnycastle's description of the plot is confirmed from Mackenzie's papers:' It had been arranged by correspondence carried on with Mackenzie, that a rising should take place in Canada when the expedition crossed. Fort Henry was garrisoned by civilians; a person in the fort had agreed to spike the guns, on the approach of the Patriots, and at a concerted signal to throw open the gates for their admittance.'[8]

By 21 February Kingston was fortified to withstand a siege. Some militia units had been called in from Prince Edward, from Lennox and Addington, and from Hastings, and the rest put on alert. Bonnycastle had barricaded most of the roads into town with felled trees, while the others were heavily guarded. He had holes cut in the ice in the path he expected the Patriots to take crossing the river. At the fort he fitted up three blockhouses and placed militia in between. He put a dozen men as a guard at Napanee, and 'stationed outposts, vedettes of cavalry, and pickets everywhere around the town within some miles. The man who meant to spike the guns was identified and sent packing.' Bonnycastle imposed a curfew and sent messengers to every house suspected of sheltering rebel sympathizers with a warning that they should not, at the risk of their lives, stir outdoors after dark. Then, satisfied with his precautions, he went to bed:

> I was endeavouring ... to take a little rest upon an iron barrack bed ... when a Militia officer from Belleville roused me in the middle watch, by saying he had ridden posthaste to announce the rebels had commenced their march on Kingston, and that he had left the Militia in arms in Belleville, and the tocsin still ringing. I had, however, better information than that given by this ardent young man, and therefore much disgusted him by telling him it was very likely, and requesting him to let me get a little rest.
>
> The Prince Edward Militia were actually then, which he did not know, on their march in rear of this very movement, and so paralysed the rebels that but few prisoners were taken near Napanee, as the body of insurgents dispersed and hid their arms and ammunition in the woods ... Among the prisoners taken was an American armourer, or manufacturer of rifles, who had carried on a snug trade in Belleville.[9]

It was later found the rebels had abandoned a sleigh loaded with rifle and musket ammunition, including bullet moulds, a keg of powder, boxes of percussion caps and pellets, and a United States musket, one of many American militia muskets that found their way into Patriot hands. Not long afterwards a boy came across a large cache of rifle and buckshot cartridges in oyster kegs hidden in the woods near Napanee. The *Chronicle and Gazette* reported that eight hundred stand of arms had been landed near Bath from Oswego as long ago as December and that five hundred rounds of ammunition had been found on a farm near there.[10] Several people found caches of ammunition in the woods, but there is no report that anyone found the eight hundred stand of arms.

There was satisfaction in Kingston that the threatened danger had been turned aside, and indignation at the wicked intentions of people living in the towns just across the lake. An editorial advised sending one thousand 'gallant fellows' to Watertown, French Creek, and Sackets Harbor to 'inflict summary punishment.' An anonymous letter from across the line warned the editor, 'Be cautious ... we have one serjeant here that can whip a whole regiment of your British regulars ... who is waiting and hoping you would show your royal faces here. Do it and you are annihilated. Beware!'[11] It would seem that too many Americans believed this kind of bombast, and went on believing it for too long.

In the emergency the militia had responded from all around the Bay of Quinte as well as from Brockville and Perth. William Wallbridge wrote that 'Uncle Turnbull and Bonter took a sleigh load of men, arms and ammunition a little before daylight two miles this side of Napanee,' but he added that 'sleighloads of armed rebels went from here to assist McKenzie.' Two of the three Belleville companies that had been ordered out were turned back before they had gone very far, but one went on to Kingston. What happened when they got there depends very much on which newspaper reported it. On 16 March 1838 the *Intelligencer* of Belleville filled almost the whole front page with 'A Statement of Facts.' This claimed to expose the errors printed in other papers about 'the ruffian crusade against Canada.' It noted with regret 'that the Chronicle of Kingston and the Statesman of Brockville have just put forth statements with regard to the affair on Hickory Island which do not contain a single fact.'

According to the *Intelligencer*, Major Thomas Parker had received a letter on 20 February telling him that an attack on Kingston was hourly expected. Captain Wellington Murney left about five o'clock with half the Belleville Rifle Company, who arrived in Kingston barracks near noon the next day. That evening they were ordered to Gananoque to confront the 'rebels and pirates':

After a most tedious journey, they arrived at Gananoque about one o'clock, and immediately reported themselves to Captain Frazer, the commanding officer at that time. During the night several persons arrived from the country ... and received arms. No discrimination, no judgment was used in giving them out, but Captain Frazer delivered arms to all who asked for them. The consequence of such thoughtless proceedings has been, that many of the muskets are now missing. During the night, the men came and went, and many returned to their homes, promising to return, who failed in their promises.

About three o'clock Captain Hartwell arrived 'and soon gave Captain Frazer to understand that he assumed command of the post.' Apparently it was not only the Patriots who suffered from rival commanders, for according to the *Intelligencer* Major Thomas Fitzgerald, a regular officer, then came on the scene, and after some argument the others agreed that he would take charge. Obviously the editor of the *Intelligencer* did not think very highly of Fitzgerald, saying he addressed the troops and 'what he said shall be withheld, for his sake. It would add nothing to his fame.' The sun rose, and the Patriots had not yet attacked, although it appears they had begun to land on Hickory Island about two o'clock in the morning. Immediately after breakfast, the companies then in Gananoque were all mustered and ordered to be ready to attack the enemy. Nothing happened. Around noon all the officers went off to look at a steamboat tied up about six miles away, thinking the pirates would set fire to it. A report had come in that sixteen sleighs had landed on Hickory Island, but 'no particular attention was paid by the commanding officer.'

About two o'clock the rest of the Belleville Rifles under Captain Bartlett arrived, and at three the officers returned from their boat-viewing. Almost at once the alarm was given. The enemy was in motion. Ball cartridge was distributed, and the order to load was given. The order to advance did not come. The officers disagreed. Captain Murney offered to lead the Belleville Rifles under Frazer's direction to 'dislodge the enemy'; Hartwell at first consented to this plan, then was persuaded by Fitzgerald to change his mind. Instead he ordered

at 4 o'clock in the morning, the attack should be made. And all was again peace and quietness ... Four o'clock came, and still there was no call to arms. Five o'clock came, and still there was no call to arms. Six o'clock came, and Captain Hartwell made his appearance, but yet there was no call to arms. But in a few minutes a prisoner was brought in, who had been taken by the scouts. He confessed that he was on duty on the Island, and that the whole body of the pirates had left ... expecting to be pursued. He stated that during the day a large number of persons came to and went from the Island, but by nightfall there were not over 200 ... many were drunk, and a large number refused ... to make the attack on Gananoque. Dragoons were immediately sent off to ascertain the fact.[12]

While the others delayed moving out of Kingston, the Honourable John Elmsley from Brockville had carried off the honours. With his company of men he had marched straight to Hickory Island, had occupied the only house on it, and brought in a few prisoners, stragglers who had been left behind by the retreating Patriots. The cavalry who were then sent to the island saw four sleighs full of armed men approaching from the American shore and, according to the *Intelligencer*, might easily have captured them, but instead of allowing them to land 'they shewed themselves at all points, the consequence was that the sleighs turned short and went back to French Creek.'

Next day Fitzgerald ordered all the troops back to Kingston, but 'Captain Murney not conceiving that he was under the command of Major Fitzgerald' gave no orders. The artillery left with Fitzgerald. The Belleville men stayed on, and they felt justified in this decision when other troops were sent to join them because of a rumour that Brockville was about to be attacked. This fortunately turned out to be false, and it was soon apparent that the invasion had been turned back.

This was not the kind of engagement that goes down in history as a glorious victory, and Richard Bonnycastle had no opportunity to distinguish himself as a military leader. What he accomplished, however, was infinitely better, for by prodigious preparations he had kept the peace. If he did not win the battle, he deserves credit for arranging things so that the enemy was defeated without a shot being fired.

Years later the *Intelligencer* published an account of the adventures of another militia company from Belleville which was sent to Kingston at the time of the Gananoque affair. The writer, who signed himself 'Old Sergt-major,' wrote that Colonel Turnbull as commander of the First Hastings Regiment received orders in the late afternoon of 22 February to lead as many as he could muster to Kingston, where an immediate attack was expected. The alarm was rung 'from the big bell in the tower of the old Methodist church on Pinnacle Street,' and over a hundred responded. Teams and sleighs were rounded up, and by eight o'clock they were off:

Every man had come in his working clothes, in fact anything heavy he could pick up in a hurry, the cold being most intense – away down below zero. Some of us had blankets wrapped around us, some quilts, and one man, I recollect, had an old woman's red cloak which he had thrown about his manly form and, with an old rusty sword, without a scabbard, buckled about his waist, he presented a fine martial appearance, of which he was very proud. As for arms, with the exception of McKenzie's Company from Madoc, who had been on duty here for some time previous and were provided with flint muskets and bayonets, we had none but what we had picked up in a hurry.

In the Sergeant-Major's sleigh William Whiteford had an old musket and bayonet, but no cartridges. Robert Read had a pitchfork and a naval cutlass, Daniel Young, the driver, had a fowling piece which had been hanging behind his bar for the past six months. 'It would do execution', he said, 'if it would only go off'. The rest of us thought the same, but we had a lingering suspicion it would be the man behind who would suffer.

Shannonville at the time consisted of two taverns, a mill, a blacksmith shop, and two or three houses. There the party halted in order to warm up in one of the taverns, but 'the Colonel, deeming our sleigh party ... the bravest, and of course the most intelligent, ordered us to go ahead and see that the road was clear.' This was because the colonel had been told that a strong party of rebels had passed Shannonville an hour before, on their way to join the force attacking Kingston. The sergeant-major's party had not gone far when they saw three double sleighs coming towards them. Dan Young pulled to the side of the road and shouted, 'Halt! in the Queen's name.' They paid no attention 'but whipped up their horses and passed us at a gallop. As they did so, we could see that each sleigh contained six men armed with rifles.' Realization came too late:

They are rebels, shouted Dan, 'fire on them, boys!' at the same time turning in pursuit. Fortunately his gun ... missed fire, or the result might have been disastrous to the party behind. As for myself, I had previously ... stuffed cartridges in the barrel of the pistols, but as I afterwards discovered they were minus the necessary flints, my efforts to fire were not very successful. 'Bob' Read's cutlass and pitchfork were not much use ... and Whiteford's musket without cartridges was likewise valueless. Consequently there was nothing to do but to pursue the enemy and give the alarm to the main body we had left in the village, which we did. As we entered the village in hot chase, Dan shouted 'Stop them, they're rebels!' but the rebels were too quick for our friends, for before the latter could form across the road, the three teams dashed up the 2nd concession road and were out of sight in a twinkling. There were a few scattering shots fired after them by Mackenzie's company, but without effect.

Not entirely without effect. The colonel's horse, not accustomed to gunfire, took fright. He threw the colonel into a snowbank and galloped for Belleville and home. He arrived there with the saddle and holsters dangling under his belly. His appearance, as he dashed down the street, gave rise to the conjecture that there had been a fight down the road, and that the Loyalists had been cut to pieces ... the people here were kept in a fever of suspense for several hours.

Meanwhile at Shannonville a dispatch arrived, calling off the company's march to Kingston since they were not needed. When they reached Belleville, they were surprised to be given an excited welcome by a crowd 'who had not expected ever to see us again alive and well.' This account was entitled 'The Bloodless Battle of Shannonville.'[13]

The alarms and excitements of the night were not yet finished, however. At ten o'clock two 'respectable farmers' drove into town to bring perturbing news to Colonel William Turnbull. They told him that, as they were driving along a road back of Belleville, several sleighs full of armed men had galloped past them silently, no sleigh bells on their harness. These were probably men in flight after the collapse of the plan to capture Kingston. Turnbull, not waiting to consult anyone so late at night, had at once ordered the church bell to ring out again, and an excited crowd quickly gathered, anxious to know what new danger threatened. Turnbull told them what he had learned, and that they should arm themselves as well as they could and prepare to defend the town against attack. While people were still out on the street, Colonel McAnnany arrived back with the Belleville Rifles from Shannonville. His story of the sleighs full of armed men on whom they had fired unsuccessfully added to everyone's fear, and many residents must have spent a sleepless night. But whatever danger threatened Belleville there were no further alarms. The big Methodist Chapel bell was silent the rest of the night.[14]

A few days later Billa Flint wrote from Belleville to the adjutant general's office that

a conspiracy in which a large number of persons of the county of Hastings were Engaged was discovered by the Magistrates: That it was made known to the Magistrates of the county on the twenty third of the same month that a very considerable number of the persons engaged in that conspiracy were under arms on the night previous some of whom had been arrested between this town and Bath. That arrests of persons Engaged in that conspiracy have continued up to a very late period and that there are many of the same persons lurking within or adjacent to the county ... your memorialists have every reason to believe; That [they] have gone through a long and tedious investigation of the circumstances attending that Conspiracy and Examination of the persons arrested and ... were not a little surprised at discovering from testimony before them that so long ago as last November, discussions had taken place at secret meetings within the county as to the signal for burning this town.[15]

The magistrates went on to describe the part played by Hastings militia in the defence of Kingston, and that they wanted to keep one hundred of them on duty to protect Belleville 'considering the number of disaffected persons and known traitors then at large in the county (many of whom are still at large).' This is one of several requests made by the magistrates for a permanent guard, and this is one that brought a 'harsh and uncourteous' reply from the adjutant general, who seems not to have shared the magistrates' apprehension. Thoroughly alarmed by the events of 22 February and what they perceived to be a widespread conspiracy in Hastings, they did their best to protect the area by arresting those they suspected of taking part, at least thirty-two within a week after the projected attack and another twelve in March.

The most colourful of those arrested was Nelson Reynolds. It was widely believed that on the night of 21 February he had led rebels from Belleville to assist in the capture of Kingston; but the only known fact is that he ignored Bonnycastle's curfew and was arrested in Bath, where he was taken before the magistrates and charged with high treason. He denied the charge, and when the guards tried to confine him before taking him to Kingston, he threw them off and escaped. Early in the morning he arrived at the home of Jacob Shibley to see his sister, who was married to Jacob's son John. This was some miles away in Portland. His visit was to bring suspicion and harassment to the Shibley family members, although in several letters that outline the family's involvement they maintained they knew nothing about the arrest. According to their account, Reynolds arrived at the Shibley house just as Jacob was leaving for the blacksmith's shop, and they exchanged only a few words in passing. Absalom Day had gone to the blacksmith's on his sleigh, and he offered to drive Jacob Shibley home. There he was introduced to Reynolds, whom he next took up on his sleigh. As they drove along, Reynolds told Day that he had been brought before the magistrates at Bath but had cleared himself, and Day said that, not knowing of any rebel activities in the area and Reynolds being a stranger, he had not liked to inquire further how the young man had got into trouble, and in any event had not thought the matter to be of any importance.[16] The authorities rejected this explanation. The correspondence does not state where Day took Reynolds, but it may have been to the home of John Shibley's brother Henry.

Meantime John Ashley, formerly constable of the Midland District, was hot in pursuit of the fugitive. He had no doubt whatever about the guilt of all concerned. He stated unequivocally that Reynolds had led the insurgents from Belleville on 22 February, expecting to meet up with the Patriot invaders.[17] Ashley arrested Absalom Day, went to the home of Henry Shibley, arrested him, then on to Jacob Shibley's where he arrested

John, who, according to his father, had not been at home when Reynolds came there. None of them was confined for long, but during the next weeks Ashley several times had a military escort bring his suspects in to be questioned; he searched the Shibley house for incriminating papers; and he tried to cajole Reynolds's sister to confide in him. Both Jacob Shibley and Day wrote at some length to deny Ashley's accusations, but without persuading John Macaulay,[18] Alexander Pringle,[19] or of course Ashley himself, even though all of them admitted they could find no proof of any guilty knowledge. Macaulay gave his opinion of the reason for Day's 'disloyalty' when he wrote to Bullock: 'I fear that the whole neighbourhood of Jacob Shibley is tainted with disloyalty and it is only by reason of Ensign Day's removal from the front concession of Kingston where he was brought up in correct principles, to the Shibley settlement in Portland, that I can account for his present disaffection.' While Day's letter reveals that he had no love for John Ashley there is nothing to show that he was 'disaffected,' which at the time meant disloyal to the Crown.

The adjutant general's correspondence adds a curious appendix to the affair. Henry Shibley was a lieutenant and Day was an ensign in the Lennox and Addington militia, and both had been recommended for promotion. Since their superior officers, Pringle and Macaulay, believed them guilty of such a serious offence as concealing a traitor and fugitive from the law, it might be expected they would immediately expel the young men from the regiment. Instead, while it was considered best to hold back their promotions, both men were kept at the head of their respective ranks. Macaulay was opposed to anything more because 'I would not consider it politic absolutely to dismiss them, as by such a proceeding a feeling prevailing in the extensive families to which they belong, and which may not amount to anything more than indifference about the Government, would most probably be converted into a sentiment of resentful hostility.'[20] Bullock took his advice. All remained free and continued to serve in the militia. Meantime Reynolds had slipped over the border and had taken refuge in the United States. He stayed there for a time; then returned voluntarily to stand trial at the assizes in July. Absalom Day was also tried there, but there is no mention of John or Henry Shibley being held or standing trial. It is easy to believe Reynolds was the kind of enterprising, adventurous fellow who might find it exciting to take part in a conspiracy, and perhaps he and the other men who were on the road near Bath and Napanee on the night of 22 February were trying to join up with the Patriot force. Or perhaps, being young, they did not want to be left out of the excitement everyone expected that night around Kingston. The magistrates had some ground for their accusations, but they were not impartial, nor do we know what answer Reynolds and the others made to the crimes with which they were charged.

8 Danger round the Bay

After they left Navy Island, the Patriots had tried to establish themselves at the western end of the province, where most of the settlers had come from the United States and where the neighbouring states of Michigan and Ohio were openly friendly to them, the governor of Ohio in particular making no secret of his support.[1] During the year 1838 many Ohio men joined the Patriot ranks along with others from Kentucky, Michigan, New York, and states farther afield. General Hugh Brady of the United States Army, who had his headquarters in Detroit, was in charge of defence along that frontier, and he did his best to put down Patriot operations; but in February, when he called together the militiamen of Michigan to help end Patriot lawlessness, he found he could not trust them with arms. They 'unblushingly declared that if arms were put into their hands, they would hand them over to the rebels.'[2]

After the failure of the raid on Gananoque there was a breathing space for Upper Canadians, although vigilance could not be relaxed while Patriot preparations south of the border continued, apparently unchecked. As well, some rebellious Canadians at home recovered their defiance. A militia officer wrote from Brantford that people there were 'extemely insolent and abusive.' They heckled and taunted his men, saying their friends had left only to show others the way. He complained that the magistrates were too frightened of the people around them to be of much help, and the same was true of the guard of twenty men stationed at Port Dover, who 'might just as well be in Toronto, they all go to bed at night and told me if a landing was made they would all run away.'[3] People in Upper Canada were repeatedly given disquieting news as the Patriots and their supporters continued to be active in a number of ways and at a number of places, some of them in the Midland District.

In April the new governor, Sir George Arthur, ordered the sentence of hanging to be carried out on Samuel Lount and Peter Matthews, two leaders of the rebellion.[4] This brought widespread protest from across the province, but Arthur would not be swayed even though his act soured his relations with many in Upper Canada and gave an added boost to recruitment for the Patriot army in the United States, where the cruelty of Britain's rulers provided an effective rallying cry. In fact the Colonial Office registered disapproval when news of the hangings reached England, but by then it was too late. And British policy seems ambiguous. If the colonial secretary wanted to reconcile the parties in Upper Canada, why did he choose as governor a military man who was at the time in command of a prison colony?[5] Arthur was not one to listen to pleas and petitions, and if the deaths of Lount and Matthews increased the sullen mood of the province he was unmoved, determined only to deal firmly with the unhappy situation.

In May a group of Patriots formed a plan to seize a steamboat on the St Lawrence in order to ferry armed men to a landing on the Canadian shore. Twenty-eight of them, said to be all from the Midland District, gathered on the night of 29 May on Wells Island on the American side below Gananoque. Having scouted the ground during the day, they went into hiding well in advance of the arrival of the *Sir Robert Peel*, which docked at midnight to take on wood for her boilers. The pirate band had darkened their faces and made some attempt to disguise themselves as Indians. What they lacked was the Indian ability to find their way in strange territory. The night was very dark, and as they advanced towards the wharf, they got lost. Eventually thirteen of them found their target, but they waited in vain for the rest. Leaping out suddenly and uttering war whoops, however, the thirteen were able to scare off the boat's crew. The sleeping passengers were then ordered off, many in nightclothes and without their luggage, and the pirates took command of the steamer. At this point they discovered that none of them knew how to work the ship's engine. After some debate and with dawn approaching, they decided the only solution was to scuttle the ship. They got it away from the dock and set fire to it.[6] The Patriots always referred to this as revenge for the *Caroline*, but the only result of the escapade was to anger Canadians and increase their determination to defeat these renegades. It had occurred on the same day Lord Durham arrived at Quebec, serving as a fiery symbol of the conflicts he had come to resolve.

Before people had recovered from this outrage there came further alarming news, that Patriots had effected a secret landing in June across Lake Erie south of St Catharines. About thirty men made the

the Short Hills area, where they were joined by some local inhabitants. Altogether they numbered nearly seventy when, a few days later, they attacked a small detachment of militia cavalry at a village near Pelham. The militiamen ran back into the tavern where they were lodged, but the Patriots made short work of their defence by setting fire to the building and captured them as they ran out. Meantime the alarm had been raised, and a heavier force of militia, bolstered by some of their Indian allies, closed in on these freebooters. Most of them escaped back to the States, but of those who were captured some were transported and one man was hanged.[7]

Lord Durham, one of those responsible for the passing of the Reform Bill of 1832, had been sent out earlier that year by the British parliament to report on the state of the colonies of British North America, particularly on Upper and Lower Canada, and to make recommendations for their future. He paid his one brief visit to Upper Canada in June.[8] When they knew he was coming to Fort Henry, some of the prisoners there prepared a petition, hoping for the same pardons he had granted so freely in Lower Canada. Whether he was given the petition or not, Durham left without seeing them and, faced with the horrors of transportation, fifteen of them agreed they would try to escape.[9] They were helped to this decision by someone in the fort who managed to convey information to one of their number, John Montgomery, owner of the inn on Yonge Street where the rebels had gathered in December. This unknown friend told him that although the walls around the room where he was being held were four and a half feet thick, they had been built just a few weeks earlier and the mortar was not yet hard. With only a nail and a ten-inch length of iron the prisoners were able to tunnel through it within a week, cleverly masking both the noise and the rubble. Then at night, using a map their benefactor had smuggled to them, they made their way outside, though not without mishap. In the dark Montgomery fell into a pit and broke his leg before they had scaled the last wall. Two of their number deserted at this point, including John G. Parker, who was the only one acquainted with the area and who was to have been their guide.[10] With all the odds against them they still managed to cross the St Lawrence and to avoid the naval boat that was patrolling the river to capture them. They had to keep hidden as they crossed a Canadian island, carrying their boat. All this time Montgomery was in great pain from his broken leg, and the party was hampered by having to help him along. In spite of all the hazards, however, they reached the American shore and were brought in triumph to Watertown, where they received a heroes' welcome. The two men who had left them at the fort were recaptured and later transported, a fate that would undoubtedly have befallen the thirteen who escaped.[11]

The news of this prison break caused a sensation, and not only in Kingston, although it did have its greatest effect where the officers and men serving in Fort Henry were known. Lieutenant-Colonel the Honourable Henry Dundas of the Eighty-third Regiment, commandant of the garrison, ordered John Ashley, who was acting as jailer, to be arrested. At some point the men had dropped their map of the fort, and its discovery indicated treachery among those employed there. It was not Ashley who was to blame, however, as Dundas soon realized. He apologized, but Ashley was deeply offended and, anxious to vindicate himself, charged Dundas with false imprisonment. Although John A. Macdonald exercised his skill for the defence, the jury awarded the plaintiff £200 damages.[12]

A few days after the burning of the *Sir Robert Peel*, Hastings County residents learned that the pirates had struck even closer to home. From the statements that were sent to the lieutenant-governor it is possible to reconstruct the sequence of events. They began late at night on Amherst, or Tonti, Island, which lies just south of Bath. In the farmhouses the candles would have been pinched out, most of them long before the disturbances began. One of the last was in the Preston house, where Isaac Preston had gone to bed after eleven o'clock. His wife, his two sons, and the 'two young females of the family' had already retired. Isaac had not been long in bed when he was roused by someone knocking at the door of the house, and he got up again. When he asked who was there and what they wanted, he was told they wanted provisions. He opened the door, and two strangers entered, 'Americans by their tone and accent.'

After some conversation Isaac, perhaps becoming suspicious, went to the door, looked out, and saw there was a man standing outside each of his windows. At once he shouted to his family to get up. The intruder who seemed to be in charge yelled, 'Quick!' to his party and sprang for the two guns that were hanging on the beams of the house. The Preston sons James and David hurried into the room where their father was battling the leader of the raid. Shots were fired and a considerable struggle ensued. One raider went into the bedroom where the two girls slept and threatened to cut their throats if they stirred. A little later, however, amid all the confusion, they made their escape through the window and across to their nearest neighbour.[13]

This was John Spring, a shoemaker. He stated that he was awakened sometime between one and two o'clock in the morning 'by the cries of some persons in distress.' The girls were no doubt terrified, for they told him their family had been murdered and robbed. Spring at once roused his family, and arming themselves, they went directly to the Preston house.[14] They found the family alive, although Isaac had been hit on the head by the ball of a large pistol and was badly bruised, one son had a finger shot off, and the other was severely cut on the cheek. The raiders had stolen the two guns, two silver watches, a quantity of wearing apparel, some valuable papers, and 174 dollars.

They had gone on to the home of William Patterson, where they robbed his elderly father, although the report does not say what was taken. From the McGinnis mill at Mill Creek they got a quantity of flour. David Tait, another resident of the island, was probably their last victim. He said he was wakened in the middle of the night by several men. When he let them in, they asked him a good many questions, perhaps to learn how much he was likely to possess. This seems to have been very little. They asked for bread and pork. He replied that he had no pork, but he gave them a loaf of bread and two or three pounds of butter. As the raiding party went out, one of them stepped back inside and offered to pay for what they had taken, and when Tait refused the money the man threw fifteen pence down on the table. Looking through the window after them, Tait thought he could count about thirty men making off, and other observers saw a boat pulling away.[15]

From Kingston, Colonel Dundas sent off two armed boats, hoping to capture these pirates, but they made good their escape. Kingston magistrates notified the lieutenant-governor at once, fearing other places might be attacked in the same way. The Bath magistrates appealed for protection, pleading that they were 'absolutely destitute of Arms' with which to defend themselves.[16] Bill Johnston cast a long and threatening shadow over the whole Quinte area, and many were convinced he had been involved directly or indirectly in the raid. The Belleville magistrates prepared a petition, for which they asked His Excellency's immediate attention:

A nightly guard has been kept up in Town, ever since the pirate Johnston has been on the waters, but men who have their labours to attend to during the day cannot attend to their watchings at the same time ... [The magistrates] consider it to be their duty to lay before Your Excellency a statement of the disturbed state of the County and Town, and of the Great danger that is incurred by allowing it to remain without the protection of a permanent military force.

The pirate Johnston who is now upon the waters, is carrying on the same system of depredation which he pursued so successfully and continually during the late war with the United States. It is not necessary for me to furnish to Your Excellency, any particular facts to establish the danger that is to be apprehended from so desperate a being as well as from the disaffected residents of this portion of the Province.

Johnston, as it is pretty generally supposed, has taken up his quarters at the mouth of the Upper Gap, and from there, with the boats which he has manned he could reach this place in a few hours, he might lay it in ashes, and be again among the Islands before the guard could reach Kingston. The people of this neighbourhood know what he has done, know what he is capable of doing, and know that he has many acquaintances in the affected parts of the Province, and many of them residing on the borders of our Lakes, who would shelter rather than expose him.

In addition to this, the County and the Town are in a most excited state, and the property of persons who attented court to witness against the rebels taken in arms, and others who had conspired against the government, is no longer secure from the depredations of the men who have been returned to the bosom of society with all their rebellious properties redoubled, instead of being allayed by the clemency which has been extended to them. Instead there is a certain appearance of uneasiness amongst that class which is opposed to the Government, which is far from tending to allay the apprehensions, which are generally entertained in this County, that another and a more vigorous rising is contemplated ... In short we feel impressed with the belief, from what we see happening around us, that the peace of this County is in danger, and that it requires the aid of Government to allay and keep down the tumult that is evidently rising –

We are far from wishing to create an Excitement, but excitement must be created, if in every treasonable alarm, the well affected portion of the people are to be called to arms, and taken from their homes night and day and stand upon their guard against an insidious and an invading foe. This however may be obviated by Keeping constantly on duty a 'company of troops' or militia in the Town, by which means the excitement would be kept down, as their vigilance would be constant ... to allay fear and establish security.[17]

The governor was not yet prepared to establish a guard in Belleville. Although Arthur shared the magistrates' fear of an invasion by way of the Bay of Quinte, he always thought Presqu'ile was the most likely point of attack. He ordered a camp of 250 men to be established there, and to augment this he sent down an armed boat, which did not arrive until late autumn. In November his secretary wrote that 'H.E. is very sorry to find that the armed boat has arrived so unprovided ... But if volunteers have come forward well at Belleville probably you will be able to detach a few men for that purpose.' Alexander Petrie, who ran a ferry service from Belleville to Ameliasburgh, was recommended in the same letter for the reactivated Provincial Marine, so that he may have served on the Presqu'ile boat.[18]

Sometime in the spring of 1838 a network of secret societies known as Hunters Lodges was initiated across the northern states, and to an unknown extent in Canada. Their structure seems to have followed that of the Masonic Order, with members advancing through several degrees. Before the year was out a membership of twenty, forty, and even seventy-five thousand was claimed for them – almost without fear of contradiction. Since they were secret societies there were no authentic records, but whatever the true figure there is no doubt they were very popular in the United States and, it was feared, in Upper Canada. They were founded to promote and assist the Patriots' aim of independence for Canada. The obvious date for such independence was the fourth of July. In the weeks leading up to it, Patriots from a broad area in the States made their way to the border, a movement of which people were very much aware on the Canadian side. There was apprehension everywhere, but in the London District fear rose to insupportable heights as rumour followed rumour that it was to be the point of attack. From the surrounding countryside, families left their houses and farms to take refuge in the village of London, hoping the regulars stationed there would be able to protect them. The militia was strengthened by units from other places, and all were put on alert. News of the preparations that had been made for their reception travelled readily back to the Patriot leaders. Discretion proved to be the better part of their valour, and they let the fourth of July pass without a blow. If the rebels on the Canadian side had been planning a combined operation, as was feared, they were unable to act alone. The country sank back with a great sigh of relief. People were scarcely able to believe they had escaped without a shot fired. The next day Arthur wrote to Colborne that the disaffected had been held back 'from rushing to open violence and renewed rebellion by the presence of the Troops.'[19] He hoped they would now abandon their wicked intentions. 'There can be no doubt there was to have been a general rise throughout the Province on this day and tomorrow, but, in every district such Militia as have arms were promptly turned out by their Commanding

Officers and have assumed an attitude that has answered every purpose. I could not have supposed it possible that such a panic could have been so universally felt.'[20]

It could only have increased the anxiety of people around the Bay of Quinte if they had seen the contents of a letter Clifton McCollom sent to Mackenzie on 19 July. McCollom was full of ideas for assisting the Patriots. First he assured Mackenzie that those of Johnston's men who had been arrested for their part in burning the *Sir Robert Peel* were again free, and that Johnston would soon 'be both heard and felt.' Then he asked why several magistrates should not be captured, threatened, tortured, and if possible kept as hostages for some of the jailed rebels. They 'may be taken off at night far into the woods & there kept as food for the musquetoes [sic] unless *redeemed*.' This seems like a bad joke, but no doubt he meant it. His next suggestion was just as fantastic: 'the British Steamers are constantly carrying Troops & must have wood at every stopping place & many of the sticks or logs of wood are large enough to contain from five to twenty pounds of Powder – when put into the flames, what a grand report they would make; I have suggested these things to my friends at Kingston & Bath & perhaps the thing could be accomplished as well at Toronto & other places – Should the British boats stop at French Creek they may be accommodated with *light* wood.'[21] It is strange to think that the man who proposed such schemes to Mackenzie had recently been a member of Belleville's first board of police. Fortunately there is no reason to believe they were ever tried out.

One of the complaints in the Belleville magistrates' petition concerned men who had been released from prison, and who came back to Hastings County with bitter feelings towards those who had sent them down to Kingston. A number of cases of vandalism were laid at the door of these ex-prisoners. Two houses burned down in Trent Port, believed to be the work of rebels, and the magistrates offered a reward of £100 for the arrest of the culprits. Of the eighty or more Midland District men who were arrested in the months after the rebellion just nine were brought into court at the July assizes, and these were all men accused of treasonable acts around 22 February, the time of the Gananoque affair. They were Nelson Reynolds, Absalom Day, Christopher Lafontaine, Pierre Lasage, Asa Lewis, Samuel and Charles Marsh, Peter Orr, and Tobias Meyers. For all the trouble that had been taken to recapture Reynolds and all that had been said about him, nothing could be proved. According to the report of the trial that appeared in the Kingston Reform newspaper, the *British Whig*, he was charged 'with being the ringleader of a party of men who came from Hastings to assist in the attack on Kingston but the evidence against him was loose and given unwillingly, and the result was the acquittal of the prisoner after a very short consultation.'[22] Meyers's case was not heard 'because others charged with the same offence have been acquitted,' and the charge against Pierre Lasage was dismissed because all the witnesses had absconded. Absalom Day had to be discharged because Nelson Reynolds being acquitted of being a traitor, Day could scarcely be guilty of 'aiding the escape of a traitor.' The other trials proceeded and the accused were found not guilty, although in the case of Lewis, Orr, Lafontaine, and one of the Marsh brothers, who were all charged with conspiracy, the jury deliberated over the weekend. It was said arms had been found in their possession and there was the strongest evidence against them. The verdicts therefore came as a surprise, according to the *Chronicle and Gazette*, since 'few people have any doubt about their guilt.' The editor criticized the judge, saying that 'unfortunately for justice' he had allowed the accused so many challenges to jurors that they had in effect been able to pick their own jury. In addition some witnesses had failed to appear, and some of those who did appear contradicted each other. The favourable outcome of the trial, said the editor, was due above all to 'the skill and ingenuity of their young lawyer,' that rising star of the legal profession, John A. Macdonald.[23]

The magistrates worked hard to identify rebels, to arrest and punish them, but the result of all their efforts was inconclusive. For instance, the following item from Rawdon appeared in the *Chronicle and Gazette*:

It was reported some time back, that a Block house had been constructed in the rear of this County, by many of the persons implicated in the late insurrection. Major Thomas Parker, of the 2nd Hastings, had given instructions to an Officer of that Regiment, resident in Rawdon, to examine the ground and ascertain how far this was correct. On Monday, Capt. E. Fidlar and Lieutenant Barry arrived in town with four persons taken in a shanty, in the Township of Rawdon. Two of them, Philo Smith and Samuel Starr, are conspicuous leaders of the late insurrection, they were examined by the Magistrates and fully committed. They were sent to Kingston this morning, under the charge of Lieutenant Noble Barry.[24]

Did the blockhouse turn out to be a shanty? And how did the writer know the two men were leaders of the 'insurrection,' presumably the threatened attack on Gananoque? He may have had reliable information, but if so he failed to give it to his readers and, it must be assumed, to the court as well, since both men were released in May when the jury did not find sufficient grounds to indict them. This is part of a more general problem. Was Hastings County full of 'a traitorous association' of rebels? Were there any rebels at all in the county?

The magistrates arrested an unknown number of men and laid charges of treason and other serious crimes against many of them. Between seventy and eighty men of the Midland District were sent to Kingston to the district jail or to Fort Henry; others were detained locally for short periods.[25] Almost certainly they were Reformers, supporters of the party opposed to that of the magistrates. It is worth mentioning that a number of them were in conflict with one or more magistrates over other matters, such as religion or church property, and some were rivals in business. This raises questions about the motives in some of the arrests, like that of Hiram Baragan mentioned earlier. John Macaulay regretted 'the apparent harsh use' of the Belleville magistrates' powers. John Macaulay, however, lived in Kingston, where the military presence was always apparent and there was little reason to fear hostile neighbours. This was in contrast to the residents of Belleville and the rest of Hastings County, where insecurity was a factor that made for overreaction in those uncertain times. Between December 1837 and the end of 1839 many people in Hastings County were afraid some of their neighbours were stirring up violence and plotting against them; but, particularly when nothing was ever proved, to arrest so many does seem like crying 'Wolf!' too often.

Which does not mean there were no wolves. Many who lived through those years in Hastings County had no doubt there were people around them ready to cooperate with the enemy and secretly carry out acts of violence. While they may have exaggerated the danger, no one can say that all of them were wrong. There are the letters of Clifton McCollom to William Lyon Mackenzie and the evidence that Mackenzie corresponded with people in the Quinte area. There is Colonel Bonnycastle's description of events surrounding 22 February 1838, as well as the hidden arms that were discovered afterwards. Later in the year there is the case of Cornelius Parks.[26] While there is no proof, there is a lot of evidence pointing to the fact that there were indeed rebels in Hastings County, even if there is not enough to say exactly who they were.

Except for the nine who were held until the assizes in July, almost all prisoners were released by the middle of May, usually on bail to ensure their appearance for trial. But although some had to return as witnesses, none of them was ever given his day in court. In Oswego, Clifton McCollom was kept informed of events on the Canadian side, and he was able to tell Mackenzie that 'all the Belleville Prisoners have been acquitted ... but an attempt was made to *mob* N.G. Reynolds on his return [to Belleville] by the Tory Orange men but they were met by the Catholics and Reformers in such a way as to urge them home faster than a common walk.' He went on to say that 'never was Hastings in better condition to assess their rights,' and if the Patriots could gain a foothold the men of Hastings would 'hasten to that spot without delay.'[27] He may have been wrong, but the local magistrates as well as many other residents were very much afraid he was right.

PLOT

9 Excitement at Belleville

In early 1838 William Wallbridge wrote to his sister that he was kept busy in his law practice because 'people are suing each other like the devil.'[1] It would seem that Bellevillians were acting in the spirit of the times which saw division and discord everywhere. This did not improve as the year went on. Sir George Arthur wrote, 'It would be impossible to give you any just conception of the state of feeling here [–] for many years it was smothered, but the animosity now existing between Loyalists and Reformers is quite shocking.'[2] There were more than political reasons to set people quarrelling. Religion was one source of bad feeling although, as we have seen, religion and politics in Upper Canada were never completely disentangled. John Wedderburn Dunbar Moodie, who came to Belleville in December of that year as paymaster for the militia, wrote:

> The people in this part of the country are split into some three or four factions – The Catholics harbouring dark designs under a hypocritical profession of loyalty and Orangemen goading them on to rebellion by claiming all the loyalty in the country to themselves, – while the native Canadians are hugging the loaves and fishes as their own peculiar perquisite, agreeing with the others on hardly any one point but in hatred of the Scotch and their Church – whose determined spirit and proud independent mind will never become the slaves of any party, nor give up one particle of their rights as British subjects in a British colony.[3]

Such admirable determination nevertheless shows his own bias, although

Moodie was a moderate man who deplored the ill-will that marred political discussion. He went on to say that he tried to mediate between the two local doctors. George Ridley and Anthony Marshall, who were normally well-disposed men but at daggers drawn over politics, 'ready to give and take offence on every occasion.'

During 1838 there was occasional encouragement for Reformers, and some of it arose from an unexpected source. This was an article by Egerton Ryerson, who now came to the defence of Marshall Bidwell's reputation. This was too late to help Bidwell, who had been exiled by Sir Francis Head, a man destined to cause friction in Upper Canada from the time he arrived until after he left. It was the manner of his going that added to the ill-will he left behind him. The Colonial Office replaced him with Sir George Arthur not because of the rebellion – his resignation was accepted in November 1837 – but because of his treatment of Marshall Bidwell. The Colonial Office had instructed Head to install Bidwell as a judge; Head objected, and the Colonial Office repeated the instruction. Head, who had never forgiven Bidwell for criticizing him at the time the executive council resigned in 1836, then said he would resign before he would carry out the order. It seems he had used this threat before in order to get his own way, but this time the colonial secretary accepted his resignation in a letter that rebuked him at some length. It also detailed Bidwell's admirable qualities and suitability for the bench.[4] Even before this letter reached him, the rebellion offered Head a weapon to wound his adversary.

When the rebel camp at Montgomery's Tavern had been overrun, a banner bearing Bidwell's name was captured. It has been said this was left over from a previous election, and in any event Bidwell was not responsible for its presence. Sir Francis, however, was happy to infer from it that Bidwell had been guilty of fomenting rebellion, or at least of cooperating with the rebels. He told Bidwell that, if he remained in the country, there was nothing he, Sir Francis, could do to prevent him from being arrested and jailed. Although there seems to be no evidence of the truth of this threat, in the confusion of those days Bidwell accepted Sir Francis's word and left the country. Many people, and not only Reformers, thought his going was a great loss and did not believe he had anything to do with the rebellion. They admired him as a gifted man who had great public spirit, and in Lennox and Addington and around the Bay of Quinte they had been proud of his attainments. Not that everyone held him in the same regard. John Macaulay of Kingston wrote to his mother, Ann, in Picton that Sir Francis 'surely deserves the thanks of this community' for saving it from the indignity of having Bidwell on the bench. 'A democrat in the very marrow of his bones, what an opprobrium it would have been to the British Ermine.' His mother regretted the departure of Sir Francis, saying, 'If he had done nothing else but ... ridding the province of such a man as Bidwell he would have deserved the thanks of every British subject ... for preventing the disgrace of having a foreigner and a traitor to hold a high office in our parliament.'[5] The exile of Bidwell, the brightest star on the Reform horizon, was just one more cause for the Reformers' dejection after the rebellion.

Egerton Ryerson had dismayed them in 1836 when he withdrew his support before the election. Now, in May 1838 in an article published in the *Upper Canada Herald* of Kingston, he criticized Sir Francis for sending Bidwell into exile and denounced the persecution of Reformers, insisting that the great majority of them were in no sense rebels.[6] Ryerson had written under a pseudonym, but the name of the author soon became known, and the article was carried in newspapers throughout the province. This brought down a barrage of criticism on Ryerson's head, the *Chronicle and Gazette*, for one, printing several lengthy articles and letters which denounced his stand.

Another element was the revival of some Reform newspapers in the spring and summer of 1838, giving hope of better days to come. Of course, those who did not distinguish between Reformers and rebels detected renewed danger in this and increased their militancy. Ryerson's change of stance was no doubt influenced by what was happening among the clergy. After the rebellion when their Reform opponents were in disarray, Strachan and his supporters had seen a grand opportunity. They loudly pressed the claim of the Church of England to be the established or, as they sometimes called it, the National Church. Strachan persisted in trying to control education as well as the proceeds from the clergy reserves, and his insistence that his church must be at the helm of the proposed publicly supported university continued to stir up bitter debate, even though construction for that institution was not begun for another five years.

Colborne's secret order to set apart twenty-two thousand acres for the endowment of fifty-seven rectories of the Church of England had to be approved by the British government, and it was not until 1838 that it became law, having generated all the heat that might be expected. It is interesting to see that John Macaulay wrote in March of his satisfaction that the question was finally 'set at rest,' only to find in August that it was likely 'to convulse the whole country.'[7] Among the fortunate parishes were these around the Bay of Quinte and its neighbourhood:

Adolphustown	incumbent	Job Deacon	164 acres
Bath	"	none	400 acres
Belleville	"	John Cochrane	418 acres
Cobourg	"	A.N. Bethune	400 acres
Fredericksburgh	"	Job Deacon	250 acres
Hallowell	"	William Macaulay	400 acres
Kingston	"	The Archdeacon	700 acres
Port Hope	"	J. Coglan	436 acres

In these communities it was natural that members of other churches should feel resentful at this additional preference shown to the Church of England, and Church of England members often adopted the same attitude of superiority as their clergy. The following year John Moodie, who attended St Andrew's Presbyterian Church in Belleville, wrote to his wife that when the minister was away, he would instead go to services in St Thomas, 'the English Church,' but his feelings were deeply hurt when he found members of that church who were his good friends would not set foot inside the 'kirk.'[8]

Certain newspapers were responsible for adding fuel to the fire, and two of them were published in Cobourg, the *Star* and the *Church*. The *Star* wanted to hang everyone who had been involved in the rebellion. The *Church*, edited by a Church of England priest in Cobourg, attacked in uncompromising terms the other denominations in order to uphold every one of Strachan's claims for the supremacy of his own church. The Methodists came most often under his fire, probably because they presented the biggest target. All the efforts to make Methodism acceptable to the governing party, first by separating the Methodist Church from the American body, then by union with the English Wesleyans, had not redeemed the sect in the eyes of the Tories. As Egerton Ryerson said, 'It is rather humiliating, that we, who have never done anything to forfeit our claim to the confidence of the government or of the public should have our motives continually misrepresented.'[9]

For instance, in January 1839 there was a revival organized by the Methodists in Belleville. Hannibal Mulkins, a member of the Methodist clergy, later reported to the *Christian Guardian* that he had gone to the militia barracks to speak to any of the men he found there, and had left a number of religious tracts for them. Soon afterwards the Reverend John Cochrane, priest of St Thomas Church, also visited the barracks. Seeing the Methodist tracts, he demanded that they be handed over to him. He then made a bonfire of them, telling the men that such things were without doubt the cause of the rebellion. Mulkins complained that 'men of such christian and catholic liberality of views should receive every few years fifty-four thousand dollars of Upper Canada public money.'[10]

The post-rebellion difficulties faced by the clergy of nonconformist churches, such as Baptist, Episcopal Methodist, and a number of others including some branches of the Presbyterian Church, were described by a minister in the London District. He wrote that it was a time of privations and difficulties, that 'our Churches being all known to be voluntary, have been the object of particular dislike to the Tory party, and as that vile faction has gained for the present the ascendancy, they have in this district particularly done everything in their power to hurt our cause.'[11] Another preacher said he sometimes felt afraid to continue, that 'there is very little preaching now in the country with the exception of the Established churches ... Many are affraid [sic] to preach, and indeed some would not be allowed the privilege.' This man felt compelled to stay a little longer 'to blow the gospel trumpet,' but soon he too gave in and went back to the States.[12] He was one of several thousand people who left the province between 1837 and 1839.

The eastern part of the country suffered less from emigration than did the western districts, having been settled longer and not having been directly involved in the uprising. Nevertheless there was considerable movement out of the area. In April 1838 the *Chronicle and Gazette* reported the departure of Dr Armitage of Kingston, Dr Richard Van Dyke of Belleville, and the Reverend James Murdoch of Bath, adding 'and we could enumerate a hundred more.'[13] In February Murdoch had come under attack from the *Intelligencer* in an article that implied he was involved in the Patriot raid planned for Gananoque, and he had answered with a vigorous rebuttal in the *Chronicle and Gazette*. However, it seems likely that harassment was at least an element in the departure of all three men, who had undoubtedly come from the States.[14] In May, John Macauley wrote to a friend in Kingston that there was a fall in the price of land 'as a result of the late rebellion and a great exodus of people.' In October a letter from his mother illustrates one of the fears that accounted for some people moving out. She wrote that prices of supplies were rising daily, and she was laying in a store of provisions since war with the United States was becoming every day more likely.[15] The next year John Moodie wrote that many people had left the Quinte area, making it a favourable time to buy land; he added that the population was 'very much disaffected but the *worst* are clearing out as fast as they can sell their farms.'[16] The whole country was affected. It was said that some townships in the London area lost half their population.

The steamer *William* IV from Cobourg to Lewiston carried at one time 150 emigrants from the eastern part of the province, and small towns like Port Hope and Pickering were almost abandoned.[17] An editorial in the Brockville *Recorder* reminded the governor that 'you and your emissaries, by their taunts and persecutions, were goading innocent men to fly from the Country.'[18] In July the Kingston *Spectator* carried a news item copied from the Brockville *Statesman*, headed 'Moving Off':

> We have had occasion frequently to allude to the constant emigration which is taking place from this District to the Far West. It seems, however, that the moving spirit, which has taken possession of so many of our inhabitants, is no longer to be confined to individual or isolated cases, but has seized them *en masse*.
>
> A public meeting has been held within the last few days, at Portland, in the Township of Bastard, at which, we have been informed, not less than the heads of sixty families subscribed their names as intended immigrants. The sum of 400 dollars was subscribed to defray the expense of sending the two agents to the 'land of promise,' in order to lay out the site for the intended location of the emigrants.
>
> Coupled with this there was a report from the *Spectator* of Mount Morris, N.Y. Emigration from Canada. – Sixteen covered wagons, mostly drawn by oxen, passed through the city of Buffalo on the 6th inst. carrying the persons and effects of about 20 families of Canadian emigrants, on their way to the 'far west.' They were all from one town in the Brockville District.[19]

The Mississippi Emigration Society was organized to move a whole colony of people from Upper Canada to Iowa, which at the time was opening for settlement. Peter Perry was one of the agents sent down to try to secure land, but it proved impossible to arrange for the members to move in as a group.[20] Then, hearing that Lord Durham had responded favourably to Robert Baldwin's proposals concerning responsible government, the society abandoned its plan. These people and many others wanted to leave the country because of the rebellion and the subsequent upheaval, social, political, and economic. The general turmoil had brought commerce almost to a standstill.

Just occasionally someone moved away from a bad situation at home but went only to another part of the country. William Purdy, a miller who lived near Lindsay, was one of these. 'He had been speaking rather plainly about the Family Compact,' so that after the rebellion a militia officer laid a complaint against him. He was arrested and taken to jail in Cobourg. After a few weeks no charge had been laid, but he was told, 'Go home and mind your own business.' This treatment so angered Purdy that he took his younger son Jesse and moved down near Bath, leaving an older son to run the Lindsay mill.[21] And undoubtedly there were still other reasons for flight. Clifton McCollom wrote to Mackenzie about two men who had arrived in Oswego, claiming to be Patriots. He warned Mackenzie against them because he had made inquiries of 'our worthy Friend H.W. Yager and of several other of our friends from Bellville, all of whom have watched both Wells and Richmond during the past 12 months.' Wells claimed that 'he (Wells) was obliged to leave Canada because he had published "a *Libel* on one of the Tory *Gang*" but the plain truth of the matter is that he obtained 100£ in cash from the Bank for the purpose of establishing a *Library* in Bellville & thought no doubt it was better to sport upon the money than be pestered dealing out Books to the good people of Bellville. J.H. Samson & H.W. Yager were the indorsers & had the note to pay.'[22]

It did not help an uneasy situation that there was uncertainty about British intentions concerning the future of the Canadas. The loyalists or Tories held the essential test of loyalty to be a belief in this country's continued existence as a colony of Great Britain. This was the often quoted 'British connection.' It is a strange fact, however, that some important British parliamentarians were by no means sure they ought to keep these unruly colonies. There were several reasons for this, but the principal one was economic. The Canadas had turned out to be a disappointing investment. The British taxpayer was burdened with the cost of administration and defence, and during the rebellion years these mounted alarmingly as several regiments had to be sent in and thousands of militia employed and supplied. All this was happening against a background of economic depression that continued and deepened at home in Britain.[23] One historian has written that the best London hoped was that colonies such as Canada and Australia should separate on good terms, and that there was no difference among British parties on this question except in the degree of reluctance or enthusiasm with which they contemplated the break.[24] Some had for a long time believed separation was inevitable.[25]

Canada's vacant land was useful to absorb unemployed Britons, of whom British politicians were becoming increasingly aware. The Industrial Revolution was displacing more and more people from their age-old occupations, very often leaving them without work and restless in the towns. Good relations with Canada were necessary so that Britain could be assured of a place for this 'surplus population' to which politicians often referred, but quite a few thought such relations could continue even if the British connection were cut and the Canadas made independent, which was, it should be noted, the aim of the rebels. This opinion was expressed by Lord Aberdeen when he said in parliament that the separation of the Canadas from Great Britain was inevitable, and should be made an easy as possible. His speech was widely reported here and must have sent a cold shudder down the spine of many a loyal Canadian.[26] Probably needlessly, for two factors operated at the time against this view. One was British pride, which would be hurt if it appeared the Canadas were being surrendered to rebels; and the other was fear of having them annexed by the United States, thereby increasing American power, which was something already causing apprehension among the trading British.

Hard times were one factor that had encouraged rebellion, and the rebellion served to make hard times worse. The government of Upper Canada was at the time involved in the construction of three major canals, for although the Welland Canal was in operation it was so poorly built that it needed considerable rebuilding. The other two were at Burlington and the Long Sault near Cornwall, and work had also begun on the Trent. The colony did not have the capital to complete them and was, in fact, on the verge of bankruptcy. In London, Upper Canadian bonds became unsaleable and, of the two companies which handled them, one failed.[27] In April John Macaulay wrote to Christopher Hagerman that he had just been confounded by the information that the country's estimated deficit of £7,000 for the year had been revised to £20,000. He wished 'we could put our Legislature *to sleep* for two or three years. The saving in money would be great, as well as in needless legislation. The propensity of the age is to excessive law-making.'[28] It is hard to know what measures he thought the legislature could have omitted in order to improve its financial position.

Hastings County was suffering as much as other places. William Wallbridge wrote that money was very scarce because the one chartered bank of the area, the Commercial Bank of the Midland District, was taking in money but not issuing any, and 'all through Belleville we have to take Uncle Turnbull's notes for cash.'[29] Trade of every kind had been in trouble ever since the bank failures at the beginning of 1837, and there were still more bankruptcies and foreclosures in 1838. Some prominent Hastings citizens experienced severe financial loss. Billa Flint had all his stock repossessed by the Montreal suppliers, and in May was said to be 'dished up, done for.' Others were no doubt already in trouble since, by the following year, the bankrupts included Henry Baldwin, William McAnnany, Thomas Corbett, and Thomas Parker. As well, 'Dougall has gone down, all his property is in Bleeker's hand.'[30] All these disturbing developments did nothing to improve the temper of Hastings County residents, and Arthur sent a member of his staff, Captain George, Baron De Rottenburg, to Belleville while he went on to inspect Fort Henry. De Rottenburg seems to have found a difficult situation in the village and sent word of it to Arthur in Kingston. Arthur wrote to Sir John Colborne, 'I have determined to proceed to Belleville tomorrow, and see the Magistrates, and I hope to get them in a good humour again, – but, as I have before mentioned to you, there is a very general dissatisfaction in this Province in consequence as it is asserted, of delay and ultimate injustice, in settling the accounts after the last outbreak.'[31]

That was on 14 October. Three days later he wrote from Cobourg on his way back to Toronto. He had found in Belleville 'great discontent and great excitement.' His visit had, he thought, been successful, helped by the presence of Mr Cartwright, whom he had brought along from Kingston to act as peacemaker.[32] They had met all the Belleville magistrates and found

> the discontent proceeds from some non-adjusted accounts of expenses incurred in turning out the Militia last winter. These accounts were rendered some time since to the Commissariat, many items were disallowed, and even the residue has not been paid. I will call upon Mr Clark the Comt Officer for an explanation ... If the statement of the Magistrates be entirely correct, there is cause for remonstrance no doubt, but none for disaffection. From the trials that took place at Kingston, there cannot be a question that there were well grounded apprehensions entertained that the disloyal people of Hastings would go to extremes, and the Magistrates were fully borne out in adopting the measures they did – the expenses ought therefore to have been defrayed.

There is no evidence, however, that Mr Clark paid any more attention to this demand than to any of the others Arthur made to the commissary department. Down in Quebec he was protected by distance, and silence. More than unpaid bills were bothering the Belleville magistrates, however, as Arthur discovered:

> The existing alarm is occasioned by the information received of the doings on the American side. Every Magistrate, I found, had heard something which he considered conclusive.
> Frequent communication was kept up with the States and several meetings had recently taken place among known disaffected people.

'The menaces of these people and the revenge they felt towards them by whom they had been arrested last winter were matters of notoriety and yet the Government had offered no protection.' The conference lasted two hours and a half, during which time I was overwhelmed with all sorts of fears and grievances.

Some weeks ago, I had heard from Mr. Boswell ... who defended the Traitors who were tried at Kingston, and thereby got into their secrets, and he assured me he had no doubt they were acting in concert with a great body of persons on the American Frontiers with whom they conspired to attack and seize upon Kingston – It is his opinion that a very considerable number of persons are still residing in Hastings, who would take up arms against the Government, if they saw any prospect of success ... No time should be lost I am of opinion in calling out a much larger force.[33]

This time Arthur finally responded to the Belleville magistrates' fears by setting up a permanent militia guard in the town. A force of a hundred men was embodied 'to whom a bounty of £2 is to be given per man, with clothing and army pay, without reduction for rations. Captain Warren, late of the 66th Regiment, an active, intelligent officer, is to have the command.'[34] Captain Warren's intelligence, however, appears to have been no match for the troublemakers in Hastings, for Arthur was soon reporting to Colborne that Warren was 'unable to manage the people in that quarter' and had to be replaced.[35] Warren's difficulties can be understood from a report he prepared for the assistant military secretary in Toronto:

[F]rom what I can learn it appears that the population of the two frontier townships Sidney and Thurlow including the town of Belleville are inclined to rise against the government and I believe they frequently hold meetings and carry on a correspondence with ... the States for the purpose of arranging plans to that effect. The two Townships in the immediate rear of these Rawdon and Huntingdon are I understand better affected. Huntingdon is I believe tolerably loyal and about one half of Rawdon might be trusted. Marmora and Madoc are again in the rear of these. Marmora is not much settled but the few who are there are loyal. Madoc is also thinly inhabited and generally loyal. The townships Tyendinaga and Hungerford may be looked on generally as loyal although there are some bad characters in them. Then again to the Westward in the Front joining Sidney lies the Township of Murray which might be looked upon as loyal with the exception of the village of Brighton and Presqu'ile and from there to the Carrying Place distant ten miles where there are violent Reformers if nothing more.[36]

William Ketcheson would have agreed with this assessment. He had earlier sent a confidential letter to Colonel Bullock to which he attached a list of those Sidney residents whose loyalty was not to be relied upon, stating,

It is my opinion that nearly all, of those marked not to be trusted, have arms, others Rifles, or shot guns, and their refusing to [forfeit?] them, is another proof of their disaffection ... altho' there are many in the Township of Sidney who may be relied upon, yet there is a large Number that I am Confident, would at any time turn out and join a party for the purpose of establishing republican institutions, and who only wait a convenient opportunity, to be aided by their friends, whom they expect will yet be able to make a bold stand, openly and vigorously to defend their Republican principles.[37]

Unfortunately the marked list has not survived. People in Sidney must surely have reacted in some way to the magistrates' suspicion, whether or not it was deserved. This hostility within the district, as well as fear of invasion, required a continuing military presence. The following is a list De Rottenburg sent to Henry Dundas at Fort Henry of 'the distribution of the Volunteer force and Sedentary Militia, which are to be employed in your District.' The numbers are impressive:

Major Warren	Presqisle [sic]	100 men 3rd Northumberland
	"	100 men 3rd Prince Edward
	Belleville	100 men 1st Hastings
	Bath	100 men 1st Addington
	Gannoque [sic]	200 men 2nd Leeds
	Brockville	200 men 1st Leeds
	Prescott	200 men 2nd Grenville
Col. Van Koughnet	Cornwall	400 men 3rd Provisional Batt.
Col. McDonald	Charlottenburg	600 men 4th " "
	Belleville	2nd Hastings Cavalry
	Kingston	1st and 2nd Frontenac Cavalry
	Brockville	1st Leeds - the whole Troop
	Stormont	1st Stormont - the whole Troop

In addition a battalion of incorporated militia was ordered to be raised at Kingston.[38]

The figures look very well on paper, but given the difficulty that was being encountered everywhere in getting men to turn out, it is questionable how well the list corresponded to the numbers who actually served. Arthur even proposed at one point to give every volunteer fifty acres of land in order to fill up the ranks, since 'better will it be to give up a million of acres in this way, than to let the Traitors have them.'[39] One of the rumours that was flying about, adding to the general state of anxiety, is described in a letter from the military secretary to Henry Dundas. He said he had information that the rebels were intent on getting possession of the steamboats by putting some of their number on board as passengers 'with arms concealed, so they may seize the boat unawares.' The lieutenant-governor ordered 'that no Steam Boat may be allowed to proceed up the Bay of Quinty, or in any other direction from Kingston, without an armed party being on board – and that all Passengers – sailors – and others may be searched carefully, before being allowed to embark.'[40]

Throughout October there was mounting fear all along the front that there was soon to be an outbreak of hostilities. Every traveller who crossed the border brought tales of the thousands of men who were gathering at a number of points, and who made no secret of their intention to invade Canada. The situation sounded an ominous echo of some recent American history. Arthur wrote to Colborne, 'My opinion has been throughout that the Americans have acted with bad faith – All the people of the Northern States, it cannot be otherwise, would wish to see the Canadas Republican States; and altho Respectable Citizens would not perhaps take an active part in subverting our Monarchical Institutions, they will do but little, if anything, to prevent the aggression by that class of persons who would pour in on us as they did upon the Texas.'[41]

The reference was to the Mexican district known as the Texas. In 1828 the Mexican government had given permission for three hundred families from the United States to move into this territory, but others quickly followed until by 1835 there were thirty thousand Americans living there. Then, in a time of political turmoil in Mexico, they declared themselves a separate republic. The Mexicans had just defeated the Spanish to gain independence, but they were unable to meet this challenge to their authority. By 1838 the Republic of Texas had applied for admission to the United States, and there was unofficial but open recruiting in the States for men to go to Texas and join these rebels. Many in Canada saw a parallel situation developing in their own country. The frequently expressed fear was that a thinly populated Upper Canada, forced into independence by the secret plotting of American settlers with their fellow countrymen across the border, would very soon be annexed by the United States.

In early November De Rottenburg sent a message to Henry Dundas at Fort Henry. It indicates that Arthur's earlier measures had not been as effective as he hoped:

> The Major General regrets to find, from intelligence received this day, that great excitement and alarm prevails at Belleville and its vicinity. Instructions will be sent to Captain Swan ... to proceed there immediately and assume Command of the Volunteer Corps and Sedentary Miltia to be employed for its defence. –
>
> His Excellency is very desirous that you should exert yourself to calm the state of alarm and excitement, which you report prevails at Kingston. The ample means of defence placed at your disposal, His Excellency had hoped, would have quite tranquillized the inhabitants of that place and its neighbourhood.[42]

Arthur replaced Major Warren by De Rottenburg, who could, he hoped, get both militia and public under control, and after bringing him back to headquarters during November and part of December, then stationed him in Belleville until the spring of 1840. De Rottenburg was given charge of the militia in Presqu'ile and the counties of Prince Edward, Hastings, and Lennox and Addington. If the lieutenant-governor's letters at this time show a degree of despair, it is not to be wondered at, for the Bay of Quinte was not the only area to cause him grave concern. West of Toronto may have been the worst, but he had little reason to trust any of the stretch between Kingston and Toronto. He had proposed stationing a detachment of militia at Whitby, and in September Colborne replied that he had 'no doubt from the character of a portion of the settlers of Whitby, Reach, and Pickering, that those townships should be closely watched.'[43] Even before the rebellion Anson Green, a prominent Methodist clergyman, after a tour of that part of the country had said 'I believe in Haldimand and Cramahe Townships there are twenty rebels to one sincere loyalist.'[44]

Arthur's informants told him that Patriots were passing the frontier in small parties, intending to join up with the disaffected and establish themselves in the rear of important posts. 'We are,' he said, 'at this moment, on a mine which I expect may spring every moment.'[45] As it turned out, there were several mines. The first, however, exploded in the lower province.

10 The Windmill

The British regiments were to some extent outside the controversies of the rebellion, so that they were able to maintain the peace with a certain amount of impartiality. It was different with the militia regiments, whose members as Canadians had their own political allegiance. This was particularly unfortunate in Lower Canada, where political differences were intensified by nationalist bias. Reformers and rebels alike were almost all French, the government party almost all English, and the militia belonged to the government party. If there had been enough regulars to police the districts around Montreal after the battles of 1837, much trouble might have been avoided. Instead, most of the policing had to be left to the militia, particularly the cavalry militia, and they were given a free hand. Their officers acted as judge and jury, and, as an observer wrote, they allowed no one to hold an opinion contrary to their own. If they thought the inmates disloyal, they ordered houses and barns to be burned. Occasionally men were shot standing in their own doorways.[1] During 1838 the *patriotes* made a few ineffective raids across the border from Vermont; otherwise the province was quiet. Violence smouldered just below the surface, however, and in November it blazed up in a major attack on the Eastern Townships.

Sir Charles Grey was with his regiment on 2 November in Montreal, where he found 'all the excitement of a besieged town.' Reports were coming in that there were rebel concentrations in many centres, and it appeared that 'the People are up on the whole line of the Richelieu, and that an attack is meditated on Sorel in the course of the evening.'[2] Beauharnois was said to be occupied by four to five hundred rebels. The leaders had their headquarters in Napierville, and when troops advanced on it fifteen hundred fled and one hundred stragglers were taken prisoner. Other pockets of resistance were soon overcome.

There were casualties among the regulars and the militia, but much heavier losses were sustained by the French, many of them after the fighting had ended. According to Grey, Colborne had at first intended to burn the homes of all rebels but changed his mind after the first few had gone up in flames. This did not prevent the militia from carrying on after he left off. Having been without supplies for three days, the regulars joined in the work of destruction by pillaging the barnyards of the defeated *canadiens*. The Glengarry Regiment from the bordering county in Upper Canada had taken part in the fighting, and they had 'left a trail of plundering six miles wide on their return from Beauharnois – carried off their spoils from houses and farms by the cartload – especially horses – of 600 men only fifty went home without one.' Grey wrote, 'Colonel Fraser, who commands the Glengarrys, says they are looked upon as savages, to which I could not help answering that I thought by his own account they rather deserved it.'[3]

Before the smoke had cleared away from this outbreak there came news of an invasion of Upper Canada. Since December 1837 loyal forces, mostly militia, had met and turned back every raid the Patriots had launched into Upper Canadian territory. It seems strange, therefore, that Patriot leaders could still believe there would be a welcome for them if they attacked Prescott, and yet they recruited a small army by fervently preaching that Canadians would rise up to free themselves from British tyranny as soon as Patriot liberators landed among them. Prisoners later named prominent men in Auburn, Ogdensburg, Oswego, Sackets Harbor, and Salina as organizers. One young man claimed he had joined, not expecting to fight, only to bring liberty to the people; that to him it was God's work for he had heard ministers of the gospel encouraging the people to support the 'Patriot Hunters.'[4] More than one of the invaders said he had been influenced by Henry Pendergast. This was the American who had been a partner in the iron works at Madoc. According to Richard Bonnycastle he had carried on subversive activities in Canada, organizing men and gathering arms. When he tried to get a contract to cast cannonballs for the military, Bonnycastle said he realized the man's only purpose was to discover the strength of Fort Henry and its ordnance.[5] Early in 1838 Pendergast went to Ogdensburg where he continued his activities among the Patriots. One resident of Sackets Harbor said he had been persuaded to join the expedition by Pendergast's assurance that there would be no fighting because two thousand Canadians would join them as soon as they landed, and that many of the British regulars had already signed up.[6]

News and rumours of all this activity in upper New York State caused great anxiety north of the border. There was widespread fear among the inhabitants that some blow was about to fall, not only from invasion but also from treachery at home. At the beginning of November John Cartwright wrote to John Macaulay that authority should be given to arrest several persons suspected of conspiracy, and habeas corpus should be suspended 'since we are surrounded with Spies and the state of the garrison is known – an order in council to be used in these dangerous times – we have a guard every night.'[7] One can only speculate on the need for such measures in Kingston, but Cartwright was a sensible man and that was his evaluation of the danger. According to the following letter, men were reluctant to do militia duty, and this would cause uneasiness to those responsible for defence. On 2 November Clifton McCollom in Oswego was writing to Mackenzie: 'Our friend H.W. Yager has been with us for a few days, in order to ascertain particulars of what is going foward and assures me that the organization has been carried on to a greater extent, than when I left Hastings & Lodges have been established among the Catholics who have heretofore opposed us. Arthur is trying to get up companies of 100 ea. in Kingston, Bath, Fredericksburgh, Adolphustown, Hallowell, Napanee, & Bellville, in the Mid-Dis. but it is no go, having been engaged 4 weeks, & enlisted but 40 to 50 men.'[8]

On 5 November De Rottenburg wrote to Henry Dundas at Fort Henry that there was reason to believe arms were being brought in and secreted and that 'information has lately been received, that the Brigands from the other side are passing the Frontier in small parties, with the avowed object of joining the disaffected here, and of establishing themselves in the rear of some of our important posts.'[9] In Oswego, Patriot General John Birge drilled the men, who crowded the rooms where he harangued them, assuring them they would be among the twenty to forty thousand who were about to liberate Upper Canada. In the feverish rush to take part in the enterprise, 'labourers left their employ; apprentices their masters; mechanics abandoned their shops; merchants their counters; husbands their families; children, their parents; Christians, their churches; ministers of the gospel their charges to attend these meetings.'[10] Prosperous merchants offered steamboats for the transport of troops, no doubt with an eye to the free land that was promised to all. On Sunday 10 November about four hundred men embarked at Mullins Bay.

A steamboat took two schooners in tow, and men and arms were loaded onto them, under the command of General Birge. Against the wishes of most of the men, Birge put in at Ogdensburg, saying they would pick up more volunteers. Instead, Birge stayed ashore, claiming illness, and about forty men stayed with him. It was not a good beginning, for 'the men lost courage on seeing their leader show the white feather.' Others had come aboard at Sackets Harbor and French Creek, so there were still about two hundred on each schooner. With Birge gone it was left to a man with some military experience, Count Nils Von Schoultz, to take charge of one of the schooners, and Bill Johnston of the other. Serious trouble began when Johnston ran his schooner onto a sandbank, and all efforts to free it proved unsuccessful. This ended any possibility of a surprise attack. Von Schoultz intended to march his men through the village of Prescott, but they refused and he ended up about a mile and a half downstream. Here the men took shelter around a number of stone buildings, including a seven-storey windmill.

In spite of all the easy assurances that had been given back in the little towns of Oswego County, the inhabitants strongly resisted these invaders. Soon all the Patriots were forced to take refuge in the windmill. Johnston got back to the American shore, promising to send reinforcements, but although hundreds of spectators lined the shore to watch, none came over. A company of the Glengarry militia arrived in Prescott; others came from Grenville, and were soon joined by three hundred from Dundas County. When Captain Sandom of the Royal Navy got word in Kingston of this invasion, he went down at once with seventy marines and regular soldiers in tow-boats, a gun mounted in one of them. The windmill, however, had walls seven feet thick and was almost impregnable. Sandom's gun proved too light to have any effect on it, and he went back to Kingston for heavier artillery. The men in the mill were in a perfect position to defend themselves, and they inflicted a number of casualties, although they also suffered quite a few when they came out to engage in close combat. On Tuesday 12 November there was a brief truce, so that both sides could bury their dead. Some of the Patriots then tried to cross to the other side in order to get medical supplies, but they were taken prisoner. Von Schoultz, seeing no hope of success, would have evacuated his men but had no boats for them. The kind of hand-to-hand fighting in these battles can be imagined from a letter sent by Ogle Gowan, who was by this time a lieutenant colonel, to his cousin James:

I received two wounds, both (Thank God) slightly, one a little below the hip, from a bayonet, when the right wing (which I had the honour to command) charged the ruffians, who were entrenched behind a Stone Wall. One inch further to the right would probably have finished me. Walter Ebbs (sexton of the church at this place) gave the fellow the benefit of his Bayonet in return and quickly despatched him to answer for his deed in another place. The other wound is in the side of my knee, and was given by a Ball fired from one of the windows of a Stone House as we advanced to drive in the doors.[11]

It was Friday when Sandom got back to Prescott, bringing four companies of the Ninety-third Regiment as well as a howitzer and two eighteen pound guns. Placing two of these in boats anchored above and below the mill, the third in a field behind it, they began to bombard the mill. Even this did little damage to the walls of the structure, but it did make the men inside realize their position was hopeless. When they tried to come out under a white flag, however, they were fired upon. Only late in the day were they allowed to surrender. In the general orders issued just after the Battle of the Windmill, fifty-two were said to have been found dead inside the mill. The prisoners were tied in single file to a long rope and made to march the mile or two into Prescott, where they were put on board the naval vessels. At their trial several expressed their gratitude to the navy men and regular soldiers who protected them from the local militia as well as from the vengeful crowds who gathered there and at Kingston, and who would not have spared them.

General orders mentions 140 prisoners, but the *Chronicle and Gazette* later gave the figure of 159, two having died in Kingston hospital, which was still treating nine others in January.[12] The trials were held in courts martial at Fort Henry. William Henry Draper, the solicitor-general, presided as judge advocate, sitting with a bench of officers, some regular and some militia. John A. Macdonald was asked to assist the prisoners prepare for their trial although, as a civilian, he could not represent any of them in a court martial. From the transcripts it appears that every effort was made to conduct the trials fairly. The sentences, however, were harsh. Eleven men were hanged, including Count Von Schoultz. He was a man who romanticized his past, making it out to be more noble than it was, but at least he played out to the very end the part he had set himself, drawing both admiration and pity from those who saw his courageous bearing at that time, in battle, imprisonment, trial, and death.[13]

It was a problem to know what to do with so many prisoners since the prisons were already full. Over fifty of them were aged from twenty-one down to sixteen; one was fifteen, and one a boy of fourteen. By spring Arthur decided they had no doubt learned a lesson they would not want to repeat. He had sixty-one of them put on board steamboats and sent them back to Ogdensburg.[14] It was a very different return from the one they anticipated when they set out to liberate Canada.

At the end of it all Draper wrote, 'Everything in this part of the country appears tranquil. I think here in Kingston there is a feeling that capital punishment has gone far enough. A very different excitement appears however to prevail to the East and blood for blood, or a criminal executed for every loyal man who fell seems to be the desire and expectation of a large number of the community.'[15] Arthur found great satisfaction in the outcome of the Battle of the Windmill. He wrote to Colborne that 'there was a little more time taken up than I expected, but it has been well done at last.' In his opinion the punishments were 'severe but just.'[16]

The executions were carried out within a few days of sentencing. Many more than the eleven were under sentence of death, but had this reduced to transportation for life, which, though it was not so final, was terrible enough. The men who were transported, some of whom had been captured in earlier encounters, were kept until spring in Fort Henry; then, clamped in heavy leg chains, they were put on board ship for England. There they were held in one of those rotting prison hulks on the Thames made infamous by Charles Dickens. After a few weeks they were loaded into the hold of an old cargo ship, crammed into incredibly confined spaces with every class of criminal. Their chains were not removed until they were well out at sea, and even then they were not allowed above deck. There followed about three and a half months of bad food, bad water, and every kind of misery as they sailed half way around the world to Van Diemen's Land. On this island off the south coast of Australia, now called Tasmania, was the penal colony where flogging and hanging were common. The governors believed the only way to control a population of convicts was with severity that erred on the side of brutality – no worse than the punishment inflicted in other prisons at the time, but no milder. Although its reputation was well known to the Canadians, they went ashore thankfully after the horrors of the prison ship, and in fact for most of them it was a great improvement. Some were put to such work as road building; others were hired out as convict labour. Some worked for settlers who treated them reasonably; others were not so fortunate. Not all survived the harshness of these years, which lasted until amnesty in 1844.[17] Most of them, however, made their way home again, usually to the United States. They had to hope for passage on a cargo ship or whaler calling in at Hobart since no transportation was provided to bring them back.[18]

There was no comparison between the punishment of those transported and those who were kept in Canadian prisons, but even here the treatment they received was sometimes inhumane. Some men later wrote about the unheated cells and food that had already been sampled by rats and vermin. In this respect it is interesting to note that in John Montgomery's account the men in Fort Henry seemed to be on good terms with their guards. As for the district jail, at the 1839 quarter sessions the grand jury 'made the following presentiments – That having Examined the Gaol during the present Sessions beg leave to report that they found the prisoners confined therein in possession of Every Comfort and Convenience,' although they did add, 'consistent with their situation,' which left the matter a little open to question.[19] Still, in all the Hastings claims later submitted, while men asked compensation for imprisonment, none of them mentioned any ill treatment in Kingston.

News of the invasion had encouraged those Hastings residents who were in league, or even in sympathy, with the Hunters, but it sent a wave of fear over the rest of the population, already nervous about the possibility of attack by 'pirates.' It was a tense situation when Arthur wrote to Durham that the 'frontier is now swarming with these Ruffians & every hour I expect to hear of their having made descents on various parts of our Territory. In Michigan they have thousands well drilled & completely equipped with plenty of cannon.'[20]

When the regular troops left Fort Henry for Prescott, Henry Dundas, the commander, wrote to John H. Blacker, the militia officer who lived near Shannonville, that 'the rebels and Sympathisers are now in possession of Prescott [–] it is now important that every loyal man should be up and doing – Give orders for every disposable man to march to Kingston without a moment's delay.'[21] Blacker sent the order on to Captain De Rottenburg. It was endorsed by the adjutant general with the comment that this would 'deprive the whole line of Country along the Bay of Quinte of every disposible [sic] man.' It does not appear that any Hastings men went down to Prescott, or even to Kingston to bolster its defence. According to the *Chronicle and Gazette* of 11 November, that duty was undertaken by the First and Second Regiments from Addington, the First and Second of Lennox, the Frontenac militia, and three troops of cavalry including the First Addington Dragoons under Captain Fralick. Some of them may have been intended for the Windmill battlefield. On 17 November John Cartwright of Kingston sent to John Macaulay a report on the men who were called out to go to Prescott, but he said the militia 'proved deficient for lack of system, the best of them were inefficient for want of organization, and Frontenac and Addington could not get them into order.' It seems as if muddle prevented any men of the Midland District from taking part in the Battle of the Windmill, but there were adequate forces in the field. Meantime there had been apprehension of trouble at home. Anthony Manahan sent a message about impending danger for Belleville because of suspicious rebel gatherings in Lennox and Addington. In consequence of this, two troops of dragoons were sent to Camden and Richmond to make a sweep through that part of the country. Manahan was always inclined to think plots were being hatched. Cartwright, taking a calmer view, said he had reason to believe 'it is a portion of the disaffected who have gathered to prevent their being assembled to do their duty as Militia although there may be foundation for the report that it is their intention to attack Belleville.'[22]

From Oswego McCollom wrote to Mackenzie on 28 December:

One of the young men from the county of Hastings U.C. who was confined at Watertown in consequence of the *Peel* affair, was here on Monday last, in good spirits, says that *All* were released, without Bail, and are now ready for any expedition which may be got up with the least prospect of annoyance to the Canadian Tyrants; I do think that if the last expedition had been got up for Prescott and all things ready on Board as though bound for that Port, with a perfect understanding to land at Presq Isle harbour, and carried this understanding into effect, It would have answered a double purpose, in the way of deceiving the torys and at the same time have taken our friends to a defenceless port, within twenty miles of Belleville, where a very good accession, to their force was at hand Tolerably well armed and prepared. The new Court house (a very strong building) would have answered ... for a fort, being situated upon the highest ground, within 5 miles of the place and I am credibly informed by H.W. Yager that from 1000 to 1500 men were waiting the arrival of the People from this side, that it was very difficult to prevent a rising there.

McCollom then suggested that in future the Patriots should keep their targets secret, except from the few who had to know them, and let the public believe something different. Even if anyone had taken this advice, it came too late. However, it seems many of the Patriots and Hunters had not yet conceded defeat. It may have been said only to console Mackenzie, but his letter continued: 'My friends on the other side are in no way disheartened but are using every means consistent with safety, in organizing and procuring temporary implements ... No one has yet been arrested in Hastings & I think this shows plainly the state of that County. Several have been immured at Coburgh, at Kingston, Brockville, Perth, Cornwall for refusing to shoulder the Queens Musquet, others for refusing the Oath of Loyalty.'[23]

There was a widespread belief that Hastings County sheltered many rebels, men who were believed to be Hunters, holding meetings and drilling in secret. Since there are few documents to substantiate such claims, the case of Cornelius Parks of Thurlow is of particular interest. His conduct certainly left him open to suspicion. Three men, neighbours of Parks, swore out depositions against him, and the magistrates examined him in January 1839. From these statements Parks appears to have been too loud and boastful to make a very good conspirator. Nevertheless the evidence tends to show that this member of a United Empire Loyalist family was a Hunter, or at least a Patriot sympathizer of some sort. William Embury swore that, on one occasion when he had agreed to take some wheat from Parks to settle a debt, Parks asked him to wait for an hour or two 'as he had to call the rest of his company out.' Since Parks was not a militia officer, this was taken to mean a company of Hunters or rebels. When Embury went over for his wheat, Parks said he was authorized to inquire into his political character and, deciding that Embury was a Tory, informed him that as soon as the Patriots arrived he would be killed. In a shop where several people were present, Parks had cheered for Bill Johnston, something that would be very unpopular with many Bellevillians. Embury's statement mentioned Joseph Canniff, Samuel Robinson, and James Sheffield as being visitors to Parks's house, implying that they were fellow conspirators.[24]

John Grewey stated that about the time of the invasion at Prescott, Parks advised him to join the Patriot party because in less than a month anyone who did not join 'would have neither house nor home.' Grewey was well placed to observe Parks since he rented part of the same house. He said many people came and left again, in great haste and at all hours of the day and night. He thought they were messengers 'carrying some kind of information through the country.' At the same time as news of the invasion reached Hastings, 'a person arrived in great speed' at Parks's house, and as a result of the information this stranger brought, Parks told Grewey he and others might as well sell their farms for whatever they could get, for they would have to give up the province almost at once, the British having failed to drive the Patriots from the mill after making two attempts, and 'they [the Patriots] would now keep a footing.' Grewey's statement implies that the person who 'arrived in great speed' was coming post-haste from the Windmill battlefield, suggesting the organized messenger service the Hunters were thought to have.[25]

About the same time, Abram L. Bogert was returning from Belleville to his home on the fourth concession of Thurlow when he met Parks, who asked him what news he had heard in town. Bogert told him the talk was that Captain Bonter's company as well as the Rifle companies had been ordered out, and there would soon be drafting. Parks said that they, meaning the government party, 'might as well go to the devil since the province was already lost ... the Americans would come over, and with the force that would join them here, they would walk thro' the Province, and there would be no fighting, and said the witness would be glad to shoulder a musket & march under the American Eagle, or flag of Liberty. Witness said he should never be glad to do it, that Parks then said, that he would soon be under the sod, and that his days were short.'[26]

Much of Parks's talk was full of bluster, but with all the uncertainty of the times it is understandable that it worried his neighbours. When he heard that Captain Bonter intended to arrest him, he boasted that 'if he attempted it he was a dead man.' He claimed to have his musket loaded and ammunition in his pistol, that those in authority dared not take a prisoner, and so on. Bogert said Parks was 'pursuing a course of intimidation to drive the loyal people of the neighbourhood from their farms.' Parks mentioned Billa Flint and Edmund Murney as being among the first who would be put to death, along with 'all those who had any hand in sending them [the men arrested in Hastings] to prison last winter.' Parks had been one of the prisoners, and on 6 January 1839 he was again committed, and the above depositions sent to the attorney general. In his later claim for compensation he said he had been acquitted both times, although on this evidence he seems to have been guilty at least of sedition. It may be that by the time Parks was tried the prosecutors were no longer eager to convict men who had only talked revolution but had done little or nothing to bring it about. By 1839 there was not much left of the rebellion except talk.

The last invasion by any large number of Patriots had occurred in early December, when about four hundred crossed on the ice to Windsor. They burned a steamboat at the wharf and set fire to the barracks where a militia guard was housed, killing several men. From there they marched to Sandwich, but by then the militia under Colonel Prince had gathered, and they were soon put to flight. Most of them made their way back to the American side of the river, but a few were later found frozen to death in the woods. Five men were taken prisoner. Prince disarmed them and then told them, one at a time, to run for their lives. At the military inquiry which followed, the bizarre scene was described. The prisoners tried to dodge and hide behind fences while Prince ordered his men to fire at them. When four were dead, some of his officers intervened to save the fifth, all this taking place in full view of people on the street.[27] Regular army officers were shocked, and the Duke of Wellington asked why Prince had not been court-martialled. Not to condone Colonel Prince, but to put these reactions into some sort of perspective, it should be noted that the men in the windmill had their white flag twice ignored, and at St Charles in Lower Canada men were not allowed to surrender even when the building in which they were trapped caught fire. In both cases British officers were in charge of British troops. Knowing this, it is not so surprising that Prince had his admirers. In Toronto he was given a public dinner, and Lewis Wallbridge wrote, 'That man is a Prince by nature as he is by name.'[28] Deplorable as that statement may seem, it indicates the degree of exasperation Canadians were feeling after a year of lawless raids and attacks.

11 More Excitement at Belleville

The alarm of the Belleville magistrates and the fear of attack which they had relayed to the lieutenant-governor when he came to town in October had in November proved to be well founded. The invasion had not come as they feared on the Bay of Quinte, but the battle at Prescott was too close for comfort. The people of Hastings waited fearfully through that week, all the time casting nervous glances around the neighbours, wondering who might betray them to the invaders. Even when the Windmill prisoners were safely lodged in Fort Henry there was still a constant feeling of insecurity because of the Patriot army just across the lake. As always, there were rumours in which huge numbers were bandied about. It was said twenty thousand were still preparing to invade Lower Canada from Vermont, and thousands more to be concentrating in other places along the border. As a result, De Rottenburg reported, there was still an unhealthy excitement in Hastings County. Arthur's secretary replied:

The Lieut Gov has heard with the greatest regret that the Townships of Rawdon and Sydney are in such a state as you represent, upon the information of Capt. Fiddler [Fidlar] – and which must of course be put a stop to –

It gives the Lieut Gov the greatest concern to find that the Inhabitants have been placed in circumstances of so much alarm at Belleville. – And it does appear to H.E. to be extraordinary, as he certainly has information from good authority that a great portion of the Inhabitants of both Sydney and Rawdon, are loyal People. – But you have of course done quite right in making preparations for both offensive and defensive operations. Should any number of men actually have risen in arms, either in Camden or Rawdon, the only way is to march a force upon them immediately, without waiting for them to come to Belleville.

It is the L.G.'s impression however, that these people cannot be so mad as to think of moving, unless there is an attack of foreigners from the American shore upon Presqu'Ile. –

The L.G. has a report from Kingston telling him that the Lenox and Addington Cavalry have been sent down to scour the country of Richmond and Camden. –

With regard to arresting individuals, if there be information upon oath of their disloyal intentions, it would of course be proper to cause the principals to be apprehended.[1]

Whatever measures were taken, they do not seem to have been altogether effective. Ten days later Arthur was writing: 'In the neighbourhood of Belleville there is a very bad feeling, and one company of Militia formed there have acted so ill that Capt. De Rottenburg has reported to me the necessity of disarming them. Another company from Prince Edward have also behaved ill which has much surprised me.'

Arthur took a very serious view of these occurrences and sent Henry Ruttan to reason with the company of men in Prince Edward, who seem to have been in a mutinous state.[2] The message went on to approve the action of Captains Bonter and Murney, who had each increased his company to one hundred rank and file. As well, a company of the Third Hastings had been sent to De Rottenburg's relief, making it seem that De Rottenburg, too, had doubts about being able to 'control the People in that quarter.' By this time it had become a problem to find enough volunteers anywhere in the province since, Arthur said, many were indifferent to the outcome. Colborne had written that it might suit the officers to be called out, 'but the best men will become disgusted if they are kept long away from home without seeing any action.'[3] There were other reasons for dislike of army life, and one was the low pay. Arthur wanted to increase it because, although the economy was still slack, immigration was almost stopped, thousands of men were working at least part time in the militia, and there was a shortage of labour. Wages had risen accordingly and men were being offered more than army pay. In the beginning each company had taken no more than six married men, 'but now we must take what we can get.' He also wanted to give rations to the wives and children of volunteers. Finally, he was ready to offer 'fifty acres to every Militia man who stands by us during the contest – This would bring them out – and better will it be to give a million of acres in this way, than to let the Traitors have them.'[4]

Even with these attractions Arthur found there were further obstacles: 'they have come forward most lamentably ... it is a sad affair! We have no supply of Blankets, Bedding, Clothing.' He was also short of arms and those he had were in poor shape. He had procured 250 blankets for Belleville and the same for Presqu'ile, but he had to offer ten shillings to any man who provided his own, the same if he brought his own gun.[5] Throughout this time there is a note of gloom in the letters of the men in authority, for although the Patriots had been defeated again and again, they seemed to have an endless number of recruits. The governor thought Upper Canadians did not show enough interest in defending the colony, and even that they were joining Hunters lodges in increasing numbers.

From Brighton Major Warren wrote, 'I sent out a party to seize some arms that I understood to be in the house of a very suspicious character and the Party found three guns of various descriptions and brought in a person dressed in a blue uniform which I have ascertained to be the dress worn by the people styling themselves Patriots in the States.'[6] The man was held while Warren tried to find out more about him, but there is no record of his arrest. When trouble erupted in Hastings, however, it did not come from foreign interference but from a local and rowdy faction. In the reaction after the December rebellion a number of Reform papers had to stop publishing, some because of the withdrawal of business, others because angry mobs wrecked their presses. Any that survived must surely have practised discretion, at least for a time, since their critics brooked no strong opposition – none at all if it could be prevented. During 1838 there was some revival of these newspapers. One that had survived in spite of its outspoken character was the Reform weekly, the *Plain Speaker*, published by Samuel Hart, first in Cobourg, then in Belleville beginning sometime in 1838. No copies have come down to us, and most of what is known about its contents has to be surmised from letters written about it by those who disliked it and were in opposition to its politics. There are excerpts preserved in another publication from an issue printed in Cobourg shortly before Hart moved his press, and they leave no doubt that the newspaper was anti-government. There was an editorial contrasting those who work to supply the comforts and necessities of life, the 'Producers' who 'eat their bread by the sweat of their brow,' with those who wallow in luxury and 'pretend to exalted excellence, superior endowments, great personal worth and deep knowledge' and therefore 'arrogate to themselves the right of governing and directing all the affairs of the Province, of telling people what to think and how to act ... lovers of *exclusive privileges* ... high sounding titles ... given to base lucre and ... very much intoxicated with power' and who 'are not the Producing Class in any other sense than this – they produce discord – engender strife – create rebellions ... and fatten on the miseries of their fellow creatures.'

There was also an article contrasting the visit by the governor of Pennsylvania to a farm with Sir George Arthur's recent visit to Cobourg. The American had taken off his jacket and helped with the harvest, while the governor of Upper Canada was received with ceremony and given a flattering address by Sheriff Ruttan. Among the crowd 'a humble mechanic was very much maltreated because he refused to take off his hat in respect to the man who disregarded the prayers of 30,000 ... and the earnest petition of heart broken wives and daughters.[7] He left town ... cheered by the office holders and Sycophants and the boarders of the *Caroline*.' The industrious mechanic and labourer were said to have reserved their three cheers for 'a *Farmer Governor*.' That provocative statement is equalled by another calling upon 'The Farmer, Mechanic, and labourer' to pull together to bring down 'those who are hanging upon their shoulders and eating up their substance.'[8] This may not be a call to revolution, but undoubtedly it had a rebel ring to it. What would make this editorial particularly offensive to the government party was not only the praise of an American governor, but the appeal to men of the working class against those who held office or were in any position to profit from the labour of others. It exemplified that 'levelling' tendency the Tories found so detestable in American society, and if this was typical of the paper when it was published in Belleville, which seems likely, the attempt by Henry Baldwin and Christopher Hagerman to have it closed down is understandable.[9]

When Hart came to Belleville, he asked a journeyman printer in Cobourg to join him. This was a young man named James Gardiner, who had worked on the Cobourg *Star* and on the *Church*, a militant pro-Strachan paper.[10] In Belleville, Gardiner was given a great deal of responsibility. He helped to get the news and write it, set type, work the press, correct the proof – in fact, he had to turn his hand wherever he was needed. This was not unusual in a small print shop employing just a handful of men and boys. On 26 November Samuel Hart was away, and Gardiner was left in charge. According to his later account of that day, it was unusually busy. As well as all the notices and advertisements for the weekly issue, there were accounts of the fighting in the lower province a few weeks earlier, still a much discussed subject. With so much news to print, every cut in the shop was pressed into service. One showing the Queen's Arms was placed upside down 'at the head of a proclamation by one of Papineau's officers.' Some people came into the office to pick up their copies hot off the press, and when the Reverend G.D. Greenleaf came in for his paper, he pointed out the error. Gardiner claimed that very few papers were on the street at that time, and he corrected the mistake for the rest of the run.[11]

Meanwhile a number of people had seen the offending page, and they must have spread the word about the misplaced royal insignia. Some chose to see it as a deliberate insult to the Crown. By evening, inflamed with patriotism and strong drink, a noisy crowd burst into the shop just before Gardiner closed up for the night. They attacked the press and threw away the types. De Rottenburg wrote the next day:

[T]he Printing Office of the 'Plain Speaker' newspaper in this town, was forcibly entered last night by a body of men, and the Printing press nearly destroyed and the Types scattered about the street.

Upon the first intimation of this outrage ... I at once repaired to the spot and found that captains O'Reilly and McAnnany, of the 2nd Hastings Militia, had posted sentries in the house, and were using every exertion to maintain the peace. At the request of the owner of the house, I continued sentries throughout the night for the protection of his property.

Two companies of the 1st and 3rd Hastings, were stationed close to the printing office, but I am given to understand, that the attack was conducted so suddenly, that the Press was destroyed before the troops could act. This event has caused great excitement in this town and neighbourhood ... The paper was fast sinking into the insignificance it so justly merits, and I have purposely abstained from acting hitherto on Mr Hagerman's letter, regarding the arrest of the Editor, because I saw clearly the influence he possessed in the Country was slowly declining ... The Magistrates assembled this day, and issued a Proclamation offering a reward of one hundred dollars for the discovery of the perpetrators of this act.[12]

Thomas Parker wrote the same day to the attorney general to say that the magistrates had discussed the riot, but there was nothing to identify those responsible for it.[13] If this was so, it seems remarkable in such a small community. James Gardiner said afterwards that he recognized some of the militia among the vandals. No one, however, claimed the reward. De Rottenburg received the following reply from the military secretary:

I am directed by H.E. to acknowledge yr communication of the 27th inst. & express his great regret 'that an outrage, such as that which you describe, should have been perpetrated at Belleville, particularly at this moment, when it is desirable to avoid exciting the feelings of the people of doubtful loyalty. – This rash act (committed no doubt through mistaken ideas of zeal) will, perhaps be the means of restoring to the 'Plain Speaker' its former popularity.[14]

His Excellency perfectly approves of the steps you have taken in this matter, and has heard with great satisfaction of the course the magistrates have pursued. –

With respect to your suspicions of the views of some of the Militia soldiers and the sergeant – His Excellency is confident that you will take all the necessary precautions against the probable danger from their disaffection, and is desirous that you should make what arrangements should appear best to you under the circumstances. – Should your suspicions be confirmed, prompt measures would of course be the most effectual. –

With regard to your opinion of the state of the neighbouring Townships – His Excellency cannot but hope, that the reports you have received of their readiness to rise may be greatly exaggerated.

Colonel Campbell, who resides in Seymour ... stated positively, that the inhabitants of his Township are loyal, and that in Percy and the neighbouring country,[15] half the bad feeling represented does not exist, – at Rawdon it certainly is bad. – Some discreet person should be sent to the latter place and its vicinity, to ascertain as accurately as possible the real state of that country.

His Excellency is desirous, that, while all due precaution is taken, and the utmost vigilance exercised, the greatest forbearance both in word and deed should be observed, for much bad blood and irritation is always created by taunting and insulting expressions; and open suspicion often drives people to acts which otherwise they would not venture upon.

With regard to the general rising you expect, His Excellency agrees with you in thinking, that if it should ever take place in the District under your command, it will be regulated by assistance from the other side ... Should any such movement take place at Presqu'ile, the Inhabitants of Prince Edward must be called upon to lend their aid. His Excellency is much gratified by the effect that his measures for the defence of the country have produced upon the Loyal Inhabitants of Belleville – and is glad to hear that confidence, so necessary at present has been restored. – With regard to the still unsettled claims of the Militia and Inhabitants – the Asst Military Secretary has been directed to write again to Mr Clarke upon the subject – and to forward a copy of his answers to the Commander of the Forces. –

His Excellency is perfectly confident, that every means in your power will be used, and all your attention will be directed, not only to defend your District against our enemies, and to quiet the apprehensions of the people, but, to avoid any unnecessary collision with such persons as may be only under suspicion.[16]

From his militia post at Presqu'ile, Major Warren reported to De Rottenburg that he strongly suspected some of the men belonging to Henry Ruttan's regiment who were stationed there and at Consecon had volunteered 'for the purpose of betraying our cause, and that treachery was intended.' He was ordered to send Captain McDonald's company from Madoc to replace the men at Presqu'ile, and if he found that the report was correct he must use 'strong measures.' As the letter continues it is plain that De Rottenburg, like Warren, found the whole area unreliable:

I am obliged to confess to Your Excellency that the state of the neighbouring townships continues most unsatisfactory –

Combination to an alarming extent prevails, but so much secrecy is observed by those implicated, that I can never get information with respect to the precise time and spot where a meeting is to be held; in fact I never hear of it until after it has taken place.

That a rising on an extensive scale is contemplated I have no doubt whatever, but I do not think this will occur unless the Americans invade this neighbourhood.

Major Warren seems to apprehend some movement in his vicinity in the course of a few days.[17]

In spite of the satisfactory outcome of the Battle of the Windmill it is clear that Arthur's troubles were not at an end. He believed the turmoil in the province was due to the baneful influence of concessions made earlier to Reformers, and that 'if this Province be eventually saved from going into a Democratic State, it must be by the special intervention of Divine Providence.'[18] Luckily for Arthur he did not know this appeal would prove no more successful than the many he addressed to Mr Clarke at the commissary office.

Turmoil continued into 1839. The Belleville magistrates' petitions for the protection of the town had brought them a militia guard, but now in the following winter they must sometimes have wondered if the cure was worse than the disease. The men were billeted in different houses rented for the purpose. Discipline under local officers was slack, and there was little for the militiamen to do since none of the feared attacks on Belleville ever materialized; with free time and cheap whiskey, it was not remarkable that they would create their own trouble. Various cases of vandalism were reported,[19] and one was later described in some detail.

John O'Carroll and his wife, Margaret, were Irish Roman Catholic immigrants to Belleville in 1834. John taught for a time in the little school recently opened by the Catholic church, but perhaps because the pay was not enough to support his family the O'Carrolls soon opened a grocery shop in part of their house. Since grocery shops were licensed to sell liquor which could be drunk on the premises, they were sometimes called public houses. In 1838 the Roman Catholics of Belleville were trying to raise money to pay for their new church, and John undertook to write letters asking for donations. This apparently roused the suspicions of some of the militia, who thought so much letter writing must mean he was in correspondence with the Patriots. They started a campaign of harassment, intimidating customers, breaking the windows, and vandalizing the shop. The O'Carroll claim under the Rebellion Losses Bill was supported by testimonials from three residents, men who had been at that time ranged on opposite sides. Two were Reformers: Nelson Reynolds and Peter Robertson, both of whom had been put in prison after the rebellion. The third was Billa Flint, one of the magistrates who had been eager to put them there. The excitement of the rebellion was past, and by nature Flint was a fair-minded man who could not condone the excesses he had observed. The statements of Reynolds and Robertson are also sympathetic, as one would expect from men who also felt mistreated, although by 1845, when they were writing, they were no longer regarded as dangerous rebels but apparently were accepted as successful businessmen. Reynolds testified that

> O'Carroll is a sober, peaceable and industrious man. – That his shop was frequently attacked and broken, in the dead hour of the night by large parties of volunteers having their side arms, and threatening all sorts of injury – that the said O'Carroll frequently applied to the civil and military authorities for protection but either for want of power or inclination on their parts, but little protection was rendered to said O'Carroll's premises [–] in fact from the frequency with which his house was assailed it would appear that there was an organized plan

by the volunteers headed by some of the junior officers, to demolish said O'Carroll's building and leave his family without a shelter. They continued this system of annoyance until said O'Carroll was obliged to quit his house, but not until very great damage had been done to the building & the lives of himself wife & children frequently endangered. The constant state of alarm in which his family was kept had the effect of injuring his wife's health ... said volunteers while on duty were so united and combined together that it was almost impossible to arrest any of them without danger to the person or persons attempting to secure them, & being composed of a wreckless [sic] and poverty stricken class of people no damage could be obtained from them.

Each letter placed ultimate responsibility for the men's behaviour on Captain De Rottenburg since he was in command of all the militia in the area, and this may be an indication that the baron's stay in Belleville was not appreciated in all quarters. Those in immediate control were local militia officers. Flint's letter supporting O'Carroll's claim said in part:

[D]uring the winter the said O'Carroll's house was repeatedly broken into and himself and family abused and I believe by the volunteers then on duty under Colonel De Rottenburg, that further O'Carroll used means to try and bring the persons who were injuring him to justice, that as a Magistrate I took up and fined one man ... five pounds, but as O'Carroll was the prosecutor I could not pay the fine to him ... I also granted a warrant for another person (a volunteer) who evaded its execution by leaving his company and going away (as I have every reason to believe by consent of his captain) to avoid punishment. I further believe the men were encouraged to treat O'Carroll in the way that they did on account of religious faith and politics (O'Carroll being a Roman Catholic) the other parties Orangemen. I also believe there was a laxity on the part of the officers in endeavouring to find out the offenders and bring them to punishment. I further know that it was impossible for any Magistrate to do anything with these men then on duty who were inclined to be abusive (and there were a great many of this kind) and what was done was at the risque of personal safety as well as risque of loss of property. I also believe that the conduct of the men engaged in disturbing O'Carroll, was the means of breaking up his keeping a public house in this town.[20]

Another witness was Peter Robertson, who at the time lived nearby and had plenty of opportunity to see the repeated assaults on the O'Carroll house, which, he said, had finally driven O'Carroll out of business.[21] To add insult to injury, O'Carroll was arrested and imprisoned for eight weeks, as shown by his claim for compensation. It is ironic that it was loyalists who constantly feared violence, but it was others who were subjected to it. Whatever the volunteers of 1838–9 were guarding, it does not seem to have been the peace. As Flint's letter indicated, the magistrates were not always able to enforce the law when opposed by those who were ostensibly protecting the interests of the government, and this was true not only in Belleville. In Cobourg a farmer named Mallory was a victim of some of these nominally loyal men. He may have expressed his Reform sentiments too often, for he roused some local Tories to take action, which they did by seizing him, putting him into a large crate in which china had been shipped, and stuffing it with straw. They carried their captive to the lake and threw him in. He was lucky that a few of the more rational citizens witnessed the dangerous prank and rescued him before he either drowned or suffocated.[22]

In 1839 Cobourg also experienced a sequel to the riotous occurrence in Belleville at the *Plain Speaker*. This was the rather bizarre case known as the 'Cobourg Conspiracy.' After his press was wrecked Samuel Hart, the publisher, left Belleville and went to the United States for a time. There he published the Lockport *Telegraph*. The following summer he turned up in Cobourg in the company of several men, Canadian and American, who were accused of trying to steal money for the Patriot cause. They were caught hiding out in the home of an elderly couple when one local member of the gang lost his nerve for the enterprise and decided to become an informer. This was Henry Moon, who spent some time in Cobourg but who had previously lived in Ameliasburgh. Half a dozen of his companions were promptly arrested. The story told at their trial was that they were planning to rob one or two banks around Cobourg and, according to Moon, were ready to do murder if need be. He claimed they also intended to kill the lawyer George Boulton, yet it was Boulton who represented them in court. A witness at the trial said some of them had already attempted robbery at one bank but were foiled when the banker's wife thrust most of the bills down the front of her dress. Although they were robbers, plainly they were also gentlemen. They expected to do better at the next location because there the banker was known to keep the money in a milk churn.

To challenge Moon's credibility, which was not rated very highly in Cobourg, several witnesses were brought forward. One was Moon's brother-in-law, who said Moon had been 'first a Baptist, then a Methodist, next an infidel, and now a traitor.' Nelson Reynolds testified that he 'would not believe anything Moon said if he swore on a stack of Bibles,' and the other witnesses from Belleville, Samuel Stephens and Jacob W. Meyers, agreed with him.[23] The court, however, decided there was evidence of a conspiracy to commit a crime, and the accused men were convicted. Hart was sentenced to seven years in prison.[24]

The rebellion had pretty well run its course, although in the next months there were some minor incidents. De Rottenburg reported the 'plunder of arms' from the store in Belleville,[25] and this, like some other crimes, was attributed to 'the disaffected' or even to Patriots, but there is no real evidence that they were in fact connected with politics. They are echoes of the rebellion, and it would be a long time before the reverberations died away.

12 Afterwards

The year 1839 was in the nature of an interregnum. By the beginning of that year the rebellion had almost run its course, but the new order was not yet established. Meantime there was uncertainty and anxiety about what the future held for the Canadas, particularly when, during this year, the Durham Report was published and the British government adopted the recommendation in it for the union of Upper and Lower Canada. This began the process that resulted the next year in a bill establishing the new Canadian state, divided into Canada East and Canada West but with a single legislature. News of this change by no means quietened the clamour of discord. The province was still suffering from all the conflict of the past two years, and business was at a low ebb. The Durham Report caused furious and sometimes violent controversy, many Tories and Reformers being as hostile as ever to one another. In addition, arguments pro and con the proposed union cut across all groups and all political opinions. There was to be no quick resolution of the sore questions that afflicted Upper and Lower Canada.

The rebellion did bring one benefit to the country, and that had been the Durham Commission. Nothing less than a rebellion would have jolted the British parliament into energetic action to remedy Canadian complaints; nothing less would have induced Lord Durham to leave the political arena, where he was one of the leading contenders, in order to investigate the affairs of the British North American colonies, and probably no one else could have produced the result he did. Even before he arrived the news that he had agreed to take on the task at once began to reassure Reformers. It seemed their appeals were finally bringing a response.

When Lord Durham arrived in Quebec to begin his mission, one of the pressing problems with which he had to deal was the large number of prisoners in Lower Canada. He pardoned the great majority and sent those he considered the most guilty to do convict labour in Bermuda. He had no reason to think this decision would be questioned by the government at home. Before accepting, reluctantly, the monumental task of looking into the affairs of all the British North American colonies and making recommendations for them, he had asked for, and been given, unlimited powers to do whatever he thought necessary. But in London, Radicals and Tories saw an opportunity to bring down the administration, and they raised a clamour about the Bermuda order. The prime minister gave in, disallowed it, and rebuked Durham. Canadian interests were, as usual, ignored while British politicians played British politics. Durham was proud, sensitive, and in poor health. Over the protests of his friends and to the dismay of Reformers, he resigned in October, five months after he had arrived. Back in England there was keen interest in his return, many believing he would lead a revolt within his party and possibly become the next prime minister. Instead he and his assistants retired for two months to write their report.

Because of the rebellion in the Canadas and the British government's precarious position at home, the report created an unusual amount of interest in England when it was published in February 1839, and when it reached Canada in April it caused a sensation.[1] The Tories had been gratified when Durham left after such a short stay but were apprehensive of the report he was to present to parliament. When it came out, it fulfilled their worst fears, for it was harsh in its treatment of the Family Compact men, and the recommendation for responsible government forecast the end of Compact rule. When Egerton Ryerson published the first excerpts from it in the *Christian Guardian*, he brought down the wrath of the Tories on his head. An open letter in the Kingston *Chronicle and Gazette*, signed by forty persons, said they had cancelled their subscriptions to the *Christian Guardian* because of this, and because the editor seemed to approve of the report.[2] The following paragraph gives an indication of the style of editorial criticism in the *Chronicle and Gazette*: 'History does not afford a more striking example ... of being made the victim of the ill-digested experiments of an imbecile ministry, undertaking to remedy our grievances without possessing any knowledge of them, and relying for their information ... upon individuals without either character or talents.'[3]

Such language is in sharp contrast to the loyal admiration usually expressed in this newspaper regarding every action of the British parliament and its representatives. In Cobourg the grand jury at the assizes of the Newcastle District 'presented the Report of Lord Durham as a libel on the Province of Upper Canada.'[4] Several newspapers referred to Durham as 'the Lord High Executioner,' copying the *Times* of London. There seemed no limit to the excesses of the partisan press. The Cobourg *Star* printed a letter addressed to Lord Durham, condemning one of his assistants, Charles Buller. It called him 'Your chief scavenger,' and said he had been 'incessantly employed in searching the *cesspools* of discontent, disloyalty and sedition, for filthy manure to promote the growth ... of the pestilent crop of falsehoods' he had written into the report.[5] But T.C. Wheeler, a schoolteacher in Whitby, wrote that people had great hopes of 'the democratical Lord Durham, and the Tories hate and fear him as the devil does holy water.'[6] He probably hit the mark, for it was the widespread popular approval of the report that was causing such extreme reaction on the part of those who opposed it. Some members of the Compact expressed anger not only over the nature of the report but over the fact that it had been made public. They seem to have hoped that, like many another royal commission report since, it would be buried in a decent silence. Instead, as they complained, it was soon being read by every Tom, Dick, and Harry.

Durham meetings were held in many centres with the object of explaining the report and gaining public support for it. That there was a meeting in Belleville seems certain,[7] although no record of it survives, and there may have been others in Hastings, home of so many Reformers. The *Chronicle and Gazette* reported meetings 'at Brighton, Haldimand, Demorestville, and Cobourg ... under the Durham and Responsible Government Flag,' calling them 'the puny efforts of a clamorous faction of rebels and traitors.'[8] The meeting at Grafton, however, is said to have brought out eight hundred people, which would scarcely deserve the adjective 'puny.'[9] Just how many turned out for some of the meetings is impossible to say since the newspapers were always ready to sacrifice fact in the service of faction. One of numerous examples is the treatment in the press of the meeting in Cobourg. The Cobourg *Star* said the promoters were 'determined on insulting the Conservative Town of Cobourg' by a meeting of 'a crew of the most ill-favoured, Yankee visaged democrats,' presenting a most sorry and despicable appearance, and whose 'audacious display of insolence and rebellion' was opposed by loyal citizens.[10] The *Star* mentioned the violence that often erupted at these meetings, although it implied this was always the fault of the Reformers, saying 'persons coming to these meetings, secretly armed, are actually guilty of high treason ... they are in arms against the Queen; and it is the duty of the Sheriff ... to put them down – and even if the people do so without any warrant from the authorities' the editor assured them they were justified. The *Star* described the

Cobourg fracas as follows: 'A few spirited old countrymen, principally Irish ... some with shellelaghs and some without, advanced to the hustings and demanded the surrender of the flags ... the standard bearer presented his pistol, stones were hurled,' and apparently a free-for-all ensued, causing the Durhamites to flee. Francis Hincks's *Examiner*, on the other hand, called it 'a peaceful meeting, disturbed by a band of Orange ruffians.'[11] Hincks was present at a meeting in Scarborough where Dr William Baldwin was one of the speakers; a man was killed, and Baldwin was lucky to escape. He was pulled off the wagon that had been his platform, and a man lunged at him with a knife. He got away only because he was dragged back up by others on the wagon and the driver at once drove off at a good clip.[12]

These Durham meetings continued over the summer, causing quite a few broken heads, but a large meeting at Hamilton in the autumn seems to have been the turning point.[13] It had become clear that a majority of Upper Canadians approved of the report and welcomed its principal recommendations, particularly the one for responsible government. With the British parliament preparing to unite Upper and Lower Canada, opposition died down to a grumble. It was better to prepare for the change that was coming than to waste any more time fighting it.[14] In the Midland District there had been a demonstration of local feeling in June, as Sir George Arthur wrote:

There has been a serious unpleasantry in the Midland District when the militia turned out for muster on the 4th Inst – they brought Lord Durham's flag, and an American flag and some speeches were made not very much in favor of Monarchical Institutions. 'Lord Durham and a responsible Government' appear now to be the watch words of all the radicals and republicans. I have such an address signed by fourteen Magistrates of the District as would leave me to expect rebellion every day. The disaffected have, I believe, displayed a good deal of rancorous feeling, and talk largely, but I cannot believe matters can be as bad as the Magistrates have represented. It is however, as you well know a very bad neighbourhood, overstocked with Americans.[15]

Since Durham's report dealt with all six British American colonies, it made many recommendations. It went badly wrong in the section dealing with Lower Canada. Upper Canadians may have agreed that French Canadians could be turned into Englishmen, a change the report predicted would take place within a generation when Lower Canadians realized the superiority of the other culture. Whatever their reason, Upper Canadian

newspapers took little notice of this part of the report. The recommendations of particular interest in Upper Canada were the one for political
union and the other for responsible government.

Many ways of securing responsibility in government had been proposed
over the years, such as an elected legislative council, or making executive
members liable to impeachment, or sending Canadian members to sit in
the British parliament. Robert Baldwin, adapting ideas of his father, had
taken a workable plan to the Colonial Office in 1836, and there it had been
ignored. The objection was always the same: how could the governor be
responsible to the Crown, and at the same time follow the advice of an
elected colonial assembly? How could the governor obey two masters? The
Baldwins' solution was simple. The governor should be guided by the advice
of the Canadian cabinet on all domestic affairs and by the Crown, through
the Colonial Office, in all external matters, leaving defence, trade, and
foreign relations to the mother country. When Baldwin explained his solution to Durham during the latter's brief visit to Toronto, Durham recognized its importance, discarded the proposal he had been considering, and
adopted Baldwin's instead, both modifying and expanding it.[16] It was to
make possible Canada's continued membership in the British Empire while
the country worked towards independence. As Baldwin wrote to Durham,
'Your Lordship has been the first British statesman to avow a belief in the
possibility of a permanent connection between the colonies and the Mother
Country ... I truly feel grateful.' Chester New, biographer of Durham, wrote
admiringly, 'It is a matter of pride that the principle on which the British
Commonwealth of self-governing nations has been built ... was in its conception a Canadian idea. Without Lord Durham's advocacy, however, the
voice of Baldwin would have been lost in the Canadian woods.'[17]

Another recommendation of the report was welcomed in the Midland
District, although it was not put into effect for some years. This was the
recommendation for municipal government. Elected local councils were
set up in 1845 with very limited responsibility, but the Municipal Act passed
in 1849 expanded the power of these councils so that they could levy taxes
and control the spending of them on public works. Writing in the 1850s
Samuel Strickland said, 'The formation of the County Councils, though
much condemned at the time, must now be admitted to have done more
to promote the prosperity of the country and satisfy people than any
other measure that could be adopted.'[18] The appointed magistrates had
vigorously opposed the transfer of power to elected local officials, but
with responsible government established in the colony the change became
inevitable. That people wanted local government was evinced by the old

town meetings, but originally these had little power and no money to spend. Nevertheless they gave the residents a forum where they could discuss town business and regulate such things as straying cattle and the location of public pathways. They were the forerunners of municipal government.[19]

It has often been taken for granted that there was a straight line of development from the rebellion to the Durham Report to responsible government. The first two cannot reasonably be separated, but quite a few historians refute the idea of a close connection between the report and responsible government. Liberalization in the British political system is given by some as the reason for believing that permission for Canada to have responsible government was inevitable. British adoption of free trade in 1846 is also cited as sufficient cause for allowing the colonies to practise a wide degree of self-rule since Britain no longer needed to rely on them for products of farm and forest, and so no longer needed to control their trade.[20] It has been said that responsible government would therefore have been granted to Canada just as soon, or even sooner, without the rebellion, and presumably then without the report. Such suppositions ignore the other possibilities that existed if there had been no rebellion to put extreme pressure on Britain, for there is no assurance that Upper Canadians would have gone on as they were, discontented but putting up with their many and increasing grievances. The province might instead have drifted into independence, which a section of the British parliament thought a natural progression.[21] In that case it is hard to see how it would have avoided being absorbed or annexed by the United States. It is, however, useless to imagine any events but those that unfolded, for history does not show us its alternatives. It would indeed be strange if such a fundamental shift in policy in these important colonies had any single, simple cause. This one came about when it did because of a number of events and developments, including the rebellion and the Durham Report.

The process began soon after the principal recommendation of the report was put into effect, the union of the Canadas. The report had foreseen this union to be a first step: 'as I am of opinion that the full establishment of responsible government can only be permanently secured by giving these Colonies an increased importance in the politics of the Empire, I find in union the only means of remedying at once and completely the two prominent causes of their present unsatisfactory condition.'[22]

While the British parliament adopted the recommendation for the union, it was not prepared to approve such a degree of self-government as Durham proposed. The first governor, Charles Poulett Thompson, later Lord Sydenham and Toronto, was determined to defeat responsible government and work with a cabinet made up of men of various political opinions. He wanted no political parties because he believed they inevitably led to corruption, and he was sufficiently adroit to succeed in his policy. His successor, Sir Charles Bagot, had to admit partial defeat. Reform members from both Canadas made an alliance that was firm enough to prevent him from forming the representative cabinet he needed. Here was the beginning of a basic change in relations between Upper and Lower Canada. The Reformers of Canada East, most of them French, had recognized in the Act of Union a move to submerge them and their interests. Still smarting from rebellion wounds, and the Durham Report, they were reluctant to play any part in the new government. It was the determination of Reform leaders in Canada West, notably Francis Hincks and Robert Baldwin, that after a time drew Reformers like Louis LaFontaine into a coalition. Once convinced that Reform goals were identical on both sides of the provincial border, there developed a strong and friendly alignment of French and English Reformers of a kind that could not have existed without the union. As a result, during Bagot's administration they refused to take part in the cabinet until the governor-general appointed men who were all agreed on their political policy. Bagot was finally forced to accept a cabinet of LaFontaine, Baldwin, and their associates. 'Whether the doctrine of responsible government is openly acknowledged or is only tacitly acquiesced in,' Bagot admitted, 'virtually it exists.'[23] The Colonial Office was not ready to give in, however, and instructed the third governor, Sir Charles Metcalfe, to reverse this process. He made appointments without consulting his cabinet, giving office to men who were in opposition. Patronage was important to the government as a means of rewarding and ensuring the continued loyalty of government supporters. (This was demonstrated after the 1841 election when Anthony Manahan became member for Kingston, and then obligingly accepted a salaried office and resigned his seat. This was done so that the governor could get into his cabinet a former provincial secretary who had not been elected.[24] Kingston was such a safe Tory seat that the success of the governor's nominee in the by-election was assured.) Metcalfe persisted, his cabinet resigned, and he was able to get a slight Tory majority, but the result was a disappointingly weak cabinet.

By 1847 the Colonial Office had recognized that government in Canada could be carried on only if the principle of responsibility were conceded. By this time passions in both Canadas had cooled; some of the earlier politicians were now superseded, and other men of moderate views had come into prominence. When the Reformers overcame the governor's claim to make what appointments he wanted, it was the culmination of the drive towards government by responsible cabinet ministers, a drive which owed much of its momentum to the encouragement the Durham Report had originally given Baldwin and his followers, and then to the perseverence with which they moved towards their goal.

The report was flawed in important ways, most notably in its total misunderstanding of the French in Lower Canada, but it did accomplish a great deal for Canada. Lord Durham would have liked to see a federation of all the colonies from St John's to Windsor. For the time being he had to compromise by uniting just two of them, but when the new parliament met in Kingston in 1841 the first step was taken on the road to Canadian confederation.[25]

During this time the United States had several times threatened to invade the country to secure some border territory to which it laid claim. The Canadian government had little say in these matters since they had to be negotiated by the British, who in each case surrendered the territory in dispute. So peace was preserved after 1839. The Patriot War, as it is still known in the northern United States, was at an end, but while this can be seen from a comfortable distance of more than a century and a half it was not apparent at the time. For several years people in Upper Canada felt continuing anxiety over the threat of invasion from abroad and treachery at home. There were some filibustering raids at several places along the border, although there was no further incident of any importance. The governor at Quebec wrote to Sir George Arthur that there was a general expectation 'of another descent ... at either end of Lake Erie or in the neighbourhood of Belleville on Lake Ontario. Would it not be as well to have a good Block House at Presqu'ile with some guns upon it and good accommodation for a Military Station [?]'[26] Nothing came of this, and fortunately it turned out to be unnecessary. Nevertheless the militiamen continued to be stationed in Belleville throughout the year even though, as we have seen, they were without enough to do.[27] Meantime there was a new government in Washington, and in many American centres growing opposition to the Patriots. This had no doubt been accelerated by the Patriot defeats at Windsor and Prescott, especially the heavy loss of life at the windmill and the severe sentencing afterwards. On 22 December 1838 'one of the largest and most respectable meetings ever held in Oswego, composed of the substantial residents of the village' voted 'to condemn, all movements and secret associations tending to disturb the tranquility of the frontier, to invade the peace of the Canadian Provinces.' On 29 December, however, there was a 'county-wide mass meeting of Hunters in the Oswego Market Building.' The Canadian situation was to trouble the waters of local American politics for another two or three years.[28]

Having so many men active in militia units throughout the Midland District required organization, and this involved the presence of two men who were of some significance to Hastings County. One of them stayed for about a year and a half, but the other was to spend the rest of his life in Belleville and to make his own place in its history. The first was Captain George, Baron De Rottenburg, who came to Belleville during the excitement of October and who was sent back there in December 1838. He remained in charge of all militia around the Bay of Quinte until some time in 1840. It would be interesting to know what effect the presence of a young, titled bachelor in a handsome red coat had on Belleville society. No doubt many a local hostess put her best foot forward, but some of the young men may have felt as Lewis Wallbridge seems to have done. His opinion of De Rottenburg is evident in a letter to his sister: 'He is a German Baron whose title in England is considered about equal to a JP in this country, and I believe he has nothing but his half pay as a captain. He is one of those officers who left the British army to go into the Spanish Legion and in fact the country is pretty well filled with those kind of military Gentlemen – fattening on the Queen's money.'[29]

This shows some prejudice on Wallbridge's part. De Rottenburg spent his active life in the British army. It is not known what basis there was for saying he had been in the Spanish Legion unless this was a popular name for a British regiment that had been sent for a time to Spain and in which De Rottenburg had served. Retired officers were on half-pay, but De Rottenburg was a serving officer and therefore on full pay; nor is it likely Wallbridge knew whether or not he had private means.[30] While his title placed him only among the minor nobility, this was of a different order from that of an Upper Canadian magistrate.

John Moodie was the second important newcomer to Belleville in 1838. He arrived at the end of the year as paymaster under De Rottenburg and for a time shared rooms with him.[31] In several letters to his wife, Susanna, he described De Rottenburg. For instance: 'A more amiable and delightful companion I have never met with. He is full of wit and talent united with the soundest judgment and decision of character.'[32] He was also, according to Moodie, slight, active, and very handsome. His only fault was that he occasionally displayed a passionate temper, which Moodie excused because he had red hair.[33] When the baron rented a house in the spring of 1839, Moodie wrote that he intended getting a wife to keep it for him. Of this

Moodie approved, saying, 'he is rather too combustible to be trusted in a state of single blessedness.'[34] During 1839 De Rottenburg married Louisa Mary Ridley, the sixteen-year-old daughter of Dr George Ridley. This may not have been a particularly romantic match since Moodie wrote of the engagement, 'I think he might have done better every way, but he is not in very good health and wants a young person to nurse him.' To celebrate his coming marriage a militia dinner was held in De Rottenburg's honour. This was a lively affair, which Moodie came through safely 'with the exception of a little wine in my face from a bottle on its passage to another head.'[35] The same dinner was described by Lewis Wallbridge:

> There was a grand dinner given here the other day ... at which Henry Meyers attended ... He and Thomas Parker when in their cups arguing of the different problems of Sir Francis and Sir George had to make use of their fists whereupon a most serious overturning of tables, breaking of dishes, etc. ensued and the dinner ended just as all such dinners do end which are exclusively military, namely in a tremendous row, all drunk and a few challenges the next morning after which a few compromises are made and each thinks he has accrued perfect satisfaction for all insults.[36]

This affords an unusual sidelight on some Hastings County residents, and the prominent place of the military because of the disorders of 1838. Half the militiamen were dismissed in May 1839, the rest by the end of the year. While he was still in Belleville, De Rottenburg was promoted to the rank of major, and when he left, he continued his army career in Canada West as assistant quartermaster general. In 1852 at a farewell dinner in Toronto, when he was about to leave for England, having been made colonel of the Prince of Wales Regiment, it was the lieutenant-governor, Sir Edmund Head, who made the principal speech, giving high praise to De Rotten-burg's work and character.[37]

Almost all the Hastings men who had been imprisoned after the rebellion returned home and continued their occupations. Two known exceptions are Clifton McCollom, who settled in Oswego, and Anson Hayden. Soon after his release from prison Hayden disappeared, taking along all the notes and bills of the business he shared with Elijah Allen.[38] It is not known where he went, but his name was remembered for a long time in the community of Hayden's Corners, renamed Corbyville only in 1882. The names of many of those who had been in jail during 1837–9 appear in positions of trust and respect in later records – as do the names of many who put them there. Nelson Reynolds became extremely wealthy and around 1850 moved to Whitby. He was prominent in several kinds of business activity, especially those related to transportation and finance. He speculated a little too much, lost his large fortune and his mansion, but he served for some years as sheriff of Ontario County.[39] Billa Flint, an active magistrate, enjoyed a long and successful career in Hastings as a miller, merchant, and mine promoter, interested in church, education, and politics. He seems to have been a generous, buoyant individual with a talent for coming out on top, even when ventures failed. His political stance changed after 1840, and he became a Reformer, ending as a Clear Grit during the 1850s. Joseph Lockwood, Reformer and member of the Mackenzie-sponsored political union, was elected moderator of Sidney Township in 1838 not long after he was let out of jail, which points up the often extreme difference between the politics of the appointed magistrates and that of the majority of voters. The same year Reuben White was again made a warden.

The rebels who fled to the United States, with the exception of Mackenzie, were all given amnesty by 1845. Many, such as Dr Charles Duncombe and Marshall Bidwell, had become established in the States and remained there, but some prominent rebels came back. Dr Rolph was one, and he was soon practising medicine again in Toronto, where he established an academy of medicine. He went back into politics and was elected to parliament in 1846. Donald McLeod, the soldier-teacher-publisher from Brockville who became a Patriot general, got a position with the Canadian Department of Agriculture, which he held until retirement. John Montgomery came back and served the public life of his country by again opening a tavern on Yonge Street, just as he had promised.

Mackenzie spent a year in jail in Albany for inciting Americans to take up arms against a foreign country. After that he eked out a living in various ways connected with writing and publishing. The best job he had in these years was given him by Horace Greeley on the New York *Tribune*, and later Greeley generously offered him a position as Washington correspondent. Hard up as he was, and there were times when his family went hungry to bed, Mackenzie characteristically refused because he could not get along with the editor in charge of the New York office. He was finally pardoned in late 1849. By then his ideas had undergone a change. He wrote to his son, 'After what I have seen here, I frankly confess to you that, had I passed nine years in the United States before, instead of after, the outbreak, I am sure I would have been the last man in America to be engaged in it'.[40] To test the waters he went first to Montreal, where he visited the parliament building. Colonel Prince offered to throw him downstairs; otherwise, no one took much notice of him. In Kingston he saw himself being burned in effigy; in Belleville there was a riot; and in Toronto there were two nights of rioting outside the house where he stayed. City authorities took charge and gave him protection, so that he was able to bring his family over to join him. Two years later he was elected to parliament as member for Haldimand, a seat he retained until he retired in 1859. A public subscription raised $7,000 to buy him the house on Bond Street that is now the Mackenzie museum, a notable gift for a rebel who would have been hanged from the highest tree if he had been captured in the country a few years earlier.

He still found cause for complaint. He would not have been Mackenzie if he had been satisfied with what had taken place. There had been a revolution – a new form of government, new men – but, as is the way of revolutions, this one had not turned out exactly as the rebels had hoped. To do Mackenzie justice, those who had predicted that party politics would bring strife and corruption were proving to be quite correct. But while some of Mackenzie's criticism was often justified, more and more it was simply contrary and came to be disregarded. Politically self-righteous, he was often in the position of voting even against good legislation because it did not come up to his arbitrary standard.

Perhaps the most remarkable return was that of John Berry, who owned land in Brockville. He had been arrested soon after the rebellion, and when released had gone to the States. He joined the Patriots in the Battle of the Windmill, was taken prisoner, and condemned to transportation to Van Diemen's Land. Prisoners could be hired by the settlers, and Berry went to work as a sheepherder in a remote part of the island. He was pardoned in 1843, and in 1845 there was a general amnesty, but nothing was heard of this in Berry's distant location. Finally in 1857 a visitor brought the news. The prisoner at once left for the coast, and after some delay was able to find a whaling ship on which he could work his passage. Two and a half years later he arrived in New York. From there he made his way to Kingston, where he boarded the steamboat going down to Brockville and found himself in the company of William Henry Draper, the judge who had ordered him transported. Draper is said to have helped him on this, the last part, of his journey home. He arrived back in Brockville in 1860.[41] He came back to a very different Canada than the one he had left. While there were some contentious issues, they were altogether different from those that had driven men from the country. Nor did they arouse the same passion.

This had not immediately changed with the new politics of 1840. The community needed time to recover from all the disruptions of the rebellion years, trials and imprisonment for some, militia service for others, and the considerable loss of settlers. The province's economic depression lasted until 1841, and when immigration picked up again it took time for the benefit to be felt. Meantime many residents continued to be in financial difficulty. In January 1839 the quarter sessions for the Midland District noted that it had been put to considerable expense because of the rebellion, with prisoners having to be brought in, housed, and fed in the jail. The members decided to appeal to the government for the cost at least of the gallows they had had to erect for hangings after the Battle of the Windmill. They also reported 'the astounding Fact that there are arrearages due by Collectors of the District amounting to the sum of £4456/13/0 and several of them since the year 1836, a sum adequate to the full discharge of the District Debt and to all the other Expences of the District, Especial for the Gaol surrounding wall.' It would also have paid for a bridge the residents wanted built across the Trent River at Cold Creek, a request that had to be refused with the laconic comment, 'on the ground of no funds.'[42]

Anyone today who sees the busy urban centres of Hastings County – Belleville, Trenton, or any of the smaller communities – or anyone who drives along the quiet country roads through farmland and woodland will find it hard to believe that the county was ever involved in a rebellion, or that any of the people who lived here conspired to bring about the violent overthrow of the government, particularly that they were encouraging foreign invaders. The local museums and other memorials to the past display the loyalty of Hastings people to Great Britain, both at the time United Empire Loyalists had to find refuge in Canada and during the long years of Victoria. There are no monuments to the rebellion. To some, even if they knew of the involvement of Hastings, this is how it should be. Anything else would destroy the myth of unfaltering loyalty on the part of the people of the district, who, according to tradition, follow in an unbroken line from the United Empire Loyalists. This begs the question, loyalty to what? Many were loyal to the Crown, that idea of British connection and protection, without being loyal to the Upper Canadian government. Some at least of those who had come from the United States must have been less impressed by the somewhat sentimental nature of this loyalty, but they were ready to defend their homes and property against invaders and welcomed the security provided by the presence of the Queen's soldiers. To some people loyalty to their province meant doing all they could to give it a greatly improved constitution and government. During the rebellion years these people were often called rebels. And some of them were.

One positive result of the rebellion was that the threat from outside the country had given common cause to a large section of the population. They had shared the same fears and the same triumph when at last they repulsed their enemy. They were proud that they had accomplished much of their defence by their own efforts, but they were also aware of the protection of the British regiments and British officers. Coming at the beginning of Victoria's reign with the sentiment she inspired, the danger the colonists had faced and their success against it greatly stimulated feelings of loyalty. This was much more a loyalty to Great Britain or the British Empire, however, than it was to Canada. The threat posed by their expansion-minded neighbour continued to remind them of their need for British protection. It was a long time before they would become Canadian citizens and share a distinct nation of their own. Meantime the Union Jack waved over them and the cult of Victoria flourished, especially in the flood of immigration from the British Isles during the rest of the nineteenth century.

There are those who see nothing positive, only suffering and destruction, as a result of the rebellion years. And no one would deny that in Upper Canada they brought a great deal of both. One way and another more than a hundred men died, some in battle and some at the end of the hangman's rope. The number of wounded is unknown. More than 850 were imprisoned. Many, often with their families, were driven from the country, some because they were rebels, others because politics or economics, aggravated by the rebellion, made life in the colony impossible. Again, there is no way of knowing how many, but they must number in the thousands. Hastings County had men imprisoned and lost a number of residents it could not easily spare. Even those doing militia duty often found it a hardship, a burden in addition to the heavy labour of their daily life. Apart from these individual trials, the rebellion affected the social climate of the province. The divisions that already existed between various groups over questions of politics and religion had now been driven so deep it would take years to bridge the chasms. Hastings County was no different; it experienced the same difficulties that faced the rest of the province. To overcome these needed purpose and cooperation. Instead, too many people could not work together because of quarrels and feuds, many of them occasioned by, or at least made worse by, the rebellion. De Rottenburg, in the spring of 1840 before he left Belleville, wrote to Arthur about the discontent that persisted there. A military man, he thought first of militia commissions, one recognition of a man's standing in the community. Too many of these, he believed, had been given to 'clerks and shopkeepers' while many 'prosperous and respectable farmers' were ignored. In addition, 'the violent and high handed proceedings of the Magistrates of the County of Hastings during the outbreak of 1837 has [sic] alienated and disgusted many.'[43]

Mrs Moodie described the situation in Belleville when she came to live there in 1840:

> The state of society when we first came to this district was everything but friendly or agreeable. The ferment occasioned by the impotent rebellion of W.L. Mackenzie had hardly subsided. The public mind was in a sore and excited state ... The town was divided into two fierce political factions ... The Tory party, who arrogated the whole loyalty of the colony to themselves, branded, indiscriminately, the large body of Reformers as traitors and rebels. Every conscientious and thinking man who wished to see a change for the better in the management of public affairs was confounded with those discontented spirits who had raised the standard of revolt against the mother country ... the odious term of rebel, applied to some of the most loyal and honourable men in the province ... gave rise to bitter and resentful feelings, which were ready, on all public occasions, to burst into a flame. Even women entered deeply into this party hostility, and those who ... might have been friends and agreeable companions, kept aloof, rarely taking notice of each other, when accidentally thrown together.[44]

It was to prove an uncomfortable community for the Moodies. As Moodie was a half-pay officer, they belonged naturally to the upper level of society, one that was expected to be Tory, and at first they unquestioningly were. But they had also been people of liberal convictions, sensitive to injustice, and they were soon convinced of the need for reform. They became close friends and allies of Robert Baldwin, an allegiance which earned them the enmity of those who considered themselves loyalists. Yet no one could have been more British, more devoted to England and its institutions, than the Moodies. The issue of loyalty had certainly become very confused.

A man who, as a schoolboy, had heard the distant gunfire at Montgomery's Tavern later wrote, 'The worst of the direct results of the rebellion was not in the tearing of men from their families. It was the feuds lasting for years, which originated at that time. Years afterwards, "You are a rebel" or "the son of a rebel" was the signal for a fight. When men gathered at grist mill or for the annual "training day" the whisky hardly started flowing before a fight commenced in some corner, and in a short time the row was general.'[45]

A strong anti-American feeling was to be another long-lasting result of the rebellion years:

No slave shall ever breathe our air,
No lynch laws e'er shall bind us;
So keep your Yankee hordes at home,
For Britons still you'll find us.[46]

The above is part of an editorial in verse that appeared in the Cobourg *Star*, and many Upper Canadians fervently echoed the sentiment. In February 1839 Sir George Arthur wrote from Toronto, 'It is impossible to imagine a people more divided. In one only point do the Loyalists seem to agree, and that is in detestation of the Americans – and certainly well they may if the ruin which has befallen the Province be any justification for such a feeling.'[47] This may have been the sentiment of the loyalists, but presumably there were others who had warmer feelings towards the republic which, for a time, they had sought to emulate. One way or other, Canadians have never been able to avoid the influence of their populous neighbour.

An effect of the rebellion already mentioned was the greatly increased power of the Orangemen. They were to influence politics in Upper Canada and beyond, and to sour relations between Catholic and Protestant well into the twentieth century. The scale of fighting in the lower province also adversely affected the attitudes of English-speaking Canadians and their French compatriots, and that had a religious component as well.

When the men of Hastings met at Hayden's Tavern in November 1837, they pledged themselves to strive for various reforms. According to Billa Flint, who said he had read one of their papers, their aims were just the kind of thing that caused the rebellion, yet neither the rebellion nor the results of the Durham Report brought them 'purification of the magistracy,' an ambiguous ambition. Nor did they create 'universal suffrage,' then or for many years to come. An elected legislative council turned out to be incompatible with responsible government as that was created. But underpinning all their demands was the desire to get control of the government into their own hands. They wanted to elect representatives who would make the laws the electors wanted, collect taxes, and spend them as the electors wanted. This was not just to give power to the people; it was to provide them with good government, often defined as government that was 'honest, efficient, and cheap.' In theory, since this was what people wanted, after they got control of the executive as well as other arms of government, they should have been able to put it into effect. Instead they found themselves beset by many of the same problems as before. Beginning in the 1840s, and increasingly in the 1850s, they were into the age of railways and the railway promoter. Sir Allan MacNab stated it plainly when he said, 'Railways are my politics.' In 1853 six of the directors of the Grand Trunk Railway were cabinet ministers.[48] One of them was Francis Hincks, the inspector general. He awarded the contract for the line east of Toronto, and in return was given a block of railway stock worth over $50,000. The temptation was great, both for those who sought railway charters and contracts and those who had the power to grant them, and there were opportunities for insiders 'to speculate in land, railway stock, and municipal railway bonds.'[49] Bargaining for some advantage, by the party or the individual member, was to a large extent taken for granted. What would now be regarded as a criminal conflict of interest was attacked by the opponents of whatever party was in power, but was exercised by each in turn. As before, government officials and employees did not always obtain their jobs because of their ability. There was no independent civil service, few standards, and even the lowliest government employee might be out of work when there was a change of government. But there were improvements in administration, many of them due to the good business sense of the first governor-general after the union, Lord Sydenham. While these made government more efficient, they were counterbalanced by other factors, such as local interests that often outweighed the national good; the self-interest of members, or of parties; and the proliferation of government departments and employees. The country was soon making great advances in every material way, but while the rebellion and the resulting Durham Report exerted strong pressure on the British government to make changes, encouraged the Reformers, and laid a foundation for some of the future developments – municipal rights, a wider federation – they did little to solve the puzzle of good government and how to get it. The old system had been used by a small group to their own profit. As one of the first councillors said, 'I found our Executive Government disposed to calculate their measures as much with a view to patronage and private endowment as the prosperity of the country.'[50] But if the Family Compact had not supplied the solution on any of the three counts, honesty, efficiency, or cheapness, neither did party government.

This comes as no surprise, of course, to modern readers, who, 150 years later, are still looking for a solution to the question the Reformers addressed, and the rebels tried, and failed, to answer.

Appendix 1:
Rebellion Losses
Claims

In 1839 in the last session of the old Upper Canada assembly, members passed a Rebellion Losses Bill, and one of the first acts of the new union legislature was to enact it. Its purpose was 'to ascertain and provide for payment of all just claims arising from the late Rebellion and Invasion of this Province.' It was to include 'any loss, destruction, or damage of property occasioned by violence on the part of persons in Her Majesty's service, or ... persons acting or presuming to act on behalf of Her Majesty, in the suppression of the said Rebellion, or for the prevention of further disturbances, and all claims arising under or in regard to the occupation of any houses or other premises by Her Majesty's Naval or Military forces, either Imperial or Provincial.'

A commission of local men was to sit at two places in each district to examine all the claims that were presented. It was not until five years later, however, that any money was voted to carry out this order. The total amount was £40,000 for the whole province. In December 1845 commissioners sat in Hastings County, which had been separated from the Midland District and was known as the Victoria District during 1839–49. The commissioners, 'having carefully and diligently ex[am]ined the undermentioned persons, or their witnesses and evidence' rendered judgment on 23 January 1846. With few exceptions, the written claims have survived, as well as the commissioners' report, and are available on microfilm. Unfortunately there are no records of the hearings or the evidence presented at them. When the governor-general signed the Rebellion Losses Bill for Lower Canada in 1849, an angry mob stoned his carriage and burned down the parliament building in Montreal. There was no such outburst over the Upper Canadian bill, but no doubt many agreed with Samuel Strickland when he wrote, 'the loyal militia of Canada West, I fear, would have been less active, could they ever have imagined that the Rebels they were then called upon to put down, would, at the close of the Rebellion, have been compensated for losses they had themselves occasioned!' (Strickland, *Twenty-Seven Years*, 262). If the awards in the rest of the province were similar to those made in Hastings County, however, neither the militia of Canada West nor Sam Strickland should have been at all dissatisfied with the results.

The commissioners named in 1840 were Benjamin Dougall, John Low, and Anthony Marshall. The commissioners' report of 1846 is generally in good condition except for one area at the top of the document where there has been deterioration and blackening. This is where the judges' names appear, as do the days and places of sitting, but although it is hard to read, the report seems to list six commissioners and two three-day sittings held at Fanning's Hotel in Belleville and at Jonas Canniff's Tavern in Thurlow. The signatures of Benjamin Dougall, William McAnnany, and William Ketcheson are legible; another may be James MacPherson; but two are so far unreadable. One thing that can be asserted about these judges is that they were not in sympathy with Reformers. It would seem that the political climate of the province might have changed, but not that of the local magistracy. No compensation was awarded to anyone who put in a claim for loss due to imprisonment, however unjust it may seem, and with three exceptions, Reuben White, Jacob Bonter, and John O'Carroll, those who were imprisoned were not compensated for any other loss at all.

White was awarded a small sum for the loss he had sustained. It was not much, but at least it was an acknowledgment that he had suffered a wrong. His compensation appears to be an anomaly among all the others on the list unless it has something to do with his wealth and influence in Sidney Township. Jacob Bonter claimed for keeping his horses in Kingston from 10 March to 10 May while he 'defended' himself. The part of the document which seems to give the charge against him has not been deciphered. While he was detained, he hired three firms of lawyers, whether consecutively or simultaneously is not stated, and he paid for witnesses (by which, no doubt, he meant he paid the expenses for witnesses). The combined efforts of Charles Benson, (William) Henry Draper, and Strachan and Heynunder secured his freedom. His claim was not fully met but was more successful than most. O'Carroll and Bonter were imprisoned for the same length of time. For stabling his horses and paying his lawyers Bonter was allowed £27/15/3. The militia guard had terrorized O'Carroll and his family, wrecked his shop, vandalized his stock, and destroyed his livelihood. Unable to earn anything as a shopkeeper while he was in jail, he had lost the house he was buying. He was given £25. There is no way of knowing how heavily the scales of justice were weighted by origin, religion, and politics, but O'Carroll had come from Ireland, was a Roman Catholic, and was plainly not well off; while Bonter belonged to a United Empire Loyalist family, was a member of the Church of England, was a man of some means, and his son who was born in 1837 was christened Francis Bond Head Bonter.

Those who were not imprisoned but were in any way associated with disloyalty, even to the extent of appearing as witnesses at the trial of a neighbour charged with 'a treasonable offence,' had their claims refused. There are no transcripts of the hearings to furnish clues as to why decisions were made as they were, but there are certain elements in them which seem significant. As already noted, the commissioners usually paid claims for militia service or supplies, at least in part and usually in full. Prominent citizens, as long as they were not conspicuous Reformers, seem to have done better than others. More than a quarter of the funds for the whole county went to the Portt brothers of Tyendinaga for the loss of their barn, the evidence being accepted that Patriots had set it on fire. The Portts were respected Tory magistrates, and George Portt had been active as a militia officer. They were originally from Ireland, prosperous, and Protestant.

These rebellion losses claims from Hastings County are on microfilm NA, MF 971 Has., to which the page numbers refer in the following annotations. Where there are variations in spelling, the most usual form is given.

Acker, Gabriel. Services rendered during the late rebellion – nine days at 5s per day. Claim: £2/5/0. Award: £2/5/0. p. 113

Alicumbrack, Henry (Huntingdon). In November 1838 he was 'falsely accused by John Hagerty and taken prisoner at my Dwelling place in the second Concession of Huntingdon and marched like a vile Criminal to Belleville.' There he was confined for twenty-four hours until he could prove his innocence of the charge. He also served in the militia for fourteen days, but before the paylist was made up he had to leave because of illness. Claim: £20/0/0. Award: 0. pp. 134–5

Ashley, Simeon (Thurlow). Since the rebellion he had been refused a tavern licence, 'being accused of disaffection although my certificate had been most respectfully signed and strongly recommended.' Claim: £50/0/0. Award: 0. pp. 228–9

Baragan, Hiram (Thurlow). This was the man who, according to his neighbours, was the victim of a plot to get possession of his farm. The land of a convicted traitor was forfeit to the Crown. Baragan claimed for thirty-one days imprisonment in Kingston and four days in Belleville, the expense of attending court in Kingston, and 'to time and damage in consequence of attending court.' Claim: £22/0/0. Award: 0. p. 61

Bennett, Charles (Sidney). Three days service as a special constable and two days 'on another occasion.' Claim: £1/5/0. Award: £1/5/0. p. 157

Benninger, John (Thurlow). Going to Kingston as a witness at the trial of Joseph Canniff and others for treason. Claim: £2/5/0. Award: 0. p. 79

Bird, Robert (Sidney). Bird, a miller, had been persuaded by Robert Baldwin to vote Reform, and in a letter to Baldwin he said this had been the reason he was thrown in jail, to the detriment of his business. Not only had he been kept for twenty days in the Midland District jail, but he had been fined for not attending to his militia duties. Claim: £75. Award: 0. p. 129

Bonter, Jacob. Having been arrested, he hired lawyers, paid for the attendance of witnesses, and kept his horses in Kingston (see above). Claim: £37/15/3. Award: £27/15/3. p. 52

Canniff, Joseph (Thurlow). Canniff was arrested in the early days of the rebellion, and again after the threatened raid on Gananoque, when he was held for eighty days. In addition to damages for imprisonment, he listed a pair of gloves and a pistol that were taken from him and not returned. Claim: £501/5/0. Award: 0. pp. 136–50

Carscallen, David Lockwood. This claim is for moving a family to Kingston, but there is no explanation and the name of the family is illegible. Claim: £2/5/0. Award: £2/5/0. p. 14

Caverley, Joseph. His imprisonment was similar to Canniff's. The second time he was arrested he spent eighty-three days in jail. Claim: £520. Award: 0. p. 172

Chapman, Daniel (Thurlow). This is one of numerous claims for teaming, that is, driving a team of horses with a wagon or sleigh. Chapman claimed for two days teaming 'by order of Captain Frazier.' Claim: £1/10/0. Award: £1/10/0. p. 60

Chapman, John (Thurlow). Two days teaming by order of Captain Frazier. Claim: £1/10/0. Award: £1/10/0. p. 159

Chisholm, Colin. Conducting prisoners from Belleville to Kingston, probably nine days in all. Claim: £6/15/0. Award: £6/15/0. pp. 40–1

Clare, Thomas. Teaming volunteers from Hungerford to Roblin's Tavern. Claim: £4/0/0. Award: £2/5/0. p. 9

Cole, Samuel (Cramahe). This claimant had been living in Hastings County at the time of the rebellion and had served with Captain Benson's troop, which was attached to the Second Hastings Regiment. He described in some detail how he came to lose a horse while on service. Claim: £20/0/0. Award: £17/0/0. pp. 82–3

Cornell, William. Riding his horse, he had spent six days guarding the mail. Claim: £2/11/0. Award: £2/7/6. pp. 32–3

Courtney, Francis. See *McConnachy* below.

Culbertson, John (Tyendinaga). When Manahan was bringing arms from Kingston to Belleville in December 1837, the steamboat carrying them had to put in at Culbertsons's wharf, where the claimant had a tavern. He supplied the men with thirty-seven breakfasts. On another occasion he supplied sixty-seven breakfasts, both times including liquor. He had lent the militia a wagon to convey some of the arms, and when he got it back months later it was in need of major repairs. He also claimed for being shot during the Mohawks' celebrations when they were disbanded, so that he still walked with a limp. Claim: £14/8/9. Award: £8/13/9. pp. 56–8

Dafoe, Zenas (Belleville). This was the gaoler and constable. He submitted a list of thirty-four people on whom he had served subpoenas, presumably in connection with the rebellion, and the mileage for each service. It seems remarkable that even this official had not been paid in the seven years since the last subpoena. Claim: £9/2/0. Award: £9/2/0. p. 95

Davidson, Peter. He spent fifteen days in prison in Kingston, three days returning home, and eight days getting bond money. He claimed for damages to his farm while he was away. Claim: £25/0/0. Award: 0. pp. 180–3

Davis, Richard (Belleville). As a sergeant in the militia, he had gone to Kingston with prisoners. Claim: £2/12/0. Award: £1/12/8. p. 109

Elmore, Asahel. This claim is interesting as evidence that Hastings men were among those who went to Toronto when the first news of the rebellion reached Belleville. Elmore had furnished supplies to the men and baggage wagons under his command when taking arms to Toronto. He also asked compensation for loss sustained when his tenants did not pay the rent they owed because they were 'arrested as Ribbels.' Billa Flint made a similar claim, which was approved, but Elmore was not so lucky and was awarded only for the supplies. Claim: £91/11/1. Award: £4/11/1. pp. 118–20, 209

Fairman, Hugh. He was arrested and kept for three days in the Belleville jail before the magistrates released him. During that time he caught a cold, which he blamed for the loss of his eyesight. Claim: £50/0/0. Award: 0. p. 69

Finkle, Gilbert (Sidney). He had not been paid for two days in service. Claim: £0/10/0. Award: £0/10/0. pp. 192–4

Finkle, Jacob. He had spent three days 'taking prisoners by order of Esquire Bowen' in December 1837. Claim: £1/10/0. Award: £1/10/0. p. 178

Elint, Billa. This magistrate and merchant of Belleville provided a quantity of food and other supplies for horses and men in the militia, and like others, had not been paid by the commissary department. He was also out of pocket for accounts and rent not paid because the debtors ran away. Claim: £52/1/0. Award: £52/1/0. pp. 132–9

Foster, Benjamin. During the rebellion he lost a log house with its furniture, bedding, clothes, and provisions. There are no details on the written claim, neither where the house was nor how it was lost, although such complete destruction suggests that it was through fire. Foster may have blamed this on rebels or Patriots. Claim: £60/5/6. Award: 0. p. 135

Garrison, Henry (Thurlow). This was for '2 days teaming by order of Captain Frazier, February 1838.' Claim: £1/10/0. Award: £1/10/0. p. 122

Geddes, James. In 1837 he helped to take prisoners down to Kingston, by order of Major J.H. Blacker. Claim: £4/0/0. Award: £3/0/0. p. 76.

Gibson, James. As a sergeant in the militia he spent four days taking prisoners from Belleville to Kingston. Claim: £2/0/0. Award: £1/12/8. p. 92

Gibson, Ralph. This was for teaming arms in Belleville for one day with an extra man. Claim: £0/18/0. Award: £0/15/0. p. 110

Gordinier, Henry (Thurlow). He spent six days on duty and because of this claimed to have lost one yoke of oxen, two cows, and two two-year-old heifers. Claim: £28/10/0. Award: £0/7/6. p. 198

Gordinier, William (Thurlow). He also spent six days on duty in 1837, and five attending a court martial. Claim: £2/15/0. Award: £0/7/6. p. 195

Greenier, Edward. He supplied four days board to four men from the W troop of cavalry militia. Claim: £4/0/0. Award: £4/0/0. pp. 43–4, 107

Hayes, Hugh. This was for seventeen days spent with Captain Frazier's company in Belleville. Claim: £6/7/6. Award: £3/15/0. p. 105

Hearns, Aaron H. After being imprisoned for nineteen days in Kingston, he had the expense of returning to attend court, although he was not tried. Claim: £26/0/0. Award: 0. p. 175

Hicks, Philip D. There is no written claim, but this is probably for service with the militia. Claim: £1/10/0. Award: £1/10/0.

Holton, E.W. (Belleville). This was a merchant who had furnished supplies to the militia. A long list is appended. Claim: £26/0/8. Award: £1/10/0. pp. 96–7

Hughes, John (Marmora). Both Patrick and John Hughes were members of the cavalry militia under Captain Benson. Each had to stable his horse in Belleville while on service, and both mounts became infected with horse distemper. In spite of veterinary care, both died. John had the doubtful support of a neighbour's deposition to the effect that he knew the horse had died, but could not say how. However, a more convincing statement would probably not have improved the outcome. It is interesting to speculate how the court assessed the value of horses that had died years before. Claim: £25/0/0. Award: £15/0/0. pp. 67–9

Hughes, Patrick (Marmora). Patrick was an innkeeper. His claim for the loss of his horse was also £25/0/0. Award: £13/0/0. pp. 63–6

Jones, Gilbert. In July 1838 he drove a team 'from Munro's shed to Kingston.' Claim: £3/0/0. Award: £3/0/0. pp. 54–5

Jones, Nathan. This Belleville merchant supplied a great many items for the militia, including large quantities of tea and sugar, an inkstand and paper, candles, and a broom. 'Peas' in large quantities appear on the lists submitted by several suppliers. These were an old type, no longer grown, used as fodder for the horses. Claim: £21/5/6. Award: £15/6/8. pp. 105–6

Ketcheson, Henry. This claim is not entirely legible. He delivered a gun or ammunition to Richard Sagar, officer of the day in Belleville, no date given. He was not the only one who had trouble recovering his property after the rebellion. Claim: £3/0/0. Award: £2/10/0. p. 30

Ketcheson, Joseph (Sidney). He spent '3 days in a rest and search of Wheeler and Marsh 2 days in a rest of Mr. White 2 days in a rest of E. Perry and Stephens' and in addition had to pay for a team, and one gun that was lost or stolen. Claim: £5/2/6. Award: £2/5/0. pp. 188–9

Ketcheson, Thomas (Frankford). Thomas furnished a 'Cookin Stove' for the barracks at Frankford. Claim: £4/0/0. Award: £4/0/0. pp. 196–7

Ketchipaw, John (Thurlow). He was imprisoned for four days in Belleville, where he seems not to have liked the food supplied in jail since he claimed the cost of being 'sued for my billet at M.D. Young's.' He also had to go to Kingston to give evidence at another trial. Claim: £10/0/0. Award: 0. p. 85

Keys, Hugh. No written claim.

Lafontaine, Christopher. This was one of the six prisoners who were brought to trial. All were acquitted. Lafontaine claimed for unlawful imprisonment, as well as for meals purchased while he was in prison. Claim: £39/0/0. Award: 0. p. 84

Leavens, Hector (Thurlow). He provided six days board and lodging for four cavalry militiamen and their mounts. Claim: £5/19/0. Award: £5/19/0. p. 210

Leavens, Henry (Thurlow). Henry drove a team, on one occasion taking prisoners to Kingston and on another some of the Rifle Company. He had also driven Captain Bonter to arrest Bleeker Meyers. Claim: £5/19/0. Award: £5/19/0. p. 210

Lemerand, Adolphus. He claimed to have served fifteen days at the Trent under Captain Robertson. Claim: £6/0/0. Award: 0. p. 216

Larroy, John (Sidney). Some of those arrested must have been hard to catch. Larroy spent two days arresting Reuben White, three days arresting John Whalen (possibly Wheeler), and three looking for Samuel Marsh. Claim: £2/0/0. Award: £1/5/0. p. 199

Lefebvre, François (Sidney). pp. 98–103

Lloyd, Adam. This was for 'servitude done under Captain William Robertson.' Claim: £1/10/0. Award: £0/7/6. p. 187

Lloyd, Edward (Huntingdon). The items in this claim include serving a summons, attendance at a court martial, bringing prisoners to Belleville, and damage to his wagon. Claim: £5/5/0. Award: £2/0/0. p. 166

Lockwood, Joseph. This former member of parliament was arrested, then got out on bail after fifteen days, but had to spend seventeen days in Kingston waiting for a trial which never took place. Claim: £32/15/0. Award: 0. pp. 123–4

Lott, Jacob. He spent three months in prison, and as a result lost a number of his cattle. Claim: £62/10/0. Award: 0. p. 130

Lott, Peter. He was imprisoned from February to May in Fort Henry 'by the then ruling authorities, and then discharged without a trial,' a common complaint. Claim £500/0/0. Award: 0. p. 132

Lyons, Thomas. This man was a mounted militiaman who had spent six days guarding the mail. Claim: £2/11/6. Award: £2/7/6. p. 31

McConnachy, Francis M., and Francis Courtney. These two men ran a livery stable. They submitted a claim for supplying two teams and sleighs to take troops from Belleville to Cobourg, most likely when news of the rebellion reached Hastings in December 1837 and hundreds of men gathered in Cobourg and Port Hope. Claim: £8/0/0. Award: £4/0/0. p. 71

McCoy, Francis. Again, a house had been rented to the militia guard and afterwards had to be almost rebuilt. Claim: £46/17/4. Award: £25/0/0. p. 10

McCready, Thomas (Thurlow). This was for two days teaming. Claim: £1/10/0. Award: £1/10/0. p. 161

McDonald, Alpheus. This was for 'loss sustained in consequence of being called on to do military duty and not fulfilling engagements and loss of saw logs.' Claim: £6/0/0. Award: 0. p. 78

McGuire, Charles (Hungerford). He lost a horse he was using in military service. Award: £20/0/0. Award: £20/0/0. pp. 111–12

Mackenzie, Donald. Like others who rented houses for the use of the militia guard in Belleville, he had to make extensive repairs afterwards. Claim: £56/13/4. Award: £50/0/0. pp. 60–60A

Martin, William. This man was a carpenter who went to Toronto for twenty days, although in what capacity is not stated. He worked afterwards building the Belleville barracks on the west side of the Moira River. Claim: £14/13/9. Award: £7/10/0. p. 94

Melvin, Mary. This was for six days service with a two-horse team. It may not have been sexual discrimination, but this is the only claim for teaming which was reduced in this way. Claim: £4/10/0. Award: £3/0/0. p. 75

Meyers, Bleeker. He sent eighty-two days in prison and was then discharged without a trial. Claim: £50/0/0. Award: 0. p. 153

Meyers, George W. This claimant suffered an obvious injustice. George was waiting for a steamboat to take him across to the States when a man asked him why he was going there. He said he was going to look for Mackenzie, which the man promptly reported to Judge Draper. He was then arrested and imprisoned, without being told why. It took two weeks to get word to his brother, who came to the prison and demanded to know why George had been arrested. The prison official told him about George's reason for leaving the country. Thereupon the brother asked the official to look in George's pocketbook, where he would find a note signed by Sheldon Mackenzie which George had been going to try to collect. George was freed, with an apology. He claimed that as a result of his imprisonment he had to sell a house worth £75 at less than value. In addition, he had paid for meals for persons taken up on suspicion and confined in 'McKenzie's stone house.' Claim: £332/10/0. Award: 0. pp. 88–90

Meyers, Jacob Walden. This claim for rent of his house, used by the guard, was one that included seven years' interest. That may sound reasonable, but no one was able to collect it. Claim: £3/13/0. Award: £0/5/0. p. 84

Meyers, John G. (Belleville). His sleigh and two horses were used two days and two nights to take prisoners down to Kingston, and he had one horse damaged by foundering 'in consequence of improper treatment on the above service.' Claim: £16/6/8. Award: £6/10/0. p. 42

Meyers, John L. (Frankford). He conveyed a load of prisoners to Belleville. Claim: £3/5/9. Award: £2/5/0. p. 70

Meyers, Tobias W. One of the men who was tried in July 1838, he claimed for 139 days of unlawful imprisonment. Claim: £139/0/0. Award: 0. pp. 86–8

Mitts, James. The claim was for a team to convey a prisoner 'from my place to John McCoy's Inn.' Claim: £0/10/0. Award: £0/10/0. p. 200

Moore, Jacob. He claimed he had spent four months in arresting prisoners and conveying them to Kingston. Claim: £20/0/0. Award: £15/0/0. p. 171

Morton, William. He acted as a special constable between 15 December 1837 and 20 February 1839. Claim: £3/0/0. Award: £3/0/0. p. 162

Mott, Stephen (Thurlow). This was another man imprisoned for three months and discharged without a trial. Claim: £50/0/0. Award: 0. p. 200

Murney, Wellington. This was for expenses incurred in getting the Belleville Rifle Company back from Gananoque to Belleville in February 1838. Claim: £29/9/1. Award: £29/9/1. p. 91

Nosworthy, James. For ten days on the road making three trips to Kingston with prisoners. Claim: £2/10/0. Award: £1/5/0. p. 81

Nugent, Richard. He drove troops once to Shannonville and once to Kingston. Claim: £4/0/0. Award: £3/7/6. p. 108

O'Brien, Christopher. This man was captain and adjutant of the First Regiment of Hastings between December 1837 and March 1838. His claim contains testimonials and references to his military experience. There is nothing specified beyond 'To duty and expenditures.' Claim: £100/0/0. Award: £20/0/0. pp. 205–6

O'Camb, Nicholas (Thurlow). He was imprisoned for eighty days, and also had to go to Kingston as a witness at the trials of Joseph Canniff and John Bonter. (There is no record of a trial of John Bonter. It may have been a magistrates' hearing, but it is hard to understand why this would have been in Kingston.) Claim: £80/0/0. Award: 0. p. 158

O'Carroll, Margaret. This is the claim for the O'Carrolls' store and business described above. Claim: £860/0/0. Award: £25/0/0. p. 51

Ockerman, Elmer. He had been imprisoned for two months and twenty days in Fort Henry. Claim: £50/0/0. Award: 0. p. 32

Ostrom, Simeon. He worked for four days with a team, making two trips to Kingston with prisoners. Claim: £6/0/0. Award: £6/0/0. pp. 37–8

Parks, Cornelius. Parks was imprisoned fourteen days on his first arrest, sixty-three days the second time, and afterwards spent a week attending court in Kingston without his case being called. Claim: £62/10/0. Award: 0. p. 135

Perry, Robert R. (Sidney). This man spent two days gathering prisoners about the district by order of Bowen the magistrate, then three days taking them down to Kingston, and two days as a special constable. Claim: £4/5/0. Award: £4/5/0. p. 174

Petrie, Allan T. This was for taking prisoners from Madoc and Belleville to Kingston. Claim: £7/10/0. Award: £6/10/0

Portt, George

Portt, William. The Portt brothers farmed together in Tyendinaga. The harvest of 1839 was a good one, and their barn was full of wheat when, on the night of 10 October, it caught fire. Several men were wakened and hurried to it, but they could do nothing to save it or the five stacks of grain and two of hay just outside. The Portts valued their loss at £470, including in that the loss they believed they suffered on the price of cattle that had to be sold because there was no hay for them. The field around the barn had been sown to fall wheat the day before the fire, so that in the morning several men, some of them Indian, examined tracks that could be seen across it. They disagreed about the number of men who made them, but the fact that men had gone to the barn during the night and run away from it again, did indicate that the fire was the result of arson. The Portts set out to prove that it was, and that it was the work of Patriot raiders.

Both brothers were justices of the peace; so first they had their fellow magistrates, and a number of their neighbours, sign a statement that in their opinion the fire was set by Patriots. As proof this seems of little worth. Of more value was the statement of Garrett Sager of Tyendinaga, who had talked to a number of people in New York State, including men jailed in Watertown for the burning of the *Sir Robert Peel*, and from their conversation had become convinced the Patriots were the culprits. The best evidence came from the United States. William Anderson of Jefferson County said he had seen a list of their enemies prepared 'by those who style themselves Hunters,' and on it was the name of William Portt. William Davenport of Tyendinaga had seen a similar list when he was in Chamont Bay, NY. Samuel Felt of Oswego had in 1838 talked to Hunters in his town, and they had wished to burn the village of Napanee, calling it 'a great Tory Hole.' They had further mentioned the name Portt as a particular target and had even offered a reward for burning out Portt of Tyendinaga 'who lead *Indians*.' Felt had later crossed 'the Mohawk Bay' and had some conversation with a fellow passenger who was a Hunter. This man told him there had been one attempt to set fire to the Portts' property, but the matches that were being used had failed. This time, the Hunter bragged, he had himself provided good matches which would not misfire.

The Portts petitioned the lieutenant-governor for compensation just after the fire, stating:

[Y]our Petitioners rendered themselves obnoxious to [the rebels?] by their steady adherence to the established constitution ... and their activity and exertions to suppress the outbreak, one as a Militia officer, and the other as Captain and leader of the Mohawks, whose services were so often in requisition at that period, and at no small pecuniary loss to their leader. The readiness and efficiency of those services so galling to the disaffected at home [,] the dread of the Indians by the reckless band of Hunters beyond the frontiers then meditating an invasion of the Province [,] caused their leader to be proscribed and marked a doomed man and the vengeance of the party was inflicted.

All payments were deferred until 1845, when the Portts submitted all the evidence they had collected. Claim: £470/0/0. Award: £420/4/2. pp. 11–29

Purdy, David. He spent three days with his team conducting prisoners to Kingston. Claim: £3/0/0. Award: £3/0/0. p. 39

Roy, Robert. The claim is not easy to read. This man owned a foundry in which valuable patterns were stolen or destroyed, moulding boxes broken, and the house and foundry wrecked. It is not known where this happened since both Chippawa and Drummondville are mentioned, but there must have been a local connection since the claim was presented in Hastings. Claim: £73/0/0. Award: £73/0/0. pp. 217–18

Ruff, Emerson. In 1837 he was a sergeant, and some of his pay was still owing in 1845. Claim: £3/0/0. Award: £3/0/0. p. 227

Ryan, Martin (Tyendinaga). He claimed to have served for three days on sentry duty and four days a month for six months travelling back and forth to Rawdon in charge of militia arms. In addition, his house burned and he lost £300 worth of goods. No details are given. Claim: £365/1/3. Award: 0. pp. 98–107

Sagar, Garret (Tyendinaga). Another sergeant, he spent six days guarding the mail, on one occasion conducting it from Roblin's Tavern to Belleville. Claim: £4/10/0. Award: £4/10/0. p. 84

Shorts, Philip. This was the owner of the office and press where Samuel

Hart had printed the *Plain Speaker*. He claimed for the damaged press and lost types. Claim: £100/0/0. Award: £4/10/0. p. 104

Shurman, James (Tyendinaga). With a man and a team he had taken the prisoner Robert Huffman from Shannonville to Kingston. He had also collected and conveyed militia to 'the alarm at Bath,' which would have been at the time of the Amherst Island raid. Claim: £3/15/0. Award: £3/0/0. p. 121

Sinclair, Samuel. He put in four days with a team 'in Her Majesty's service,' unspecified. Claim: £3/0/0. Award: £3/0/0. p. 208

Smith, Bernard (Frankford). A log house and a quantity of corn belonging to him had been burned. He was sure this was the work of 'enemies of the Crown' because he and his sons George and Samuel had turned out at the first news of the rebellion, and faithfully served in the militia. For this they had received threats from some of their dissident neighbours. Claim: £50/0/0. Award: 0. p. 193

Smith, George (Frankford). 'Persons in the employment of the government' took away his gun in 1838 and had never returned it. Claim: £2/0/0. Award: £2/0/0. pp. 190–1

Smith, John. With a team, he spent four days taking prisoners to Kingston. Claim: £3/0/0. Award: £3/0/0. p. 53

Smith, Philo. He had been imprisoned for sixty-seven days and had the expense of returning home from Kingston. He also claimed for the loss of a hatchet and a pair of pantaloons. Claim: £41/15/0. Award: 0. pp. 172–3

Smith, Samuel (Frankford). Very little has survived about the arrest of the Hastings prisoners. From the claims it appears some, like the Marsh brothers, were not easy to find since more than one claimant spent time looking for them. This claim is for three days spent 'in a rest of Wheeler and Marsh.' Claim: £1/15/0. Award: £0/15/0. p. 192

Snider, Andrew (Huntingdon). He spent three weeks and five days on duty at the Trent. During his absence he 'hired my cattle kept.' Claim: £13/0/0. Award: £1/12/6. p. 215

Squires, Ebenezer (Huntingdon). He was a prisoner from 29 February to 16 August 1838. He claimed for keeping a span of horses in Kingston for three weeks 'in the first year of the rebellion.' Claim: £5/0/0. Award: 0. p. 212

Squires, Edward (Huntingdon). In the first year of the rebellion he served under Captain McAnnany, but in the second year he was teaching school and was fined for not reporting for duty. Claim: £3/15/0. Award: 0. pp. 213–14

Stickle, Addi. This claim is for neglect of his farm, because he had to go to Kingston to give evidence just when he should have been planting his crops. Claim: £10/0/0. Award: 0. p. 134

Stocton, [first name illegible]. There is no written claim, only the name on the commissioners' report. Claim: £26/17/81/2. Award: £17/17/81/2. p. 59

Thompson, Alexander. He made one trip to Kingston with the first prisoners, using a double team, and again with the second lot of prisoners, four days each time. Claim: £6/0/0. Award: £6/0/0. pp. 35–6

Turner, Gideon (Sidney). This was the township clerk, who was arrested in December 1837 and again in February 1838, spending almost three months in jail. Claim: £100/0/0. Award: 0. pp. 116–17

Walker, Elizabeth. There is no written claim, only the name on the commissioners' report. She probably supplied a team and driver. Claim: £3/0/0. Award: £3/0/0. p. 13

Wallace, Robert. He served as a special constable, probably in the arrest of prisoners. Claim: £3/0/0. Award: £3/0/0. p. 80

Warren, C.W. He was a captain in the militia, who had been 'doing his duty to Queen and country by taking suspicious characters to Kingston.' He acted as a special constable up until the time he enlisted in the Belleville Rifle Company. He had also on one occasion gone as a courier to Toronto. Claim: £25/0/0. Award: £10/0/0. pp. 103–9

White, Reuben (Sidney). He was one of the early settlers of Sidney, a prosperous merchant and mill owner, who had been a member of the assembly. A man named William Bane came with a guard to arrest him in December 1837 and seems to have made free with many of White's possessions, some of which were never returned. This claim is set out like a business account, with such items as '1 box or chest containing my papers with notes and accounts,' '1 silk handkerchief tied up full of papers,' and 'missing out of my Store draw when Bane were searching them for papers five pounds in cash.' Bane had also driven off in White's cutter, leaving White to pay for stabling it and a driver to bring it home again. Among other expenses were the cost of raising a £2,000 bond and the fare to go back to Kingston for eight days 'while attending court to obtain my trial and got none.' Claim: £65/19/2. Award: £2/10/0. pp. 125–6

Willard, Barry (Belleville). This is for billeting overnight one sergeant and three privates. Claim: £0/10/6. Award: 0. p. 93

Willcox, David. He spent four days going down to Kingston with a prisoner. Claim: £3/0/0. Award: £3/0/0. p. 207

Wolcott, F.C. [Chauncey] (Thurlow). He spent '11 days teaming arms and ammunition, prisoners and other commodities by order of the magistrates.' Claim: £8/5/0. Award: £8/5/0. p. 133

Wonnacott, John. With other members of the family, John had come to Belleville from England around 1834. By 1838 he was married to a local woman, living in modest comfort, and active in the militia. On 17 February he received an invitation to spend an evening with friends about ten miles west of his home in Sidney. Since he had business in that direction, he accepted. His friend seems to have lived two miles beyond River Trent towards Brighton, and Wonnacott spent the night there. When he got home, he was told by a man who worked for him that some of the Rifle Company had come to warn him to turn out for militia duty. Thinking they had meant only to remind him of the regular weekly drill, he paid no particular attention to the message. But this was at the time of the threatened invasion at Kingston, and the Rifle Company was preparing to march there. The Belleville magistrates arrested Wonnacott and asked for £20 bail.

Wonnacott claimed the magistrates treated him unfairly since they refused his note and gave him no opportunity to get the money, although they could not have expected him to be carrying so much – at the time £20 was a considerable sum. They kept him in custody for twenty-four hours. But he was landlord to one of the magistrates, who owed him £20 in back rent, and when next day Wonnacott threatened to send in the bailiff to collect, the man reluctantly gave his note for the bail money. Wonnacott was incensed. He demanded of the magistrates why they refused 'my bail who are in better circumstances than the person whose Note they took ... the answer given was that it was none of my business.' And another young man who had simply refused to go to Kingston 'never paid his money at all,' although he had no property in the county. The explanation came from one of the magistrates who later told Wonnacott's father there would have been no arrest and no bail if John had not married into a Reform family. John defended his wife's people:

> [T]he whole Family has ever devoted themselves to the British Constitution and have bled for it both in the old revolution and the late War ... Having informed your Excellency of the injustice of the punishment [you] have it at your discretion to say whether I am entitled to get my fine remitted or not ... I was one of the first to turn out on all occasions being one of the Special Constables and one that has done all in his power to get the said Company organized and to put down anything like Rebellion. (NA, RG 5, A1, vol. 197, 109750, petition of John Wonnacott to lieutenant-governor, 30 June 1838, Belleville)

Wonnacott claimed the amount of the fine, and for the guard's use of a

house he owned, plus seven years and nine months' interest. Claim: £33/
19/3. Award: 0. pp. 114–15

Yager, Henry. This claim is interesting because of the enigmatic part
played by Yager after the rebellion. He had been a Reform member of
the assembly and had contested the 1836 election as a Reform candidate.
Others with a similar background were accused of treason, and it would
not have seemed strange if Yager too had been arrested. It may be that,
while he was not a Tory, he held no strong Reform opinions, had not
attended the meeting at Hayden's Tavern in 1837, and was the kind of
man who could keep friends on both sides of politics. Whatever the
reason, he was obviously not regarded in the same light as other prominent Reformers. In 1838 when it was feared the Patriots were about to
cross the Niagara River, Henry Yager was sent with a company of men
to take arms to Chippawa. The first night, the men stopped at the Trent
where Jacob Ford had an inn. Yager offered him the usual government
bill for the men's meal and lodging, but Ford cannily refused it, insisting
he must have better security. Because of the urgency of his mission,
Yager gave his personal note. He then found, like many others, that the
government was reluctant to pay him. As he was unable to redeem the
note himself, Ford got an execution against him, and he was forced to
sell a horse at a loss of £10. Claim: £10/0/0. Award: £4/0/0. p. 170.

Appendix 2:
The Prisoners

There is no accurate record of the rebellion prisoners from Hastings County. The following is the list of Midland District prisoners in Charles Lindsey's *Life and Times of William Lyon Mackenzie*, with some corrections and additions from local documents. A few of these men came from Frontenac County; more from Lennox and Addington; but a majority can be placed as residents of Hastings County.

When a man was arrested, he was taken before one or more magistrates, who might release him, keep him in custody for a short time, or send him down to the Midland District jail in Kingston (a few men were put into Fort Henry). The jails of the province were full to overflowing, and the wheels of justice did not move speedily. Habeas corpus had been suspended at the time of the rebellion, and the judges could not cope with the number of cases, although a special commission was set up in Toronto to deal with those who took part in the Yonge Street rebellion. Local men who were released on bail had to go back to Kingston for trial, but even when they made the journey, which for many of them was a two-day trip, their cases were usually not heard. Some of them were also summoned as witnesses and again found they had made the journey for nothing. It is a recurring complaint in their claims that they were never able to have their day in court. Just nine of them were brought before the bar; six of those were actually tried, and all of them were acquitted.

The dates given are not infallible guides to the length of time the men were in prison. Some of them claimed for being in jail the whole time shown on the list, but others must have been out on bail for at least part of that time. This is shown by documents concerning Nelson Reynolds. He is shown here as being imprisoned from 26 December to 6 July 1838, yet he was certainly free when he was again arrested on 22 February, then escaped to the United States, and returned in time for the assizes in July, when he won an acquittal. Absalom Day, who was arrested 23 February, according to the statement of the constable John Ashley, and who is shown as being imprisoned from 8 March to 22 April, was probably free between these dates. This is suggested by the adjutant general's correspondence outlined earlier. After Day's arrest, when Macaulay and Bullock discussed his militia commission, they decided not to promote him but to keep him at the top of his rank. He may have been in jail at the time, but that seems most unlikely. The dates therefore have to be treated with some caution.

The following abbreviations are used:

A.G.	Attorney General
g.b.	good behaviour
L.G.	Lieutenant-Governor
magis.	magistrates
n.t.	not tried
Q.C.	Queen's Counsel

An asterisk indicates a member of a United Empire Loyalist family.

*Alicumbrack, Henry, farmer: 1 day in Belleville jail, released by magis.
Anderson, Thomas, farmer: 28 Feb.–29 Mar.; n.t.; indicted but bill ignored
Anderson, William, farmer: 19 Dec.–2 May; n.t.; indicted but bill ignored
Babcock, Samuel, farmer: 28 Feb.–2 Mar.; n.t.; released on bail
Baragan, Hiram, farmer: 30 days in Kingston, 4 in Belleville; n.t.; released on bail
Bibby, John, butcher: 26 Dec.–2 Jan.; released on security for g.b.
*Bird, Robert, miller: 27 Feb.–8 Mar.; n.t.; released on bail
*Bonter, Jacob: 2 months in Kingston; n.t.
Burley, John, gentleman: 12 Dec.–13 Dec.; released by magis.
*Canniff, Joseph, miller: 14 Dec.–1 Jan, 24 Feb.–12 May; n.t.; released on bail by A.G.
Caverley, Joseph, farmer: 15 Dec.–2 Jan., 23 Feb.–17 May; n.t.; released on bail by A.G.
Chatsey, James L., farmer: 3 Mar.–7 Mar.; n.t.; released by magis.
Collard, David, farmer: 28 Feb.–2 Apr.; n.t.; released on bail
Cunningham, William, artist: 14 Dec.–16 Dec.; released by magis.
Davidson, Daniel, farmer: 2 Mar.–12 May; n.t.; indicted but bill ignored by grand jury

Davidson, Peter, farmer: 17 Dec.–2 Jan.; n.t.; indicted but bill ignored by grand jury

*Day, Absalom, farmer: 3 Mar.–22 Apr.; n.t.; indicted but bill ignored by grand jury

*Day, Anson, farmer: 19 Dec.–7 July; acquitted by court of oyer and terminer

*Fairman, Hugh, farmer: 1 day in Belleville jail; released by magis.

Forward, William, attorney: 22 Feb.–13 Mar.; n.t.; released on bail

Getty, James, farmer: 27 Feb.–16 May; n.t.; indicted but bill ignored by grand jury

Grenier, Christopher, farmer: 3 Mar.–2 Apr.; n.t.; charged with aiding the escape of a traitor; charge dropped when 'traitor' (Reynolds) found not guilty

Hare, James G., farmer: 22 Dec.–5 Jan.; n.t.; released on bail by A.G.

Hayden, Anson, doctor: 19 Dec.–2 Jan.; n.t.; released on bail by A.G.

Hearns, Aaron, farmer: 17 Dec.–2 Jan.; n.t.; released on bail by A.G.

Herman, John, farmer: 29 Feb.–16 Aug.; n.t.; liberated by L.G.

Hickey, Edward, farmer: 27 Feb.–13 May; n.t.; indicted but bill ignored by grand jury

Holsenburgh, George, farmer: 29 Feb.–16 Aug.; n.t.; released by L.G.

*Huffman, George R., tanner: 9 Dec.–4 Jan.; n.t.; released on bail by Q.C.

Ketchipaw, James, farmer: 3 Mar.–7 Mar.; n.t.; released on bail

Lafontaine, Christopher, farmer: 22 Feb.–8 July; acquitted by court of oyer and terminer

Lasage, Pierre, carter: 9 May–7 July; n.t.; indicted but witness disappeared; case dismissed

Leslie, William, merchant: 2 Mar.–14 May; n.t.; released by magis.

Lewis, Asa, farmer: 22 Feb.–8 July; acquitted by court of oyer and terminer

Lockwood, Joseph, farmer: 17 Dec.–2 Jan.; n.t.; released on bail by A.G.

Long, Nelson, carpenter: 2 Mar.–12 May; n.t.; indicted but bill ignored by grand jury

*Lott, Jacob, farmer: 2 Mar.–16 May; n.t.; indicted but bill ignored by grand jury

*Lott, Peter, farmer: 11 weeks 5 days; indicted but bill ignored by grand jury

McCann, James, teacher: 22 Dec.–12 Jan.; n.t.; released on bail

McCollum, Clifton, merchant: 17 Dec.–20 Dec.; n.t.; liberated by L.G.

*Marsh, Charles, farmer: 22 Feb.–8 July; acquitted by court of oyer and terminer

*Marsh, Samuel, farmer: 22 Feb.–8 July; acquitted by court of oyer and terminer

Martin, John, farmer: 29 Feb.–12 Aug.; n.t.; released by A.G.

*Meyers, Bleeker, farmer: 27 Feb.–16 May; n.t.; indicted but bill ignored

Meyers, Tobias, farmer: 24 Feb.–9 July; indicted but not tried because others charged with same crime were acquitted

*Mott, Hiram, farmer: 23 Feb.–11 May; n.t.; indicted but bill ignored

*Mott, Stephen, farmer: 23 Feb.–11 May; n.t.; indicted but bill ignored

Mullins, Thomas, farmer: 2 Jan.–5 Jan.; n.t.; discharged on security for g.b.

O'Camb, Nicholas: Thurlow resident who claimed for 80 days imprisonment

O'Carroll, John, merchant: His claim stated he had been imprisoned for 8 weeks

*Ockerman, Elmer, farmer: 27 Feb.–13 May; n.t.; indicted but bill ignored

Orr, Peter, farmer: 22 Feb.–8 July; acquitted by court of oyer and terminer

Parkeymore, Samuel, farmer: 5 Jan.–9 Jan.; discharged on security for g.b.

*Parks, Cornelius, innkeeper: 19 Dec.–2 Jan, 63 days in 1839; n.t.; released on bail by A.G.

Pennock, John, cooper: 27 Feb.–14 May; n.t.; bill ignored by grand jury

Phillips, Charles, shoemaker: 1 Jan.–9 Feb.; n.t.; discharged on security for g.b

Pockard, John, farmer: 29 Feb.–16 Aug.; n.t.; liberated by L.G.

Proctor, Amos, farmer: 27 Feb.–16 May; n.t.; bill ignored by grand jury

Proctor, Benjamin, tinsmith: 24 Apr.–12 May; n.t.; bill ignored by grand jury

*Reynolds, Nelson, merchant: 26 Dec.–6 July; acquitted by court of oyer and terminer

Robertson, Peter, merchant: 27 Feb.–16 May; n.t.; bill ignored by grand jury

Robertson, Robert merchant: 27 Feb.–16 May; n.t.; bill ignored by grand jury

Robins, Vanrenslaer, labourer: 12 Mar.–13 Mar.; n.t.; dismissed by magis.

Robinson, Oliver, farmer: 19 Dec.–20 May; n.t.; indicted but bill ignored

*Roblin, Ivy R., farmer: 27 Feb.–16 May; n.t.; indicted but bill ignored by grand jury

*Shibley, Henry: 23 Feb.; arrested; released by magis.

*Shibley, John: 23 Feb.; arrested; released by magis.

Smith, Joshua, merchant: 24 Feb.–12 May; n.t.; indicted but bill ignored by grand jury

Smith, Philo, labourer: 14 Mar.–15 May; n.t.; indicted but bill ignored by grand jury

*Squires, Ebenezer: 29 Feb.–16 Aug.; n.t.; liberated by L.G.

Starr, Samuel, shoemaker: 14 Mar.–11 May; n.t.; indicted but bill ignored by grand jury

Stephens, Samuel, farmer: 27 Feb.–23 Mar.; n.t.; admitted to bail

Stickle, John W., farmer: 27 Feb.–16 May; n.t.; indicted but bill ignored by grand jury

Stratton, Harvey, farmer: n.t.; admitted to bail

Thibodo, Augustus, farmer: 12 Dec.–13 Dec.; n.t.; dismissed by magis.

Tucker, Richard, farmer: 19 Dec.–20 May; n.t.; indicted but bill ignored

Turner, Gideon, township clerk: 17 Dec.–2 Jan.; 23 Feb.–17 May; n.t.; admitted to bail by A.G.

Weaver, Francis, teacher: 12 Dec.–4 Jan.; n.t.; admitted to bail by Q.C.

Wheeler, John, farmer: 31 Dec.–12 Jan.; n.t.; discharged on security for g.b.

White, Reuben, farmer: 17 Dec.–2 Jan.; n.t.; admitted to bail by Q.C.

Wonnacott, John: 1 day in Belleville jail; released by magis.

Notes

Throughout the Notes archival sources are abbreviated as follows: Colonial Office (CO); Hastings County Historical Society (HCHS); National Archives (NA); and Public Archives of Ontario (PAO). Books cited in short form are listed in the Selected Bibliography.

INTRODUCTION

1 Creighton, *John A. Macdonald: The Young Politician*, 48
2 See Mills, *The Idea of Loyalty in Upper Canada, 1784–1850*.
3 Later Sir Richard Bonnycastle; he was at the time acting commander of Fort Henry.
4 John Moodie became sheriff of the Victoria District, which was the name given to the same area as Hastings County from 1840 to 1849. Susanna was the author of numerous books, including the widely known *Roughing It in the Bush*.
5 Buckner, *The Transition to Responsible Government*, 267, citing Bagot to Stanley, 28 Oct. 1842
6 It seems certain the men had gathered to form a political union or to sign up new members of a union branch already formed, with its constitution dictated by Mackenzie.
7 *Belleville Intelligencer*, 3 Feb. 1863. The Hastings County Historical Society has a few copies of earlier date, some of which have been quoted in this book.

CHAPTER 1 In the Beginning

1 *Kingston Chronicle and Gazette*, 20 Dec. 1837. This was the 'terrible meeting at Hayden's.'

2 The Murray Canal now connects the two.

3 They also retained three lots in the eastern part of Thurlow Township.

4 Most of these were from veteran regiments that had in effect been rented out to the British by their German, Swiss, and Low Countries allies.

5 Turner, *Voyage of a Different Kind*, 103. Van Alstine ended up at Adolphustown in Prince Edward County.

6 There is some uncertainty about the date, which could have been as early as 1811.

7 Boyce, *Historic Hastings*, 32–3

8 The governor at Quebec had the title of governor-general, but while the governor in Upper Canada was usually called lieutenant-governor, he received his instructions from the Colonial Office and reported directly to it.

9 *Chronicle and Gazette*, 3 Aug. 1839. There was a rumour that Hastings was to become Hagerman District, which the editor denied, saying it 'must be the invention of the "Responsible" journals.'

10 See Robert Saunders, 'What Was the Family Compact?' *Ontario History* 49, no. 4 (1957), 165–78.

11 J.H. Aitchison, 'The Courts of Requests in Upper Canada,' in Johnson, ed., *Historical Essays on Upper Canada*, 90

12 Both men had fought in the American Revolutionary War, and Ferguson, after establishing himself as a merchant in Kingston, had urged Bell to come to Canada. He continued to advise Bell in military matters for many years.

13 NA, M 210,000796–9, William Bell Papers, John Ferguson to William Bell, 29 Nov. 1798

14 HCHS archives, Thomas Coleman Papers

15 Mills, *The Idea of Loyalty in Upper Canada, 1784–1850*, 8. Rogers probably meant 'American' in the sense of 'North American,' in the way the British sometimes used the word.

16 NA, Provincial Secretary's Correspondence, Canada West, RG 5, C1, vol. 7, 3779–83, John McCuaig to lieutenant-governor, Picton, 13 Aug. 1837

17 Ibid., 38122–5, Edward Beeston to lieutenant-governor, Hallowell, 18 Aug. 1837. Hallowell and Picton were at that time separate villages, both now included in Picton.

18 Sidney Township Records. In 1790 Leonard Soper was elected clerk, David Simmon constable, George Meyers and Caleb Gilbert path-masters, and Matthias Marsh and William Lownsbury fence viewers.

19 'Reminiscence of Mrs. White, of White's Mills, near Cobourg, Upper Canada, formerly Miss Catherine Chrysler of Sidney, near Belleville, Aged 79,' *Ontario Historical Society Papers and Records*, 7 (1906), 153

20 *Lord Durham's Report on the Affairs of British North America*, 2:219
21 Head, *A Narrative*, 215. Sir Francis stated that the population was 450,000 in 1837.
22 One-seventh of the land granted was to be held for the Church of England, which works out at a fraction close to one-eighth since a seventh was also held by the Crown, but this arithmetic was ignored and clergy reserves were one-seventh of the land, usually every seventh surveyed lot in a township.
23 *Correspondence of John Graves Simcoe*, 5:229
24 Ibid., 4:276–7. Huntingdon and Rawdon are in Hastings County; Loughborough is just above Kingston in Frontenac County; Murray is west of Sidney, across the Trent River in Northumberland County.
25 *Lord Durham's Report*, 2:224
26 Brian Osborne, 'Settlement of the Hinterland,' in Tulchinsky, ed., *To Preserve and Defend*, 67
27 *Lord Durham's Report*, 2:222
28 *Land Registrar* 5, no. 4 (Dec. 1980), 5
29 This was the agreement with the Canada Land Company, which was given 2.5 million acres to sell, paying a percentage to the Upper Canada government.
30 Brode, *Sir John Beverley Robinson*, 189
31 John S. Moir, 'The Upper Canada Religious Tradition,' in Hamil et al., eds., *Profiles of a Province*, 189–90
32 Diocesan Centre Archives, Ontario Diocese, Kingston. The plan was approved in 1819, and the church opened in 1821.
33 See Canniff, *The Settlement of Upper Canada*, 260–307 for the distribution of religious sects around the Bay of Quinte.
34 There are many indications of the popularity of Methodism in Hastings County, but comparative figures are hard to obtain for any period before 1840. The township records for that year show the following figures for the five largest religious groups in Hastings: Church of England – 2,058; Church of Scotland and Presbyterian – 1641; Roman Catholic – 1,734; Methodist (Wesleyan, Episcopal, other) – 3,137; Baptist – 757. By that time immigrants had changed the membership of churches. The most numerous were from Ireland, no doubt adding more in proportion to the Roman Catholic and Presbyterian congregations than there would have been in the 1830s and earlier.
35 *Correspondence of John Graves Simcoe*, 1:32, Simcoe to Henry Dundas, 30 June 1791
36 Ibid., 3:91, Bishop Jacob Mountain to Henry Dundas, 15 Sept. 1794
37 'Reminiscence of ... Catherine Chrysler of Sidney,' 153

38 *Correspondence of John Graves Simcoe*, Simcoe to Henry Dundas, 28 April 1792

39 PAO, *Journals of the Legislative Assembly*, 1812, 7th Report, 16

40 Ibid., 1816, 9th Report, 297-9. Sir Francis Gore had spent most of his time on leave in England.

41 Phillips, *The Development of Education in Canada*, 112

42 Queen's University Archives, Alves Papers, Alexander Alves to his father, 1 Nov. 1834

43 See Carol Lawrie Vaughn, 'The Bank of Upper Canada in Politics 1817–1840,' *Ontario History* 60, no. 4 (1969), 185–204.

44 *Kingston Chronicle*, 22 Sept. 1818

45 His name for the church brought some criticism. There were those who said he had named it St Thomas Coleman.

46 Diocesan Centre Archives, Ontario Diocese, Kingston, Belleville records, St Thomas Church, 15 April 1819. Coleman's name reappears, however, as a warden on 24 July 1821.

47 Armstrong, *Handbook of Upper Canadian Chronology*, 30

48 Jameson, *Winter Studies*, 2:220

49 NA, RG 5, A1, 32063–5, George Medley to lieutenant-governor, Loughborough, 26 April 1819

CHAPTER 2 The Lines Are Drawn

1 Milani, *Robert Gourlay*, 102. Others were being treated more liberally. Charles Fothergill arrived in the country at the same time as Gourlay. Although he was not a farmer but an ornithologist and publisher, the surveyor general held up other applications until Fothergill had decided on a location; he was already in possession of 1,200 acres near Cobourg when Gourlay held one of his township meetings there. He printed a pamphlet condemning Gourlay.

2 *Kingston Gazette*, 17 Mar. 1817

3 This was probably a misspelling of Moses Moss, who owned land in Sidney.

4 Gourlay, *A Statistical Account of Upper Canada*, 1:470–97

5 *Kingston Chronicle and Gazette*, 16 June 1818

6 Milani, *Robert Gourlay*, 155

7 Ibid., 145

8 *Chronicle and Gazette*, 16 June 1818

9 Gourlay, *A Statistical Account of Upper Canada*, 2:615–20

10 Goldie, *Diary of a Journey through Upper Canada and Some of the New England States 1819*, 22

11 NA, M 210, William Bell Papers, Pat Strange to William Bell, York, 28 June 1818
12 Strachan, *Documents and Opinions*, 68
13 New, *Lord Durham's Mission to Canada*, 95
14 R.G. Riddell, 'Egerton Ryerson's Views on the Government of Upper Canada in 1836,' *Canadian Historical Review* 19 (1938), 403
15 See James Rea, 'Barnabas Bidwell: A Note on the American Years,' *Ontario History* 60, no. 2 (1968), 31–58.
16 After the war immigration from the United States was actively discouraged. Under Governor Francis Gore the oath of allegiance could not be administered to Americans, which meant they could not own land.
17 See Brode, *Sir John Beverley Robinson*, 126–9, 135–7; Gerald M. Craig, *Upper Canada: The Formative Years*, 114–23, 188–9.
18 HCHS Archives, Thomas Coleman papers
19 The proposals back and forth among the Colonial Office, the legislative council, and the assembly repeatedly dropped into a morass of legal questions. The bill that was enacted recognized as citizens all who had come into the country before 1820, as well as those who had received land grants, held any public office, or taken the oath of allegiance. (All militiamen took the oath.) Anyone who entered the country after 1820 could be naturalized after seven years upon taking the oath.
20 Dent, *The Story of the Upper Canadian Rebellion*, 1:108
21 Head, *A Narrative*, 60
22 Lindsey, *William Lyon Mackenzie*, 1:40
23 Altogether he was expelled five times.
24 See Robert Saunders, 'What Was the Family Compact?' *Ontario History* 49, no. 4 (1957), 165–78.
25 *Chronicle and Gazette*, 25 Oct. 1837
26 *Oxford Dictionary of Quotations*, 2d ed. The lines come from an egalitarian and revolutionary sermon by John Ball at Blackheath in 1381. This was at the outbreak of Wat Tyler's Rebellion (the Peasants' Revolt).
27 Canniff, *The Settlement of Upper Canada*, 571–2. As well as those named by Canniff a bill of sale exists for a female slave owned by the Finkle family.
28 Morton, *The Kingdom of Canada*, 222
29 Moodie, *Roughing It in the Bush*, 31. Mrs Moodie wrote, 'I was not a little amused at the extravagant expectations of some of our steerage passengers.' Mrs Moodie was always acutely aware of class differences.
30 Strachan, *Documents and Opinions*, 22–3
31 Brode, *Sir John Beverley Robinson*, 24–5

32 Romney, *Mr. Attorney*, 144–5; Brode, *Sir John Beverley Robinson*, 220
33 *Dictionary of Canadian Biography*, 5:167–72
34 Ibid., 7:156–60
35 Ibid., 7:583–5
36 Ibid., 7:365–72
37 S.F. Wise, 'John Macaulay: A Tory for All Seasons,' in Tulchinsky, ed., *To Preserve and Defend*, 185–202
38 *Dictionary of Canadian Biography*, 7:363–72
39 Jameson, *Winter Studies*, 1:150
40 This petition to the Colonial Office was sent to parliament for an 1836 debate on Canada, but the debate was not covered in *Hansard*; nor has the petition itself been located.
41 CO 42/413, RC 2205, 312
42 Ibid. 307–10. The 'sectarian party' was of course the Church of England and the 'respectable denomination' the Methodist Church. Colborne had made an insulting reply to a Methodist address.

CHAPTER 3 A Slow Fuse

1 NA, Township Records, RG 5, B26, vol. 21; *Arthur Papers*, 2:138–9, 1839. There are no accurate figures for the county at this time, but in 1836 Sidney, the most settled township, reported a population of 2,768. According to the 1839 report to Arthur, the Hastings population was 12,000.
2 PAO, Crown Lands Papers, General Correspondence of the Surveyor General, 15 Jan. 1834, Trent Port. Other names on the petition were John Grier, J. Brooks Crowe, William Robertson, John Murphy, Robert Potts, M.D. Curran, Jacob Ford, and Denis Macaulay.
3 *Kingston Chronicle and Gazette*, 15 Jan. 1831
4 Guillet, *The Valley of the Trent*, 242
5 Rolph, *Descriptive and Statistical Account of Canada*, 137. Rolph described Belleville as 'a neat village but too much addicted to lumbering.'
6 Boyce, *Historic Hastings*, 63
7 *Chronicle and Gazette*, 5 May and 16 Sept. 1837
8 *Chronicle and Gazette*, 1 Feb. 1837. The proposed mill is also mentioned in Rolph, *Statistical Account of Canada*, 154.
9 Billa Flint's practice of sometimes, but not always, adding 'Jr.' to his name has caused some confusion, making it seem that there were two Billa Flints in Hastings County. Local historians, however, are well acquainted with his career, in milling, mining, and trading, in the affairs of the Methodist Church

(including temperance societies and Sunday schools), in education, and in politics. He had one adopted son, J.J.B. Flint.

10 Mary Quayle Innis, 'The Industrial Development of Ontario,' in Johnson, ed., *Historical Essays on Upper Canada*, 142. The author thought this was probably the first such mill since weaving was usually done at home.

11 The bank had closed for a time because of a shortage of capital resulting from misappropriation of funds.

12 PAO, Wallbridge Papers, MS 93, William Wallbridge to Marianne Howard, Belleville, Mar. 1838

13 Jameson, *Winter Studies*, 2:220

14 Read and Stagg, eds., *The Rebellion of 1837 in Upper Canada*, fn., 43–4

15 CO 42/471, 203, James Macaulay's report to Sir George Arthur, 1841

16 Boyce, *Hutton of Hastings*, 46–7

17 CO 42/471, 203, James Macaulay's report, 1841

18 Haight, *Life in Canada Fifty Years Ago*, 19

19 William Riddell, 'An Old Provincial Newspaper,' *Ontario History* 19 (1922), 140–1. The newspaper was the *Plain Speaker*, afterwards published in Belleville.

20 Lawrence Kitzan, 'The London Missionary Society in Upper Canada,' *Ontario History* 59, no. 1 (1967), 40

21 NA, Me 24, B35, Henry Yager Papers, William Holmes to Henry Yager, MLA, 3 April 1835

22 *Arthur Papers*, no. 185, James Macaulay's report to Sir George Arthur, 1838

23 Moodie, *Roughing It in the Bush*, 182

24 Steamboats had transformed the movement of goods and people along the lakes. By this time they were fairly numerous on Lake Ontario, the first having been launched in 1817 at Ernestown. See Innis, 'The Industrial Development of Ontario,' in Johnson, ed., *Historical Essays on Upper Canada*, 145.

25 Guillet, *Early Life in Upper Canada*, 559

26 *Kingston Chronicle*, 10 Mar. and 17 Mar. 1832; *Chronicle and Gazette*, 16 April 1836

27 This may have been because of ill health since Samson died a few months later – 'of excessive drinking,' according to William Wallbridge.

28 NA, Mg 24, B35, 0000021–3, Henry Yager Papers, Stephen Benson to Henry Yager, 20 Mar. 1835

29 Ibid., 0000032, 2 April 1835. The constitutional societies were organized in opposition to the political unions.

30 Dunham, *Political Unrest in Upper Canada*, 10, quoting Sir John Colborne.

31 Simcoe had first proposed such a university, and the next governor, Sir

Peregrine Maitland, thought it a political necessity. Although it met with furious opposition in Upper Canada, such a university would have been on the English model.

32 Elizabeth Cooper, 'Religion, Politics, and Money: The Methodist Union of 1832–1833,' *Ontario History* 81, no. 2 (1989), 104. During the 1836 election campaign the *Guardian* did take a political stance to the extent of opposing the Reform candidates.

33 See R.G. Riddell, 'Egerton Ryerson's Views on the Government of Upper Canada in 1836,' *Canadian Historical Review* 19 (1938), 403. Ryerson was in many ways a conservative and distrustful of democracy.

34 The Waterloo Circuit included Kingston.

35 Sissons, *Egerton Ryerson*, 1:242

36 Egerton Ryerson, 'Methodist Chapel Property Case, Report of the Trial of an Action brought by John Reynolds and others on the part of persons calling themselves "The Methodist Episcopal Church in Canada" against Billa Flint, Jun., & Others, Trustees of the Wesleyan Chapel in the Possession of the Latter in the Town of Belleville Tried at the Assizes Held in Kingston, October 11th 1837 before Mr. Justice Jones with brief notes and remarks by E. Ryerson,' United Church Archives, Pam Bx 8253 B44 M47

37 The unionists won on appeal. As a result of the union and the resistance to it, two Methodist congregations continued almost side by side, the union church becoming today's Bridge Street United and the Episcopalian, Tabernacle United Church.

38 Sissons, *Egerton Ryerson*, 1:392

39 NA, Benson Papers, MG 211, 1918, C.O. Benson to John Benson, Belleville, 31 Mar. 1837

40 The nomination for McNabb was seconded by R. Davies, that of Reynolds by B. Clapp.

41 *Chronicle and Gazette*, 2 April 1836

42 Metropolitan Toronto Reference Library, Baldwin Room, *Public Document Relating to the Late Changes in the Executive Council* [pamphlet], 1836

43 This meant that the legislature would not pass any money bills.

44 *Chronicle and Gazette*, 16 April 1836, from the *Belleville Intelligencer,* n.d.

45 Peter O'Reilly was a Belleville magistrate. Nelson Reynolds was the son of the Methodist Episcopal bishop and also a magistrate.

46 *Chronicle and Gazette*, 23 April 1836. William Robertson and J. Brooks Crowe were two of the founders of Trent Port.

47 Thompson, *Reminiscences of a Canadian Pioneer*, 82

48 *Chronicle and Gazette*, 6 July 1836

49 CO 42/437, Dr Duncombe's report to the Colonial Office on the 1836 election

50 Bruce Walton, 'The Election of 1836 in Lennox and Addington,' *Ontario History* 67, no. 3 (1975), 153–67

51 See Akenson, *The Orangeman*, chapter 1. Although Dr Akenson has written this as fictional biography, he has based it on historical fact. See 'A Note on Sources' at the end of the book.

52 See Wilfred Kerr, 'When Orange and Green United, 1832–1839,' *Ontario History* 34 (1942), 34–42.

53 HCHS files, letter from Royal Orange Grand Lodge, Ottawa, to Mr W.C. Mikel, K.C., 9 April 1934

54 *Chronicle and Gazette*, 7 April 1836

55 Buckner, *The Transition to Responsible Government*, 62

56 *Arthur Papers*, no.679, J.B. Robinson to Arthur, 4 Mar. 1839

57 For a description of the extent of poverty in Upper Canada and the institutionalization of charity and relief, see Rainer Baehre, 'Paupers and Poor Relief in Upper Canada,' in Johnson and Wilson, eds., *Historical Essays on Upper Canada: New Perspectives*, 305–39.

58 *Kingston Spectator*, reprinted in the *Constitution*, 29 Nov. 1837

59 Jameson, *Winter Studies*, 1:99

CHAPTER 4 Explosion

1 Joseph Lockwood was arrested after the rebellion because his name had been found 'on one of Mackenzie's lists, the others having been torn away.' Most likely this was a list made at the Thurlow meeting.

2 Ironically, a notice by Mackenzie that this convention was slated for 19 December appeared in the *Chronicle and Gazette* for 9 December, the issue which carried news of the rebellion in Toronto.

3 Support for such a union was general among the merchant class in Lower Canada, but was by no means universal in Upper Canada. It nevertheless had strong advocates, such as the Kingston *Chronicle and Gazette*, which ran a series of editorials on it during October 1837. One good reason was to ensure a better share of the duties on goods coming into the country. The greater part of the imports were destined for Upper Canada, but Lower Canada kept most of the tariffs.

4 Ouellet, *Lower Canada 1791–1840*, 277

5 A handful of officers and men did remain in Upper Canada on what might be called custodial duty; for instance, at Fort Henry in Kingston.

6 Reprinted in the *Chronicle and Gazette*, 1 Nov. 1837

7 Ibid., 11 Nov. 1837

8 Ibid., 1 Nov. 1837

9 Strickland, *Twenty-Seven Years in Canada West*, 259

10 Moodie, *Roughing It in the Bush*, 210

11 NA, Merritt Family Papers, Correspondence of W.H. Merritt, vol.13, 002031–4, Catherine Merritt to Dr Jediah Prendergast, St Catharines, 8 Dec. 1837, quoted in Read and Stagg, eds., *The Rebellion of 1837*, 314–15

12 Metropolitan Toronto Reference Library, Baldwin Room. This was in the proclamation issued by Sir Francis Bond Head and sent by courier to inform the Queen's loyal subjects of the rebellion, call the militia to come to the defence of the government, and offer rewards for the capture of rebel leaders: £1,000 for Mackenzie, £500 for David Gibson, Jesse Lloyd, Samuel Lount, and Silas Fletcher.

13 The *Constitution*, 29 Nov. 1837; reported in the *Chronicle and Gazette*, 6 Dec. 1837

14 Lindsey, *William Lyon Mackenzie*, 2:358–62

15 *Chronicle and Gazette*, 9 Dec. 1837

16 James Fitzgibbon, 'A Narrative of Occurrences in Toronto Upper Canada in 1837,' Metropolitan Toronto Reference Library, Baldwin Room

CHAPTER 5 The Gallant Militia

1 NA, Adjutant General's Correspondence, RG 9, IB1, vol. 22, Hastings file, Coleman to Bullock, Belleville, 19 Oct. 1837

2 Jameson, *Winter Studies*, 1:300–2

3 Others are to be found in Guillet, *Early Life in Upper Canada*, 345–8, and in Lizars, *Humours of '37, Grave, Gay and Grim*, 95–7.

4 Grey, *Crisis in the Canadas*, 73, Grey to his father, 12 July 1838

5 Jameson, *Winter Studies*, 1:81

6 Fryer, *Volunteers and Redcoats*, 26

7 This may have been Fitzgibbon or, possibly, Col Nathaniel Coffin, the adjutant general. Most of those in authority were still unconvinced of the need for arming the militia.

8 Bonnycastle, *Canada As It Was*, 2:281; NA, RG 5, A1, vol. 180, 00055–9, R.H. Bonnycastle to J. Joseph, Kingston, 7 and 8 Dec. 1837

9 *Kingston Chronicle and Gazette*, 6 Dec. 1837

10 Bonnycastle, *Canada As It Was*, 2:281

11 NA, Rebellion Losses Claims, MF 89 Has, Culbertson claim

12 NA, RG 5, C1, vol. 9, 4949–51, Anthony Manahan to Col. James Fitzgibbon, Belleville, 11 Dec. 1837

13 Not only were the Mohawks long-time allies of the British and among the first UELs to land in the Quinte area, they were well aware of the Indian

Wars the Americans were waging. For obvious reasons the blacks in Canada were equally afraid of the Americans and turned out in large numbers to serve in the militia.

14 *Chronicle and Gazette,* 27 Dec. 1837, letter dated Belleville, 18 Dec. 1837, reprinted from the *Upper Canada Herald*

15 Culbertson was a cousin of Joseph Brant. Although Manahan gave him the title, it is not certain that John Culbertson was the chief of the band. Obviously he occupied a prominent position.

16 NA, RG 5, C1, vol. 9, 4949–51, Anthony Manahan to Col James Fitzgibbon, Belleville, 11 Dec. 1837

17 Ibid., 4960–1, Edmund Murney to J. Joseph, Belleville, 12 Dec. 1837

18 *Chronicle and Gazette,* 9 Dec. 1837

19 *Cobourg Star,* 27 Dec. 1837. The orders are dated Colborne, 16 Dec. 1838.

20 NA, RG 5, A1, vol. 180, 99280–3, Col Henry Ruttan to Col James Fitzgibbon, Colborne, 10 Dec. 1837

21 Ibid., 99277–9, 12 Dec. 1837

22 Ibid., 99274–6, 14 Dec. 1837

23 NA, RG 5, C1, vol. 28, Lt Col John S. Cartwright to Col Richard Bullock, Toronto, 4 Jan. 1838

24 Ibid., vol. 22, John McCuaig to Col James Fitzgibbon, Picton, 16 Dec. 1837

25 *Chronicle and Gazette,* 23 Dec. 1837

26 NA, RG 5, C1, vol. 22, Col Thomas Coleman to Col James Fitzgibbon, Belleville Park, 14 Dec. 1837

27 Bonnycastle, *Canada As It Was,* 2:105

28 HCHS Archives, Deposition of James Whiteman, n.d.

29 NA, RG 5, A1, vol. 210, 115634–6, general orders, Toronto, 22 Nov. 1838

30 Rolph, *Statistical Account of Canada,* 157. The village was Killarney.

31 It is uncertain when the Hastings men reached Cobourg. The Prince Edward contingent got there about 7 Jan. 1838, but the men who had gathered in Cobourg had moved on to Toronto the week after the uprising.

32 PAO, Macaulay Family Papers, MS 78, R3, Ann Macaulay to Helen Macaulay, Picton, 16 Jan. 1838

33 Guillet, *Early Life in Upper Canada,* 34–9

34 *Chronicle and Gazette,* 13 Dec. 1837

35 Bonnycastle, *Canada As It Was,* 2:105

36 Uniforms were not issued to militiamen in peacetime, and even during the rebellion there were not always enough for the men who were serving.

37 Creighton, *John A. Macdonald: The Young Politician,* 60; J.K. Johnson, 'Sir James Gowan, Sir John A. Macdonald, and the Rebellion of 1837,' *Ontario History* 60, no. 2 (1968), 61–4. Macdonald had been on the march to Mont-

gomery's Tavern: 'Philip Low [brother of the John Low who was a magistrate in Belleville] of Picton and I marched shoulder to shoulder.' During the week of the rebellion he was in the Commercial Bank Guard Company in Toronto.

38 *Chronicle and Gazette*, 20 Dec. 1837

39 Ibid., 3 Jan. 1838

40 Ibid., 30 June 1838

41 Ibid., 13 Dec. 1837

42 Ibid., 20 Dec. 1837

43 NA, RG 5, C1, vol. 9, 5525, Geo. Benjamin to John Joseph, Belleville, 19 Dec. 1837

44 *Arthur Papers*, no. 300, De Rottenburg to assistant commissary general, Government House, Toronto, 26 Oct. 1838

45 PAO, Wallbridge Papers, MS 93, William Wallbridge to Marianne Howard, Belleville, April 1838

46 PAO, Baird Papers, MS 393, A-6-a, correspondence, Nov. 1838

47 NA, Adjutant General's Correspondence, RG 9, IB1, vol. 28, Col Murchison to adjutant general, Tyendinaga, 23 Jan. 1838; Maj. John Blacker to adjutant general, Shannonville, 3 April 1838

48 Ibid., Col Fraser to adjutant general, Ernest Town, 9 Sept. 1838

49 Ibid., Cornet W.J. Fairfield to Col Fraser, Bath, 23 Aug. 1838. A cornet was the fifth officer in a cavalry troop, so called because he carried the banner or cornet.

50 Ibid., vol. 22, Col Coleman to Capt. McNabb, Belleville, 8 Dec. 1837

51 Ibid., vol. 28, Maj. Ketcheson to adjutant general, Belleville, 17 Jan. 1838

52 John Langton to Hugh Hornby, Blythe, 20 Feb. 1838, in Langton, *A Gentlewoman in Upper Canada*, 66

53 HCHS Archives, Bowen file

CHAPTER 6 Pirates and Brigands

1 Lindsey, *William Lyon Mackenzie*, 2:123–8

2 *Arthur Papers*, no. 220, H.S. Fox to Arthur, Washington, 26 June 1838

3 Allan MacNab was a lawyer, member of the assembly, and speaker of the house after the election of 1836. He made a fortune in land and, later, in railway speculation, enabling him to build the house in Hamilton called Dundurn Castle.

4 NA, RG 5, C1, 1284, Capt. Drew to Admiralty, 1 Jan. 1839. The Canadians had at least one casualty since Captain Drew appealed for compensation to militiaman MacCornish, who had been seriously wounded 'at the taking of the Caroline.'

5 Grey, *Crisis in the Canadas*, 73

6 Strickland, *Twenty-Seven Years*, 259
7 A complete account of the Duncombe Rising is to be found in Read, *The Rising in Western Upper Canada*.
8 Lindsey, *William Lyon Mackenzie*, 2:135
9 Read, *The Rising in Western Upper Canada*, 116–17
10 Ibid., 122
11 Ibid., 123
12 Bonnycastle, *Canada As It Was*, 79
13 NA, RG 5, C1, vol. 9, 5339, A.F. Atkinson to lieutenant-governor, St. John's Church Parsonage, Bath, 27 Dec. 1837
14 According to a letter in the *Chronicle and Gazette* of 27 Mar. 1838, Parker had been for many years a resident of Kingston, where he was a general storekeeper, known as Honest John G. He had held a commission in the First Frontenac Militia Regiment.
15 NA, RG 5, A1, vol. 180, 99380–2, Anthony Manahan to J. Joseph, Belleville, 16 Dec. 1837
16 Different names were used over the years for these officers. Commissioner is similar to the modern councillor; and moderator, to reeve.
17 This church is still remembered for it stood at Bayside on No. 2 Highway until it was demolished in 1970.
18 NA, RG 5, A1, vol. 180, 99380–2, Anthony Manahan to J. Joseph, Belleville, 16 Dec. 1837
19 It is not clear why it was two non-resident magistrates who arrested a Belleville man and placed him under house arrest.
20 NA, RG 5, C1, vol. 9, 5244, John Macaulay to Thomas Parker, Kingston, 19 Dec. 1837
21 Ibid., 5245, George Ridley to Daniel Perry, Belleville, 23 Dec. 1837
22 Ibid., 5242–3, Thomas Parker to Anthony Manahan, Belleville, 23 Dec. 1837
23 Ibid., 5256, John Macaulay to John Joseph, Kingston, 22 Dec. 1837
24 PAO, Mackenzie-Lindsey Papers, Correspondence, Clifton McCollom to W.L. Mackenzie, Johnstown, Montgomery Twsp, NY, 30 Jan. 1838
25 NA, RG 1, L3, vol. 556, Leases and Licenses, 1798–1839/128 MG9 88–12
26 NA, RG 5, A1, vol. 180, 99495–506, Paul Glasford to J. Joseph, Brockville, 19 Dec. 1837, enclosing letter of Billa Flint, Jr., to magistrates of Brockville, 15 Dec. 1837, Belleville, and Examination of Peter Robinson of Belleville by Brockville magistrates, Brockville, 18 Dec. 1837
27 NA, RG 5, C1, vol. 9, 5249, Thomas Parker to Anthony Manahan, Belleville, 19 Dec. 1837
28 NA, RG 5, A1, vol. 180, 99498, Examination of Peter Robertson, Brockville, 18 Dec. 1837
29 Ibid., vol. 181, 100303, the Queen vs. Peter Robertson, deposition of Thomas

Newton. Robertson appeared before Thomas Parker, Henry Baldwin, George Benjamin, Samuel and Elijah Ketcheson, Billa Flint, George Bleeker, Peter O'Reilly, Rufus Purdy, and Edward Fidlar.

30 PAO, Mackenzie-Lindsey Papers, Correpondence, S.C. Frey to W.L. Mackenzie, Morristown 4 Jan. 1838

31 NA, RG 5, A1, vol. 180, 99497, Billa Flint to J. Joseph, Belleville, 15 Dec. 1837

32 Ibid., vol. 181, 100094, Petition of Sundry inhabitants of Hastings on behalf of H. Baragan, 28 Dec. 1837

33 NA, RG 5, A1, vol. 189, 99520–2, Report of the Midland District School Board, 18 Dec. 1837

34 NA, RG 5, C1, vol. 22, Hastings file, 26 Dec. 1837, petition of various Belleville residents to adjutant general

35 NA, RG 5, C1, vol. 9, 5052–3, J. Allen Esq. to adjutant general, Allen's Mills, Marysburgh, 15 Dec. 1837. A further charge by Allen was that Dingman sold contraband from the United States, but it seems half the traders in the country could have been charged with the same offence. Tea was a notable instance. The East India Company had a monopoly on its sale, but this was so widely ignored it scarcely impinged on the tea trade across the lakes. Smuggled tea is said to have found its way into the houses of council members, and even of the governor.

36 *Kingston British Whig*, 3 April 1838

37 NA, RG5, C1, vol. 9, 1176, enclosure, Anthony Manahan to Col James Fitzgibbon Belleville, 11 Dec. 1837

38 NA, RG 5, A 1, vol. 180, 99874–7, enclosed with Alexander Pringle to J. Joseph, Kingston, 28 Dec. 1837

CHAPTER 7 The Bloodless Battle

1 NA, Rebellion Losses Claims, MF 89 Has, no. 79

2 Some have attributed the name of the Hunters Lodges to him, although it is more likely to be an equivalent of *les chasseurs*, the name adopted by escaped rebels from the lower province.

3 NA, RG 5, A1, vol. 181, 99966–7, George Benjamin to John Joseph, enclosing copy of affidavit, Belleville, 27 Dec. 1837. The affidavit includes the statement that 'the leading person at French Creek is one Johnson, the man who robbed the mail in the last war.' This was Bill Johnston, to the Patriots an admiral, to the Canadian loyalists a pirate.

4 Lindsey, *William Lyon Mackenzie*, 2:181. Mackenzie put a notice in the Watertown papers on 17 Feb. 1838 asking his friends 'to withdraw all confidence from him [Van Rensselaer] in matters connected with Canada.'

5 *Kingston Chronicle and Gazette*, 21 Feb. 1838

6 Ibid., 25 Feb. 1838

7 Bonnycastle, *Canada As It Was*, 2:80

8 Lindsey, *William Lyon Mackenzie*, 182; Le Sueur, *William Lyon Mackenzie: A Reinterpretation*, 334. According to Le Sueur, Mackenzie had done more than correspond, he had made a daring visit to the Canadian shore near Bath in order, presumably, to talk to those who would take part in the sabotage.

9 Bonnycastle, *Canada As It Was*, 2:89

10 *Chronicle and Gazette*, 19 Mar. 1838. The find was on Daniel Perry's farm.

11 Ibid, 2 Mar. 1838

12 This copy of the *Intelligencer* is one of the few issues that have survived from the 1830s. A photostat of it is on file in the Hastings County Historical Society archives.

13 HCHS archives. This account exists only as a photocopy of an undated cutting from the *Intelligencer*. It was probably written in the 1880s.

14 NA, RG 5, A1, vol. 185, 104216–9, William Turnbull to John Joseph, Belleville, 24 Feb. 1838. Although the order to go to Kingston had been sent to Turnbull, it seems by his report that it was McAnnany who led the Rifle Company on their march.

15 NA, RG 9, IB1, vol. 28, Billa Flint to adjutant general, Belleville, 26 Mar. 1838

16 Ibid., vol. 27, Absalom Day to John Macaulay, Portland, 24 May 1838

17 Ibid., John Ashley to Alexander Pringle, Kingston, 21 April 1838

18 Ibid., John Macaulay to Col Bullock, Kingston, 30 April 1838

19 Ibid., Alexander Pringle to John Macaulay, Kingston, 25 April 1838

20 Ibid., John Macaulay to Col Bullock, Kingston, 30 April 1838

CHAPTER 8 Danger round the Bay

1 See Francis Paul Pruchka, ed., 'Reports of General Brady on the Patriot War,' *Canadian Historical Review* 31 (1950), 56–68, and William D. Overman, 'A Sidelight on the Hunters' Lodges of 1838,' *Canadian Historical Review* 19 (1938), 168–72.

2 *Kingston Chronicle and Gazette*, 2 Mar. 1838, unattributed letter to Bishop Macdonnell from Sandwich, dated 21 Feb.

3 *Arthur Papers*, no. 153, T.W. McGrath to John Maitland, Brantford, 1 May 1838

4 Peter Matthews's father, Thomas, had lived in Marysburgh and in Sidney before moving to Pickering Township, where he married Mary Ruttan. He held two Crown grants in Sidney.

5 Sir George Arthur was governor of the prison colony of Van Diemen's Land

(Tasmania) at the time of his appointment. He arrived in Canada in March 1838.

6 M'Leod, *A Brief Review of the Settlement of Upper Canada*, 242–3. Perhaps all of them came from the Midland District, as M'Leod said, but Bill Johnston was believed to be in charge.

7 Read, *The Rising in Western Upper Canada*, 137–8, 150

8 Durham had introduced an earlier reform bill which parliament defeated. The 1832 bill was passed by parliament but became law only after mass meetings and some riots persuaded the House of Lords to give way; when the demonstrations continued, the king finally had to admit defeat. Durham was known in the popular press as Radical Jack.

9 *Chronicle and Gazette*, 1 Aug. 1838

10 He was the man whose letters to Henry Lasher, John Vincent, and Augustus Thibodeau had brought about their arrest in December (see *Chronicle and Gazette*, 9 Dec. 1837).

11 Lindsey, *William Lyon Mackenzie*, 2:369, Appendix H

12 *Chronicle and Gazette*, 19 Sept. 1838

13 NA, RG 5, A1, vol. 195, 108521–2, deposition of Isaac Preston, corroborated by James and David Preston and sworn before J. McKay and Alexander Pringle, Isle of Tonti, 8 June 1838

14 Ibid., 108523, deposition of John Spring, sworn before Alexander Pringle, Kingston, 7 June 1838

15 Ibid., 108524, deposition of David Tait, sworn before G. Baker, J.P., Midland District, 7 June 1838

16 Ibid., 108506–7, W.G. McKay to Bonnycastle, Bath, 7 June 1838

17 Ibid., 108526–30, petition of magistrates to John Joseph, Belleville, 11 June 1838

18 *Arthur Papers*, no. 477, C.C. Domvile to Col George, Baron De Rottenburg, Toronto, 20 Nov. 1838

19 *Arthur Papers*, no. 237, Arthur to Colborne, 5 July 1838

20 Ibid.

21 PAO, Mackenzie-Lindsey Papers, McCollom to W.L. Mackenzie, Oswego, 19 July 1838

22 *Cobourg Plain Speaker*, 17 July 1838, quoting the *Kingston British Whig*

23 *Chronicle and Gazette*, 7 and 11 July 1838

24 Ibid., 4 Mar. 1838

25 There is no record of the number who were arrested and detained locally, and the list of those sent to the district jail or Fort Henry is not complete. Several Hastings men not on the list later claimed compensation under the Rebellion Losses Bill for such incarceration.

26 See chapter 10.

27 PAO, Mackenzie-Lindsey Papers, McCollom to W.L. Mackenzie, Oswego, 17 July 1838

CHAPTER 9 Excitement at Belleville

1 PAO, Wallbridge Family Papers, MS 93, William Wallbridge to Marianne Howard, Belleville, 24 Jan. 1838

2 *Arthur Papers*, no. 139, private letter, Arthur to Colborne, Toronto, 25 April 1838

3 NA, Moodie-Strickland-Vickers-Ewing Family Papers, John Moodie to Susanna Moodie, Belleville, 24 May 1838. This letter greatly exaggerated the local situation, for residents of Scotch background had been prominent in various positions over the years, some of them as magistrates.

4 CO 42/439, Lord Glenelg to Sir Francis Head, London, 24 Nov. 1837

5 PAO, Macaulay Family Papers, MS 78, R3, John Macaulay to Ann Macaulay, Toronto, 16 Jan. 1838; Ann Macaulay to John, Picton, 20 Jan. 1838

6 The union of Wesleyan and Episcopal Methodists ended in 1840. Ryerson's article was no doubt a sign that the union was already in trouble since it could not have pleased the government or, presumably, the Wesleyans.

7 PAO, Macaulay Family Papers, MS 78, R3, John Macaulay to Ann Macaulay, Toronto, 31 Mar. and 31 Aug. 1838

8 NA, Moodie Family Papers, John Moodie to Susanna Moodie, Belleville, 24 Nov. 1839

9 *Christian Guardian*, 19 Dec. 1838

10 Ibid., 30 Jan. 1839

11 Rev. William Proudfoot to an unidentified commissioner of the United Associated Synod, London, 14 Aug. 1838, quoted in Read and Stagg, eds., *The Rebellion of 1837*, 422

12 Rev. James Marr to Rev. Absalom Peters, St Thomas, 5 July 1838, quoted in Read and Stagg, eds., *The Rebellion of 1837*, 421 and fn.

13 *Kingston Chronicle and Gazette*, quoting the *British Whig*, 7 July 1838

14 Doctors had to come from outside the country since there was as yet no Canadian medical academy. The nearest academies were in the northeastern States. James Murdoch was a clergyman who seems to have belonged to a branch of Presbyterians based in the United States.

15 PAO, Macaulay Family Papers, MS 78, R3, John Macaulay to John Kirby, Toronto, 1 May 1838; Ann Macaulay to John Macaulay, Picton, 7 Oct. 1838. Added to the Patriot troubles was the Maine–New Brunswick border dispute, bringing renewed American threats of war.

16 NA, Moodie Family Papers, John Moodie to Susanna Moodie, Belleville, 24 April 1839
17 R.S. Longley, 'Emigration and the Crisis of 1837 in Upper Canada,' *Canadian Historical Review* 17 (1936), 34
18 Ibid., quoting *Brockville Recorder*, 26 July 1838
19 *Kingston Spectator*, 13 July 1838, quoted in Read and Stagg, eds., *The Rebellion of 1837*, 420–1
20 Longley, 'Emigration and the Crisis of 1837 in Upper Canada,' 35–6
21 Watson Kirkconnell, *Victoria County Centennial History* (1921), 94–5, quoted in Guillet, *Early Life in Upper Canada*, 763
22 PAO, Mackenzie-Lindsey Papers, C.H. McCollom to W.L. Mackenzie, Ogdensburg, NY, 7 Mar. 1839
23 Harrison, *Early Victorian Britain*, 34
24 Burroughs, *The Colonial Reformers and Canada*, xxvi, 125–6
25 Brode, *Sir John Beverley Robinson*, 91
26 *Chronicle and Gazette*, 24 Mar. 1838. This was in the report of a British parliamentary debate on Canada which had taken place in January.
27 M.L. Magill, 'John H. Dunn and the Bankers,' in Johnson, ed., *Historical Essays on Upper Canada*, 83–100
28 *Arthur Papers*, no. 138, John Macaulay to Christopher Hagerman, Toronto, 31 April 1838
29 PAO, Wallbridge Family Papers, MS 93, William Wallbridge to Marianne Howard, Belleville, 28 Feb. 1838
30 Ibid., 6 May and November 1838. Flint's luck did not so easily run out, however, and by November he was back in business, 'stronger than ever.'
31 *Arthur Papers*, no. 357, Arthur to Colborne, Kingston, 14 Oct. 1838
32 Probably John Solomon Cartwright, son of Richard Cartwright. He was a magistrate, member of the assembly, and militia colonel. See *The Dictionary of Canadian Biography*, vol. 7
33 *Arthur Papers*, no. 362, Arthur to Colborne, Cobourg, 17 Oct. 1838
34 *Chronicle and Gazette*, 26 Oct. 1838
35 *Arthur Papers*, no. 429, Arthur to Colborne, Toronto, 8 Nov. 1838
36 CO 42, Q4 19 21 Seq 61, Major Warren to Col Halkett, assistant military secretary, Belleville, 26 Oct. 1838. It is signed 'Captain and Major commanding at Belleville.'
37 NA, RG 9, IB1, vol. 28, Col William Ketcheson to Col Bullock, Sidney, 9 July 1838
38 *Arthur Papers*, no. 523, De Rottenburg to Henry Dundas, Government House, 5 Nov. 1838
39 Ibid., no. 429, Arthur to Colborne, Toronto, 8 Nov. 1938

40 Ibid., no. 448, C.C. Domvile to Henry Dundas, Toronto, 1 Nov. 1838
41 Ibid., no. 357, Arthur to Colborne, Kingston, 14 Oct. 1838
42 Ibid., no. 523, De Rottenburg to Henry Dundas, Government House, 5 Nov. 1838
43 Ibid., no. 336, Colborne to Arthur, Sorel, 28 Sept. 1838
44 Anson Green to Egerton Ryerson, 16 Nov. 1838, quoted in Guillet, *Early Life in Upper Canada*, 672
45 *Arthur Papers*, no. 528, Arthur to Col H. Booth, Toronto, 8 Nov. 1838

CHAPTER 10 The Windmill

1 'Stewart Derbishire's Report to Lord Durham on Lower Canada, 1838,' *Canadian Historical Review* 18 (1937), 53
2 Grey, *Crisis in the Canadas*, 144, L'Acadie, 19 Dec. 1838
3 Ibid., 161, St Edwards, 13 Nov. 1838
4 NA, RG 5, B41, vol. 1, file 16, Upper Canada Courts Martial at Fort Henry, 1838–9, testimony of Jeremiah Winnegar; *Kingston Chronicle and Gazette*, 28 Nov. 1838
5 Sir Richard Bonnycastle, quoted in Innis and Lower, eds., *Select Documents in Canadian Economic History*, 2:126–7
6 NA, RG 5, B41, vols. 1–2, Military Courts Martial 1838–9 at Fort Henry
7 NA, RG 5, A1, vol. 209, 115122, John Cartwright to Hon. J. Macaulay, Kingston, 2 Nov. 1838
8 PAO, Mackenzie-Lindsey Papers, 2235, C.H. McCollom to W.L. Mackenzie, Oswego, 2 Nov. 1838
9 *Arthur Papers*, no. 351, De Rottenburg to Dundas, Belleville, 5 Nov. 1838
10 Tiffany, *The Relation of the United States to the Canadian Rebellion of 1837–1838*, 68; see also G.F.G. Stanley, 'Invasion: 1838 (Battle of the Windmill),' *Ontario History* 54, no. 4 (1962), 237–52.
11 PAO, Ogle R. Gowan Papers, MU 1147, Ogle Gowan to James, Brockville, 15 Dec. 1838. For a discussion of the results of the participation in this and other engagements of the rebellion by Ogle Gowan and the Protestant Irish, see Akenson, *The Irish in Ontario*, 196.
12 NA, RG 5, B41, vol. 1, file 2, general orders; *Chronicle and Gazette*, 5 Jan. 1839
13 Ibid., B40, Nils Von Schoultz, records re trial and execution of, 1838
14 Ibid., B41, file 16, Military Courts Martial 1838-9 at Fort Henry. This includes descriptions of the battle from the British officers' point of view. Verbatim reports of the trials were published in the *Chronicle and Gazette*.
15 Ibid., vol. 1, file 4, W.H. Draper to Sir George Arthur, Kingston, 27 Dec. 1838

16 *Arthur Papers*, no. 474, Arthur to Colborne, Government House, 20 Nov. 1838
17 See *The Wait Letters*. At least two prisoners escaped. Chandler and Wait from western Upper Canada were able to get on board a whaler in 1841 and eventually reached the United States.
18 See Mary Brown, Introduction, *The Wait Letters*; and Crowley, *Documentary History of Australia*, 1:488–9. Sir George Arthur is described in the latter as a governor who showed no mercy to prisoners.
19 PAO, Quarter Sessions Reports, Midland District. 24 April 1839
20 *Arthur Papers*, no. 458, Arthur to Durham, Toronto, 16 Nov. 1838. Arthur may have been deceived by Patriot propaganda, for the Patriots were never well drilled nor equipped with plenty of cannon. But he was pressing the point that he did not have enough men, certainly not enough with good military equipment, to defend the country against a serious invasion.
21 *Arthur Papers*, no. 444, Henry Dundas to Col John Blacker, Kingston, 11 Nov. 1838. The letter is addressed to Blacker as major of the Third Battalion of Hastings militia.
22 NA, RG 5, A1, vol. 210, 115499, John Cartwright to John Macaulay, 17 Nov. 1838
23 PAO, Lindsey-Mackenzie Papers, W.H. McCollom to W.L. Mackenzie, Oswego, 28 Dec. 1838
24 NA, RG 5, A1, vol. 214, 117158, deposition of William Embury, Thurlow
25 Ibid., 117158–9, deposition of John Grewey, Thurlow
26 Ibid., 117159–60, deposition of Abram Bogert, Thurlow
27 Ibid., B39, John Prince, records of inquiry into the conduct of, 1839
28 PAO, Wallbridge Family Papers, Lewis Wallbridge to Marianne Howard, Belleville, 28 Nov. 1838

CHAPTER 11 More Excitement at Belleville

1 Arthur Papers, no. 477, C.C. Domvile to Lt Col (George) Baron De Rottenburg, Government House, 20 Nov. 1838
2 Ibid, no. 512, Arthur to Colborne, Toronto, 30 Nov. 1838. De Rottenburg had reported the trouble in Prince Edward, but the need for Ruttan's intervention may have had something to do with the resentment Canadians often felt towards British officers.
3 Ibid., no. 389, Colborne to Arthur, Quebec, 26 Oct. 1838
4 Ibid., no. 429, Arthur to Colborne, Toronto, 8 Nov. 1838
5 Ibid., no. 458, Arthur to Durham, Toronto, 16 Nov. 1838
6 CO 42, C Series, vol. 611, 288–90, Warren to De Rottenburg, Brighton, 20 Oct. 1838

7 This refers to petitions presented to Arthur to save the lives of Lount and Matthews.

8 William Riddell, 'An Old Provincial Newspaper,' *Ontario History* 19, no. 2 (1922), 139–43

9 NA, RG 5, A1, vol. 209, 115156–7, Henry Baldwin to Lt C.C. Domvile, Belleville, 7 Nov. 1839

10 Later on he became the Rev. James Gardiner, a Methodist minister and a long-time resident of Belleville.

11 Herbert Fairbairn, 'The Night the "Plain Speaker's" Type Was Pied,' *Ontario History* 20, no. 1 (1923), 86–7; HCHS Archives, Gardiner file

12 NA, RG 5, C1, vol. 23, De Rottenburg to Arthur, Belleville, 27 Nov. 1838

13 Ibid., A1, vol. 209, Thomas Parker to John Macaulay, Belleville, 27 Nov. 1838

14 James Gardiner repaired the press as well as he could, and Mrs Hart tried to carry on with a Methodist paper, but circulation was not large enough to keep it going.

15 Percy and Seymour are townships in Northumberland County.

16 *Arthur Papers*, no. 508, C.C. Domvile to Lt Col De Rottenburg, Toronto, 28 Nov. 1838

17 NA, RG 5, A1, vol. 241, De Rottenburg to Maj. Gen. Sir George Arthur, Belleville, 24 Mar. 1840

18 *Arthur Papers*, no. 516, Arthur to Colborne, Toronto, 30 Nov. 1838

19 Several claims were filed later for extensive repair, or even rebuilding, of buildings used by the guard.

20 NA, MF 971.038 Has., 51, O'Carroll claim

21 Ibid.

22 Guillet, *Early Life in Upper Canada*, 674

23 These three men were well-known Reformers, and all three had been among those jailed earlier in the year, charged with treason. Their testimony may not have carried much weight with the court.

24 E.C. Guillet, 'The Cobourg Conspiracy,' *Canadian Historical Review* 18 (1937); *Cobourg Star*, 18 and 25 Sept. 1839

25 NA, RG 5, C1, vol. 881, 1691, Baron De Rottenburg to adjutant general, Belleville, 16 Nov. 1839

CHAPTER 12 Afterwards

1 George W. Brown, 'The Durham Report and the Upper Canadian Scene,' *Canadian Historical Review* 20 (1939), 155–9

2 *Kingston Chronicle and Gazette*, 5 June 1839. Ryerson was no supporter of

responsible government, but no doubt approved comments and recommendations in the report concerning religion and the churches.

3 Ibid., 15 May 1839
4 Ibid., 18 May 1839
5 *Cobourg Star*, 8 May 1839
6 NA, MG 11, CO 42, Q Series, vol. 419, pt 1,. 51, T.C. Wheeler to H.L. Wheeler, Whitby, 26 May 1839, enclosed in Arthur to Normanby, 21 Aug. 1839
7 Longley, *Sir Francis Hincks*, 48. Longley mentions meetings at Whitby, Beaverton, and Belleville, among others.
8 *Chronicle and Gazette*, 13 July 1839
9 Guillet, *Lives and Times of the Patriots*, 33
10 *Cobourg Star*, reprinted in the *Chronicle and Gazette*, 13 July 1839
11 Guillet, *Lives and Times of the Patriots*, 33
12 Baldwin, *The Baldwins and the Great Experiment*, 164
13 New, *Lord Durham's Mission*, 208–9
14 See Chester Martin, 'Lord Durham's Report and Its Consequences,' *Canadian Historical Review* 20 (1939).
15 *Arthur Papers*, no. 805, Arthur to Colborne, Toronto, 17 June 1839
16 Durham included the distribution of land in the list of responsibilities given to the British parliament, but in fact it was left with Canada. Much public land was already in the hands of the Canada Company.
17 New, *Lord Durham's Mission to Canada*, 98
18 Strickland, *Twenty-Seven Years in Canada West*, 269
19 Boyce et al., *Sidney Township 200*, 17–19. Because of such early expression of democracy in Hastings County, the year 1990 marked the two-hundredth anniversary of municipal government in Sidney Township.
20 A great deal has been written on this question based on a variety of opinion. For instance, see Read and Stagg, eds., *The Rebellion of 1837*, xcix–c; the authors discount the effect of the rebellion and the Durham Report in obtaining responsible government, whereas such historians as Chester New ascribe great importance to it.
21 Burroughs, *The Colonial Reformers and Canada*, 123–7
22 *Lord Durham's Report*, ed. Gerald M. Craig, 157
23 Buckner, *The Transition to Responsible Government*, 267
24 Ibid., 81
25 The first parliament was held in part of the present Kingston General Hospital, as indicated by a plaque in the entrance hall.
26 *Arthur Papers*, no. 614, Glenelg to Arthur, Colonial Office, 3 Jan. 1839
27 They were not disbanded until December 1839.

28 Edwin M. Waterbury, 'Oswego County during the Patriot War,' *Papers of the Oswego County Historical Society* (1944), 174–6

29 PAO, Wallbridge Family Papers, William Wallbridge to Marianne Howard, Belleville, 26 April 1839

30 His antecedents were well known for he was the son of Lt Gen. Frederick, Baron De Rottenburg, who had served briefly as administrator of Lower, then of Upper, Canada during the War of 1812–14, before joining General Brock's staff.

31 John Wedderburn Dunbar Moodie was made the first sheriff of Victoria District, the name of Hastings County when it was separated from the Midland District in 1840. His wife Susanna is one of the foremost writers of early Canadian literature.

32 NA, Moodie-Strickland-Vickers-Ewing Papers, John Moodie to Susanna Moodie, Belleville, 25 Dec. 1838

33 Ibid., 24 Jan. 1839

34 Ibid., 24 Feb. 1839

35 Ibid., 24 April 1839

36 PAO, Wallbridge Family Papers, Lewis Wallbridge to Hiram Howard, Belleville, 26 April 1839

37 Morgan, *Sketches of Celebrated Canadians and Persons Connected with Canada*, 699–701

38 *Belleville Intelligencer*, 8 May 1838

39 Nelson Reynolds built the mansion known as Trafalgar Castle. It was sold to be used as a school and is still in use as part of Whitby Ladies College.

40 Lindsey, *William Lyon Mackenzie*, 2:290

41 Guillet, *Lives and Times of the Patriots*, 230

42 PAO, Quarter Sessions Report, Midland District, 24 Jan. 1839

43 NA, RG 5, A1, vol. 241, De Rottenburg to Arthur, Belleville, 24 Mar. 1840

44 Moodie, *Life in the Clearings*, 35

45 'Reminiscences of Simon Miller,' in Smith, *The Pioneers of Old Ontario*, 129

46 Brown, 'The Durham Report and the Upper Canadian Scene,' 154

47 *Arthur Papers*, no. 651, Arthur to Colborne, Toronto, Feb. 1839

48 Longley, *Sir Francis Hincks*, 73

49 Ryerson, *Unequal Union*, 247–51

50 Donald C. MacDonald, 'The Honourable Richard Cartwright, 1755–1815,' in MacDonald et al., *Three History Theses*, 63

Selected
Bibliography

Akenson, Donald. *The Irish in Ontario: A Study in Rural History*. Kingston and Montreal: McGill-Queen's University Press 1984
– *The Orangeman: The Life and Times of Ogle Gowan*. Toronto: James Lorimer 1986
Armstrong, F.H. *Handbook of Upper Canadian Chronology and Territorial Legislation*. London, Ont.: Lawson Memorial Library, University of Western Ontario 1967
Armstrong, F.H., H.A. Stevenson, and J.D. Wilson, eds. *Aspects of Nineteenth-Century Ontario*. Toronto: University of Toronto Press in association with the University of Western Ontario 1974
Arthur, Sir George. *The Arthur Papers, Being the Canadian Papers, Mainly Confidential, Private, and Demi-Official of Sir George Arthur, KGH, Last Lieutenant-Governor of Upper Canada*. Ed. Charles E. Sanderson. Toronto: Toronto Public Libraries and University of Toronto Press 1959
Bailey, Thomas A. *A Diplomatic History of the American People*. Englewood Cliffs, NJ: Prentice Hall 1980
Baldwin, R.M., and J. Baldwin. *The Baldwins and the Great Experiment*. Toronto: Longmans Green 1969
Bonnycastle, Richard. *Canada As It Was, Is, and May Be*. 2 vols. London: Macmillan 1864
Boyce, Gerald. *Historic Hastings*. Belleville, Ont.: Hastings County Council 1967
– *Hutton of Hastings*. Belleville, Ont.: Hastings County Council 1972
– *The St. Andrew's Chronicles*. Belleville, Ont.: St Andrew's Presbyterian Church 1978
Boyce, Gerald, Kathy Karkut, June Sine, Robert Gay, and Lewis Zandbergen,

eds. *Sidney Township 200, 1790–1990*, Belleville, Ont.: Hastings County Historical Society 1990

Brode, Patrick. *Sir John Beverley Robinson: Bone and Sinew of the Compact*. Toronto: University of Toronto Press for the Osgoode Society 1984

Brown, George. *The Early Methodist Church*. Toronto 1938

Buckner, Philip. *The Transition to Responsible Government: British Policy in British North America*. Toronto: Greenwood 1985

Bumsted, J.M. *Documentary Problems in Canadian History*. 2 vols. Georgetown, Ont.: Irwin Dorsey Ltd 1969

Burroughs, Peter. *The Colonial Reformers and Canada 1830–1849*. Toronto: McClelland and Stewart 1969

– *The Canadian Crisis and British Colonial Policy 1830–1841*. Toronto: Macmillan 1972

Canniff, William. *The Settlement of Upper Canada*. Toronto 1869; reprint, Belleville, Ont.: Mika Silk Screening 1972

Careless, J.M. *The Union of the Canadas and the Growth of Canadian Institutions 1841–1857*. Toronto: McClelland and Stewart 1967

Clark, Stanley Delbert. *Movements of Political Protest in Canada 1640–1840*. Toronto: University of Toronto Press 1959

Craig, Gerald M. *Upper Canada: The Formative Years 1784–1841*. Toronto: McClelland and Stewart 1963

– ed. *Early Travellers in the Canadas, 1791–1867*. Toronto: Macmillan 1955

Creighton, Donald. *John A. Macdonald: The Young Politician*. Toronto: Macmillan 1965

– *Towards the Discovery of Canada: Selected Essays*. Toronto: Macmillan 1972

Crowley, Frank. *A Documentary History of Australia*. 6 vols. West Melbourne: Thomas Nelson 1980

Dent, John Charles. *The Story of the Upper Canadian Rebellion*. 2 vols. Toronto 1885

Doughty, A.G., and Norah Storey. *Documents Relating to the Constitutional History of Canada, 1816–1828*. Ottawa 1935

Dunham, Aileen. *Political Unrest in Upper Canada 1815–1836*. London 1927; reprint, Toronto: McClelland and Stewart in association with the Institute for Canadian Studies, Carleton University 1963

Durham, John George Lambton, First Earl of. *Report on the Affairs of British North America*. Ed. Sir Charles Lucas. 3 vols. Oxford 1912; abridged and ed. G.M. Craig. Ottawa: Carleton University Press 1982

Earl, David W.L., ed. *The Family Compact, Aristocracy or Oligarchy?* Toronto: Copp Clark 1967

Errington, Jane. *The Lion, the Eagle, and Upper Canada: A Developing Colonial Ideology*. Kingston and Montreal: McGill-Queen's University Press 1987

Flint, David. *William Lyon Mackenzie*. Toronto: Oxford University Press 1971

Fryer, Mary Beacock. *Volunteers and Redcoats, Rebels and Raiders*. Toronto and Oxford: Dundurn Press 1987

Gates, Lillian. *After the Rebellion: The Later Years of William Lyon Mackenzie*. Toronto and Oxford: Dundurn Press 1988

Goldie, John. *Diary of a Journey through Upper Canada and Some of the New England States, 1819*. 1827

Gourlay, Robert. *A Statistical Account of Upper Canada*. 2 vols. 1822; abridged by S.R. Mealing. Toronto 1974

Grey, Charles. *Crisis in the Canadas: The Grey Journals and Letters*. Ed. William Ormsby. Toronto: Macmillan 1964

Guillet, Edwin C. *Early Life in Upper Canada*. Toronto: Thomas Nelson and Sons 1933

– *The Lives and Times of the Patriots*. Toronto: Thomas Nelson and Sons 1938

– *The Valley of the Trent*. Toronto: Thomas Nelson and Sons 1957

Haight, Canniff. *Life in Canada Fifty Years Ago*. 1885

Hall, Roger, William Westfall, and Laurel Sefton MacDowell, eds. *Patterns of the Past: Interpreting the Province's History*. London and Oxford: Dundurn Press 1988

Hamil, Fred Coyne, J.J. Talman, and S.F. Wise, eds. *Profiles of a Province*. Toronto: Ontario Historical Society 1967

Harrison, J.F.C. *Early Victorian Britain, 1832–51*, London: Fontana 1979

Head, Sir Francis Bond. *A Narrative*. London 1839; reprint, ed. S.F. Wise. Toronto: McClelland and Stewart 1962

Herrington, Walter. *History of the County of Lennox and Addington*. 1913; reprint, Belleville, Ont.: Mika Silk Screening 1972

Howison, John. *Sketches of Upper Canada*. Edinburgh 1825

Hughes, Robert. *The Fatal Shore*. New York: Alfred A. Knopf 1987

Innis, Harold Adams, and A.R.M. Lower, eds. *Select Documents in Canadian Economic History, 1783–1885*. 2 vols. Toronto: University of Toronto Press 1933

Jameson, Anna. *Winter Studies and Summer Rambles*. 3 vols. London 1838; reprint, Toronto: Coles Publishing 1972

Johnson, J.K. *Becoming Prominent: Regional Leadership in Upper Canada, 1791–1841*. Kingston and Montreal: McGill-Queen's University Press 1989

– ed. *Historical Essays on Upper Canada*. Toronto: McClelland and Stewart 1975

Johnson, J.K., and Bruce G. Wilson, eds. *Historical Essays on Upper Canada: New Perspectives*. Ottawa: Carleton University Press 1989

Kilbourn, William. *The Firebrand: William Lyon Mackenzie and the Rebellion in Upper Canada*. Toronto: Clarke, Irwin 1960

Landon, Fred. *An Exile from Canada to Van Diemen's Land*. Toronto: Longmans, Green 1960

Langton, Anne. *A Gentlewoman in Upper Canada: The Journals of Anne Langton*. Ed. H.H. Langton. Toronto: Clarke, Irwin 1967

Langton, John. *Early Days in Upper Canada*. Ed. W.A. Langton. Toronto: Macmillan 1926

La Pierre, Laurier. *Genesis of a Nation: British Colonial Period*. Toronto: Canadian Broadcasting Corporation 1967

LeSueur, William Dawson. *William Lyon Mackenzie: A Reinterpretation*. 1907; reprint, Toronto: Macmillan 1979

Lindsey, Charles. *The Life and Times of William Lyon Mackenzie and the Rebellion of 1837–38*. 1862; reprint, Toronto: Coles Publishing Company 1971

Lizars, Robina, and Kathleen MacFarlane Lizars. *Humours of '37, Grave, Gay and Grim*. Toronto: William Briggs 1897

Longley, Ronald S. *Sir Francis Hincks: A Study of Canadian Politics, Railways and Finance in Upper Canada*. Toronto: University of Toronto Press 1943

Lower, Arthur. *Colony to Nation: A History of Canada*. Toronto: McClelland and Stewart 1977

MacDonald, Donald C., J.C. Morrison, and E. Rae Stewart. *Three History Theses*. Toronto: Ontario Department of Public Records and Archives 1961

Mackenzie, William Lyon. *Selected Writings of William Lyon Mackenzie*. Ed. Margaret Fairley. Toronto: Oxford University Press 1970

– *William Lyon Mackenzie: Canadian History through the Press*. Ed. Anthony Rasporich. Toronto: Holt, Rinehart and Winston 1972

Maclean, Allan C. *The First Hundred Years, 1877–1987*. Kingston: Tabernacle United Church 1977

M'Leod, Donald. *A Brief Review of the Settlement of Upper Canada*. Cleveland 1841; reprint, Belleville, Ont.: Mika Publishing Company 1972

Martin, Chester. *The Foundations of Canadian Nationhood*. Toronto: University of Toronto Press 1955

Milani, Lois Darroch. *Robert Gourlay, Gadfly: Forerunner of the Rebellion in Upper Canada 1837*. Toronto: Ampersand Press 1971

Mills, David. *The Idea of Loyalty in Upper Canada, 1784–1850*. Kingston and Montreal: McGill-Queen's University Press 1988

Moodie, Susanna. *Roughing It in the Bush*. 1852; reprint, Toronto: Macmillan 1959

– *Life in the Clearings*. 1853; reprint, Toronto: Macmillan 1959

Morgan, Henry J. *Sketches of Celebrated Canadians and Persons Connected with Canada*. London 1862

Morton, W.L. *The Kingdom of Canada*. Toronto: McClelland and Stewart 1972

– ed. *The Shield of Achilles*. Toronto: McClelland and Stewart 1968

Nackman, Mark E. *A Nation within a Nation: The Rise of Texas Nationalism*. Port Washington, NY, 1975

New, Chester. *Lord Durham's Mission to Canada*. An abridgement of *Lord Durham: A Biography of John George Lambton, First Earl of Durham*. London 1929; reprint, Toronto: McClelland and Stewart 1971

Ouellet, Fernand. *Lower Canada 1791–1840*. Toronto: McClelland and Stewart 1980

Patterson, Graeme. *Whiggery, Nationality, and the Upper Canadian Reform Tradition*. Toronto: University of Toronto Press 1975

Phillips, Charles. *The Development of Education in Canada*. Toronto: William Gage 1957

Plumpton, Mary. *The Rambling River: A History of Thurlow Township*. Belleville, Ont.: Thurlow Township Council 1967

Radcliff, Thomas. *Authentic Letters from Upper Canada*. 1833; reprint, Toronto: Macmillan 1952

Read, Colin. *The Rising in Western Upper Canada, 1837–38: The Duncombe Revolt and After*. Toronto: University of Toronto Press 1982

Read, Colin, and Ronald J. Stagg, eds. *The Rebellion of 1837 in Upper Canada*. Toronto: The Champlain Society in cooperation with the Ontario Heritage Foundation and Carleton University Press 1985

Rolph, Thomas. *Descriptive and Statistical Account of Canada*. London 1841

Romney, Paul. *Mr. Attorney: The Attorney General for Ontario in Court, Cabinet and Legislature, 1791–1899*. Toronto: University of Toronto Press 1986

Roy, James. *Kingston, the King's Town*. Toronto: McClelland and Stewart 1952

Ryerson, Stanley B. *Unequal Union: Confederation and the Roots of Conflict in the Canadas, 1815–1873*. Toronto: Progress Books 1983

Schull, Joseph. *Rebellion: The Rising in French Canada, 1837*. Toronto: Macmillan 1971

Shireff, Patrick. *A Tour through North America, Together with a Comprehensive View of the Canadas and the United States, As adapted for Agricultural Emigration*. Edinburgh 1835

Simcoe, John Graves. *The Correspondence of Lieutenant Governor John Graves Simcoe*. 5 vols. Ed. E.A. Cruikshank. Toronto: Ontario Historical Society 1923

Sissons, C.B. *Egerton Ryerson: His Life and Letters*. 2 vols. Toronto: Clarke, Irwin 1937

Smith, William. *The Pioneers of Old Ontario*. n.p.: George Morang 1923

Strachan, John. *John Strachan: Documents and Opinions*. Ed. J.L.H. Henderson. Toronto: McClelland and Stewart 1969

Strickland, Samuel. *Twenty-Seven Years in Canada West*. 2 vols 1853; reprint, Edmonton: Hurtig 1978

Talbot, Edward Allen. *Five Years Residence in the Canadas*. London 1824

Thompson, Samuel. *Reminiscences of a Canadian Pioneer for the Last Fifty Years (1833–1883): An Autobiography*. 1884; reprint, McClelland and Stewart 1968

Tiffany, Orrin Edward. *The Relation of the United States to the Canadian Rebellion of 1837–1838*. Buffalo 1905; reprint, Toronto: Coles Publishing 1972

Traill, Catharine Parr. *The Backwoods of Canada*. Toronto 1929

Tulchinsky, Gerald, ed. *To Preserve and Defend: Essays on Kingston in the Nineteenth Century*. Montreal and London: McGill-Queen's University Press 1976

Turner, Larry. *Voyage of a Different Kind*. Belleville, Ont.: Mika Publishing Company 1984

Upton, L.F.S., ed. *United Empire Loyalists: Men and Myths*. Toronto: Copp Clark 1967

Wait, Benjamin. *The Wait Letters*. Erin, Ont.: Press Porcépic 1976

Index